Have Yourself
a Merry Legal
Christmas

Also by David Krell and from McFarland

*Bo Belinsky: The Rise, Fall and Rebound
of a Playboy Pitcher* (2025)

*"Our Bums": The Brooklyn Dodgers in History,
Memory and Popular Culture* (2015)

Also Edited by David Krell
and from McFarland

*The New York Mets in Popular Culture:
Critical Essays* (2020)

*The New York Yankees in Popular Culture:
Critical Essays* (2019)

Have Yourself a Merry Legal Christmas

Laws and Justice in Holiday Movies and Television Shows

DAVID KRELL

Foreword by Elissa D. Hecker

McFarland & Company, Inc., Publishers
Jefferson, North Carolina

LIBRARY OF CONGRESS CATALOGING-IN-PUBLICATION DATA

Names: Krell, David, 1967– author | Hecker, Elissa D. writer of foreword.
Title: Have yourself a merry legal Christmas : laws and justice in holiday movies and television shows / David Krell ; foreword by Elissa D. Hecker.
Description: Jefferson, North Carolina : McFarland & Company, Inc., Publishers, 2025. | Includes bibliographical references and index.
Identifiers: LCCN 2025031029 | ISBN 9781476696560 paperback ∞
   ISBN 9781476656441 ebook
Subjects: LCSH: Christmas films—History and criticism | Law in motion pictures | Christmas television programs—History and criticism | Law on television | LCGFT: Film criticism | Television criticism and reviews
Classification: LCC PN1995.9.C5113 K74 2025 | DDC 791.43/634—dc23/eng/20250714
LC record available at https://lccn.loc.gov/2025031029

ISBN (print) 978-1-4766-9656-0
ISBN (ebook) 978-1-4766-5644-1

© 2025 David Krell. All rights reserved

No part of this book may be reproduced or transmitted in any form or by any means, electronic or mechanical, including photocopying or recording, or by any information storage and retrieval system, without permission in writing from the publisher.

Front cover image: Shutterstock AI Generator

Printed in the United States of America

*McFarland & Company, Inc., Publishers
   Box 611, Jefferson, North Carolina 28640
      www.mcfarlandpub.com*

In the 1960s, two young women
began a lifelong friendship
when they were legal secretaries at
Fast & Fast, a law firm in Newark, New Jersey.

For Sheila Krell, née Scherer, my mom,
who always tells me when *The Bishop's Wife*
is on television.

For Concetta "Connie" Goldman,
née Caporaso (1940–2019),
who loved Christmas.

Acknowledgments

Researchers are only as good as the material they can access. My thanks to the New York Public Library Main Branch for its outstanding archives of books, magazines, newspapers and microfilm. In addition, the ProQuest database and newspapers.com were invaluable for tracking down movie reviews, biographical information and other pertinent material in newspapers.

This book was born in the Non-Fiction Book Proposal Workshop at Media Bistro, a Manhattan-based education company with an outstanding roster of classes designed for writers. I enrolled in several incarnations of the workshop, which offered terrific camaraderie among my fellow scribes looking to take the seed of an idea, nurture it and create a viable book proposal for agents and publishers. Ryan Fischer-Harbage, a literary agent and mentor extraordinaire, helmed a few of these workshops; I got two publishing deals for books about baseball under his tutelage before pursuing my Christmas book idea.

My deepest appreciation to Ryan for his continued encouragement, critique and candor during the eight-week journey that took this project from an idea to a book proposal. Also, my thanks to Art Carine, Elissa D. Hecker and Tracey Diamond for their input on the manuscript draft. Lisa Bloomfield, Megan Purcell and Janet Zipper offered tremendous encouragement throughout the project.

Renny Temple was extremely generous with his time. His memories of a guest appearance on a crucial holiday episode of *All in the Family* provided invaluable perspective on the story's impact.

For their guidance and permission regarding photos, I'd like to highlight Michael Pinckney of the Ronald Reagan Presidential Library, Jason Tomberlin of the University of North Carolina at Chapel Hill, Sye Gutierrez and Christine Adolph of the Los Angeles Public Library, the United States Senate Historical Office and Andersen Air Force Base.

Layla Milholen, Gary Mitchem and the rest of the team at McFarland must be noted for championing this project. It's both a pleasure and a privilege to work with them.

Table of Contents

Acknowledgments — vi
Foreword by Elissa D. Hecker — 1
Preface — 3
Introduction — 7

Christmas and Money

1. Usury (*A Christmas Carol*) — 17
2. Bearer Bonds (*Die Hard*) — 22
3. Contests (*Emmet Otter's Jug-Band Christmas*) — 25
4. Private Banking (*The Beverly Hillbillies*) — 29
5. Offer (*Cheers*) — 35
6. Bank Runs, Larceny (*It's a Wonderful Life*) — 40

Christmas and the Military

7. Military Funerals (*The West Wing*) — 47
8. The Geneva Convention, Copyright Infringement (*Stalag 17*) — 52
9. Falsifying Military Records (*M*A*S*H*) — 59
10. Draft Dodging (*All in the Family*) — 66
11. Humanitarian Missions (*Operation Christmas Drop*) — 71

Christmas and the Home

12. Civil Negligence (*The Man Who Came to Dinner*) — 77
13. Subletting (*The Apartment*) — 83
14. Defense of Home (*Home Alone*) — 88

15.	Moonshining (*The Andy Griffith Show*)	93
16.	Theft of Electricity (*Deck the Halls*)	99
17.	Burglary (*How the Grinch Stole Christmas!*)	104

Christmas and Crime

18.	Witness Protection (*The Sopranos*)	109
19.	Prostitution, Narcotics, Organized Crime, Murder (*L.A. Confidential*)	116
20.	Community Policing (*Car 54, Where Are You?*)	123
21.	Resisting Arrest, Constitutional Rights (*White Christmas*)	128
22.	Self-Defense (*A Christmas Story*)	133

Christmas and Copyrights

23.	Music Publishing Rights—Recorded Songs (*Love Actually*)	139
24.	Music Publishing Rights—Public Performance (*Jack Frost*)	145
25.	Unpublished Works (*The Bishop's Wife*)	150
26.	Public Domain (*Scrooged*)	156

Christmas and Government

27.	Gifts to State Government Employees (*Parks and Recreation*)	159
28.	Gifts to the President of the United States (*Family Ties*)	165
29.	United States Postal Service (*Miracle on 34th Street*)	170
30.	Blacklisting (*Seinfeld*)	177

Chapter Notes	185
Bibliography	207
Index	209

Foreword

Elissa D. Hecker

All I want for Christmas is … this book.

Sometimes it can be difficult to bring legal issues, history and business alive so that readers can understand real-world applications. David Krell does this so well by weaving complicated topics into stories that we know and love through 20th- and 21st-century pop culture references and themes. The chapters in this book cover over a century of film and television and offer insight into what happened in those stories, as well as what could have been happening behind the scenes and plotlines—legally, business-wise and regulatorily.

I have had the pleasure of editing David's column, "Krell's Korner," in the *Entertainment, Arts and Sports Law Journal* for over 15 years and it brought me great pleasure to read this book, which was like sitting down with an old friend. David's conversational and witty writing style makes the reader feel like they are "in" on the plot, joke or sideline.

Through the lens of Christmas in legacy entertainment properties, David teaches us lessons about money, business, the military, real estate, crime, copyrights and the government. This is a great read for undergraduate or law school students and, of course, for film and television buffs.

For example, by using *A Christmas Carol*, *Die Hard*, *Cheers* and *It's a Wonderful Life* to illustrate complicated money issues, the first section of this book covers usury, which is the illegal action or practice of lending money at unreasonably high rates of interest, bearer bonds, contests (which are highly regulated), private banking, offer and acceptance and bank runs.

The next section, which includes *The West Wing*, *M*A*S*H* and *All in the Family*, is devoted to the military. It covers military funerals, the Geneva Convention, falsifying military records, draft dodging and Operation Christmas Drop. This section delves deeply into U.S. history and offers some surprising details.

Following that is the section regarding rights around one's home and real estate. David considers *Home Alone* and *The Man Who Came to Dinner*, holiday favorites that are rife with issues about home invasion and occupation. This section covers negligence, subletting, defending the home, moonshining and theft of electricity.

Next, David covers crime from plotlines ranging from *The Sopranos* to *A Christmas Story*. This section includes the witness protection program, murder, narcotics, community policing, resisting arrest, burglary and self-defense.

Of greatest interest to intellectual property junkies is the next section, which focuses on copyrights. These chapters cover music publishing, unpublished works and the public domain through *Love Actually*, *Jack Frost*, *The Bishop's Wife* and *Scrooged*.

The final section concerns the U.S. government. This includes the rules around gifts to state government employees (cue Leslie Knope, in the chapter devoted to *Parks and Recreation*), gifts to the president (*Family Ties*), the U.S. Post Office (*Miracle on 34th Street*) and, through an interesting episode of *Seinfeld*, the history behind the House Un–American Activities Committee, which led this country down the dark road of McCarthyism and blacklists.

David is a prolific writer about baseball history (*Do You Believe in Magic? Baseball and America in the Groundbreaking Year of 1966*; *The Fenway Effect: A Cultural History of the Boston Red Sox*; *1978: Baseball and America in the Disco Era*; and *Bo Belinsky: The Rise, Fall and Rebound of a Playboy Pitcher*, among others). In addition, his mind is a repository of the who, what, where and why of the film and television industries and he is able to transfer his interest from the minute details to the greater themes in a manner that captivates the reader.

This book shows the breadth of his knowledge, and application of such, as well as his appreciation and joy for the films and television series that he spotlights.

You will rejoice in the knowledge that you garner from this excellent book combining Christmas films and television series with U.S. law, history and business. If nothing else, you will absolutely increase the chances that you will be the most fascinating guest at your next holiday party.

As general counsel to small businesses, solopreneurs, and entrepreneurs in their legal and business affairs across the United States, **Elissa D. Hecker** *guides clients through strategic thought processes, teaches them how to negotiate from a position of strength, protect their brands and intellectual property, set up their businesses and legal infrastructures so that they are protected (including contracts, licensing, digital issues, trademarks and copyrights), and works on independent contractor–employee issues. She also practices in the fields of entertainment, arts and book publishing and is a repeat Super Lawyer, Top Lawyer and Best Lawyer in America.*

Preface

Jurisprudence is the foundation of America.

Law professors use the Socratic method to train future lawyers who will maintain the principles set forth in the United States Constitution and reinforced through cases, laws, codes, regulations and ordinances. In 1971, John Jay Osborn Jr.'s novel *The Paper Chase* introduced a mass audience to this staple of legal education, which not only tests a student's understanding of the material but also the crucial ability to think on one's feet. A professor asks a student about the facts of a case, the law and rationale applied by the judge, and hypothetical questions related to these topics.

Using his experience at Harvard Law School, Osborn described the plight of first-year law students as they embark on a byzantine path of learning formed by fear, ambition, and intellect with the Socratic method as a foundation. *The Paper Chase* reached the bestseller list; a movie and TV series followed.

Every first-year law student is subject to this rite of passage. Mine occurred in contracts class during the fall of 1989 in Villanova Law School with the case *Siegel vs. Spear*. The professor called my name and posed the question that he always asked to begin the interrogation: "Who's suing who for what?" My heartbeat increased and my face reddened from nerves as I spoke into the microphone and recited the facts of this 1923 case decided in the New York Court of Appeals. A customer sued a storage company after a fire destroyed his furniture; he had been assured that the facility would insure for the furniture, but it never did.

"Do you think the court decided correctly for the plaintiff, Mr. Krell?" asked the professor.

"Yes."

"Why?"

"Well, he trusted the company. There was an agreement to store the furniture and there was a bailment."

We had just studied bailments in property class a couple of weeks before, so I thought it was worth mentioning. As soon as the words came out of my mouth, I had an ominous feeling. The professor continued. "Oh, enlighten us, Mr. Krell. What's a bailment?"

"A bailment happens when you entrust your property to another person or entity. In this case, he trusted that his property would be taken care of. Plus, the company never got the insurance."

"Oh, he trusted the company. Do you trust me, Mr. Krell?"

"In what way?"

To this day, I don't know where the words came from or where I got the confidence for my response, but it ignited tremendous laughter throughout the lecture hall filled with approximately 100 of my fellow students. Even the professor laughed and said, "Good one."

The Socratic method is an effective technique that trains law students to be prepared. A law school exam is similar, except you write down your answers instead of speaking them. It's common for a law professor to create a fact pattern with fictional characters and require the students to apply a legal analysis based on the case law that they've absorbed throughout the semester.

For example, a contracts exam might use *The Sopranos*. Tony wants to sell his used Cadillac Escalade, which he claims is in great condition. Silvio tells him that he'll buy it for $40,000. Tony says that's a fair price and agrees to sell. The exchange takes place later that day. A week later, Johnny Sack tells Silvio that Tony stole the Escalade from him. Plus, the Escalade is not in "great condition": Silvio must spend $4500 for the replacement of sparkplugs, tires and a battery, plus repairs. Tony never disclosed the condition of the Escalade or its status as a stolen vehicle. Johnny tells Silvio that he wants the Escalade returned to him. What causes of action does Silvio have against Tony? What defenses does Tony have against Silvio?

The answers will involve the definition and analysis of several issues including offer, acceptance, consideration, fraud, good faith, caveat emptor (let the buyer beware) and bona fide purchaser.

In 2011, I got inspired to match my passion for Christmas culture with my legal background. My article "A Very Legal Christmas" in the New York State Bar Association's *Entertainment, Arts and Sports Law Journal* focused on three topics: *Rudolph the Red-Nosed Reindeer*, *It's a Wonderful Life* and Santa Claus.

The genesis of the Rudolph the Red-Nosed Reindeer franchise began with a story published as a giveaway for Montgomery Ward shoppers in Chicago in 1939. *It's a Wonderful Life* fell into the public domain because of failure to renew the copyright registration in the 1970s but the United States Supreme Court case of *Stewart vs. Abend* allowed a recapture of copyright protection. The well-known depiction of Santa Claus in a red suit has its origins as an advertising figure.

Preface

My experience with the article got me thinking about expanding the concept to illustrate legal principles in a book combining Christmas movies and TV episodes with the Socratic method. This motivated me to enroll in the Non-Fiction Book Proposal Class at Media Bistro. After the class, my proposal remained in a folder on my computer as I ventured toward writing baseball books. But the challenge ultimately proved too enticing to resist.

I revived the proposal in 2020 during the Covid-19 restrictions requiring Americans to wear masks in public places, work from home if possible, and adjust to isolation instead of interaction. Watching Christmas stories provided an emotional antidote to the deadly, airborne virus that upended norms, destroyed routines and frightened everyone faster than Rudolph and his eight reindeer pals tug Santa Claus' sleigh.

A turning point occurred on March 11, 2020, when the NBA announced the first seemingly radical but inevitably necessary action by a large organization or company to put public safety ahead of financial profit (given the information that we knew at the time): postponement of its remaining games on the 2019–20 schedule. A day later, the NHL took similar action.

Across the country, gathering places either closed or suffered a severe downturn. Government mandates, guidelines and restrictions (plus people's fear of being in crowded places) led to plummeting revenue in restaurants and bars, resulting in closings. Religious sanctuaries, bookstores and comedy clubs stood empty. With the closing of movie theaters came an increase in streaming movies. But watching from your den or living room—even on a 65-inch screen—is not the same as a shared experience with a hundred others.

Zoom replaced live interaction. We scrambled to set up accounts so we could virtually attend weddings, bar mitzvahs, Rosh Hashanah and Yom Kippur services, Passover seders, Easter Mass, Sunday Mass, Christmas Mass, confirmations, graduations, class reunions, birthday parties, office meetings, media interviews, business conferences, funerals, shiva calls and wakes.

Companies closed their offices, allowing workers to fulfill their duties from the dining room table or living room couch in sweatpants and a T-shirt while checking in with clients, bosses and colleagues through email and phone calls. In Manhattan, you could drive a tank up Madison Avenue or down Fifth Avenue and not hit anything for 40 blocks. A financial benefit emerged: Working from home meant a big reduction in expenditures for dry cleaning, commuting and meals. But there was an emotional cost. Isolation became stark. Loneliness intense.

In the summer of 2020, research became my refuge from news about

Covid-19's impact on public health (and also from news about riots, lootings and burnings in the name of social justice wrecking businesses in Minneapolis, Chicago, Beverly Hills and New York City). Christmas tales in movies and television provided a salve, telling us not how the world is but how it ought to be with community, kinship and warmth governing. My work continued after the distribution of vaccines and our return to normalcy.

This project allowed me to use my legal education for a new way of looking at the stories that are part of a communal background, entertaining, inspiring and amusing us every year between Thanksgiving and December 25, whether it's *A Christmas Carol*'s Ebenezer Scrooge undergoing a character transformation, John McClane saving office workers from thieves brandishing machine-guns at Nakatomi Plaza in *Die Hard*, or the characters and storylines intersecting in *Love Actually*. Complementing the legal topics are historical information, biographies and reviews because my goal is not to overwhelm with legal jargon, but rather to isolate, analyze and explain the relevant legal issues in an informative, entertaining and compelling manner so that anyone from a seasoned jurist to a layperson can enjoy the book.

For those in the legal community, it can be a launching pad for more research concerning the laws, cases, regulations and legal principles described. For non-lawyers, it provides a novel look at some of the stories that have defined the Christmas season in America.

Introduction

Christmas. It's the most wonderful time of the year.

Hollywood producers have leveraged Christmas for movies and TV, offering new stories every year to touch and inspire us, and to remind us that the chaos of events, whether they impact the world at large or our everyday lives, can be squashed for a few moments—or at least tamed—by a happy ending with a holiday theme.

Try to imagine December without the quartet of Bing Crosby, Danny Kaye, Vera-Ellen and Rosemary Clooney singing the title song in *White Christmas*; a newly elected British prime minister finding his resolve against an arrogant American president in *Love Actually*; an eight-year-old boy defending his family's suburban Chicago home against bumbling thieves in *Home Alone*; or an angel offering guidance to a frustrated clergyman in *The Bishop's Wife*.

Rudolph's red nose, Charlie Brown's tree and the Grinch's turnaround from bandit to benefactor have become annual TV cornerstones since they debuted in the 1960s. Sitcoms and dramas typically have a December episode with a Christmas theme. The Hallmark Channel has created a terrific inventory of tales with predictable plotlines, formulaic characters and warm-hearted outcomes framed by a Christmas setting comforting us like a soft blanket, flannel pajamas and hot cocoa on a cold winter night.

Are you looking for a depiction of Santa Claus as a character and not a symbol? You can absorb yourself in *Fred Claus, Red One, The Night They Saved Christmas, Santa Claus Is Comin' to Town, Santa Claus: The Movie, The Santa Clause, Mr. St. Nick, The Christmas Chronicles* and *The Case for Christmas*.

We cry with joy when the citizens of Bedford Falls crowd the living room in the Bailey abode to rescue George Bailey from financial peril, public shame and an impending prison sentence for embezzlement. A 1977 TV movie offered a gender reversal of the story: *It Happened One Christmas* starred Marlo Thomas as a female version of James Stewart's character.

We laugh at the vignettes featuring Ralphie Parker and his friends in *A Christmas Story*. Though set in 1940, it's a timeless tale of childhood desires and woes.

We cheer when a Manhattan judge rules on the legal veracity of Santa Claus in *Miracle on 34th Street*. If you're a fan of this story, there are versions besides the 1947 film starring Edmund Gwenn as Kris Kringle: TV adaptations in 1955, 1959 and 1973 as well as a feature film in 1994.

First published as a novella in 1843, *A Christmas Carol* provides an evergreen holiday template for writers and producers. Television shows have generated interpretations by plugging its characters into Charles Dickens' tale of regret, realization and redemption. *The Odd Couple, Family Ties, Sanford and Son, WKRP in Cincinnati, The Famous Teddy Z, Popular, Martin* and *The Jetsons* are among the programs devoting an episode to their spins on Ebenezer Scrooge, and Bob Cratchit, *et al*.

We search for the air dates and times when our favorite full-length version of *A Christmas Carol* will be showcased on television because Seymour Hicks, Reginald Owen, Alastair Sim and Albert Finney have become as much a December tradition as the Rockefeller Center Christmas tree.

Animation fans may lean toward *A Flintstones Christmas Carol, Mickey's Christmas Carol, Mister Magoo's Christmas Carol, Bugs Bunny's Christmas Carol* and *The Smurfs: A Christmas Carol*. Jim Henson and his team created *A Muppet Christmas Carol* with Michael Caine as Scrooge and Kermit the Frog as Bob Cratchit. For a humorous interpretation, the one-hour special *Rich Little's A Christmas Carol* displayed Little's talent for celebrity impersonations, including W.C. Fields as Scrooge, Paul Lynde as Cratchit, Richard Nixon as Jacob Marley, Humphrey Bogart as the Ghost of Christmas Past, Groucho Marx as Fezziwig, Johnny Carson as Fred and Truman Capote as Tiny Tim.

Hollywood has also provided TV movies that take Dickens' characters out of mid–19th century London. *Ebbie* stars Susan Lucci as department store mogul Elizabeth "Ebbie" Scrooge. Jack Palance plays the title role in *Ebenezer*, a Canadian production with a Western angle: Here, the miser is a land magnate. Cicely Tyson portrays Ebenita Scrooge in *Ms. Scrooge*, a modern story placing her in an executive position at a loan company. *A Diva's Christmas Carol* revolves around pop music star Ebony Scrooge, portrayed by Vanessa Williams.

Scrooge's name is not used but the plotline of *A Christmas Carol* is evident in offerings such as *An American Christmas Carol, A Carol Christmas, A Nashville Christmas Carol* and *Carol for Another Christmas*. The storyline has been used for a Jewish character on Yom Kippur in *Northern Exposure* and a womanizer at his brother's wedding in *Ghosts of Girlfriends Past*.

There are also movies where Christmas is not the overriding theme, but the holiday season is present in at least one scene and sometimes throughout the story. *The Winning Team, Citizen Kane, Goodfellas, Full Metal Jacket, Batman Returns, Rocky, Catch Me If You Can* and *Lethal Weapon* come to mind.

This book is meant to guide the reader to laws, cases, regulations and legal principles connected to movies and TV productions with a Christmas theme, but it is not a substitute for legal advice. For counsel, an attorney should be consulted to further examine the nuances described. There are six categories: Christmas and Money, Christmas and the Military, Christmas and the Home, Christmas and Crime, Christmas and Copyrights and Christmas and Government.

Christmas and Money

Ebenezer Scrooge's miserliness defines his persona. It's presumed that Scrooge is a private banker in *A Christmas Carol*, but there's no compassion for charitable endeavors or his customers. His fellow townspeople have nary a good word to say about the man who disdains Christmas and anyone who celebrates its merriment with smiling faces and warm hearts. But does he commit usury in his dealings or is he simply a hard-nosed banker acting without regard to common courtesy and social contracts?

Set during a Christmas office party in a Los Angeles skyscraper, *Die Hard* initially portrays the villains as terrorists. Their declared sociopolitical motives obfuscate the rather simple objective: stealing hundreds of millions of dollars in bearer bonds from the company's vault. A case regarding this investment asset is discussed.

Jim Henson and his team produced the TV special *Emmet Otter's Jug-Band Christmas*, based on a children's picture book of the same name. Although the characters are not nearly as famous as others in the Henson stable (Big Bird, Elmo, Miss Piggy), they offer a wonderful take on O. Henry's "The Gift of the Magi" with Kermit the Frog introducing the story and giving a wrap-up at the end. Emmet and his mother separately enter a talent contest held on Christmas Eve, which inspired me to research the legal intricacies of these types of events.

CBS's *The Beverly Hillbillies* aired for nine seasons (1962 to 1971) and existed in the same fictional universe as *Petticoat Junction* and *Green Acres*. In the first episode, Jed Clampett shoots at animals on his land in the Ozark Mountains and hits oil, which leads to a bounty of $25 million from an oil company; Beverly Hills becomes the new home for the Clampett family. Milburn Drysdale, president of Commerce Bank of Beverly

Hills, oversees the Clampett fortune and goes to great lengths to satisfy their desires, curb their impulses and retain their fortune while helping it grow. In a Christmas episode, the Clampetts head home for the holiday; Drysdale misunderstands the situation. His assessment: They're leaving Beverly Hills for good and taking their fortune with them. Drysdale appears to provide the service of private banking, which has strict rules for the financial community to follow.

On *Cheers*, the stories largely take place in a Boston bar, also named Cheers. From 1982 to 1993, TV audiences enjoyed the comedy of bar regulars, recurring characters and guest stars elevating Cheers to the ranks of its pub peers in popular culture: the Regal Beagle on *Three's Company*; Duffy's Tavern on *Duffy's Tavern*; Kelsey's Bar on *All in the Family*; the Boar's Nest on *The Dukes of Hazzard*; Danny's on *Quincy, M.E.* During a holiday season, Cheers' owner, ex–Red Sox pitcher Sam Malone, gets a gift that even Santa Claus couldn't deliver when a generous offer is extended to purchase the bar. The legal principle of an offer is explored.

It's a Wonderful Life strikes an emotional chord emphasizing community, resilience and self-worth. A key scene takes place in the early 1930s, when fears of bank collapses sent customers from Pasadena to Poughkeepsie running to withdraw their money. These "bank runs" caused several banks to fold, a scenario paralleled when the Bailey Brothers Building & Loan stands on the verge of bankruptcy until George and Mary Bailey use their honeymoon gifts of cash totaling $2000 to keep it afloat. This scene prompted me to look at the genesis, history and impact of bank runs during the Great Depression including the creation of the Federal Deposit Insurance Corporation to protect bank customers.

Christmas and the Military

The West Wing showcases the fictional administration of President Josiah "Jed" Bartlet. Government affairs became story material: calculating the census, selecting a person to be on a stamp, nominating a Supreme Court justice, invoking the 25th Amendment, and negotiating a budget with Congress are among the examples. A gut-wrenching Christmas episode involves communications director Toby Ziegler taking on the responsibility for a proper military funeral honoring a homeless Korean War veteran. The legalities are covered along with information about Arlington National Cemetery, presumably where the funeral takes place.

World War II has been—and will continue to be—a terrific source for Hollywood producers with the subgenre of Allied prisoners of war depicted in films including *The Bridge on the River Kwai*, *The Great Escape*,

Von Ryan's Express and *King Rat*. *Stalag 17* (1953), based on the Broadway play of the same name, depicts a mystery in an Allied POW camp governed by a German colonel: A spy masquerading as a prisoner inside one of the barracks feeds the colonel information about escape attempts. The story begins a few days before Christmas with the story's climax taking place on December 25. One scene involves an inspector trying to determine whether the prisoners are being treated according to the rules in the Geneva Convention, which ignited my curiosity about this landmark law protecting POWs.

M*A*S*H portrays the surgeons treating wounded patients at an Army hospital during the Korean War. Produced by 20th Century Fox Television and airing on CBS from 1972 to 1983, *M*A*S*H* introduced medical terms to a mass audience such as end-to-end anastomosis, arterial graft and Battalion Aid Station. In the Christmas episode "Death Takes a Holiday," two doctors and a nurse try to sustain a patient with a grave head wound past midnight so his kids won't have to think of Christmas as the day their daddy died. When he doesn't survive, the medical team makes a pact to falsify the record. It's a fascinating example of law in the military arena.

All in the Family premiered on CBS in 1971, captivating audiences with a raw quality combining humor with headlines. Current events were fair game for the writers. Airing on Christmas Day 1976, "The Draft Dodger" features an explosive performance by Carroll O'Connor as Archie Bunker when he realizes that a guest of his daughter and son-in-law for the family's Christmas dinner went to Canada to escape the draft for military service in the Vietnam War. In addition to being a terrific portrayal of an emotional reaction to a hot-button issue, it's also a gateway for a discussion of the legal issues surrounding the draft, the eventual withdrawal of American troops from Vietnam and a presidential pardon of draft dodgers.

Operation Christmas Drop began during the presidency of Harry S. Truman. It provides the background for *Operation Christmas Drop*, a romantic comedy on Netflix educating audiences on the creation, challenges and benefits of this venture in goodwill that drops care packages to remote islands in the South Pacific every Christmas season. The military's legal authority for this humanitarian project is examined.

Christmas and the Home

The Man Who Came to Dinner is a hilarious look at the conflict arising when an erudite, pretentious commentator of international renown visits a Midwestern family's home during the Christmas season, slips on the front steps and must recover there. It's a jumping-off point for an analysis concerning the legal implications of negligence.

The Apartment is either a comedy with dramatic moments or a drama with comedic moments, depending on your perspective. While it belongs in the genres of films about business and films about New York City, it also falls squarely into the Christmas category given the highly significant scenes taking place with the holiday aura on full display. For a legal discussion, the story inspires a look at the intricacies of subletting apartments in the city that never sleeps.

A blockbuster during the holiday season of 1990, *Home Alone* vaulted ten-year-old Macauley Culkin to worldwide stardom. When his character, Kevin McAllister, is mistakenly left behind by his family during a Christmas trip to Paris, he defends his home against two bandits who are to burglary what the Keystone Kops were to law enforcement. Kevin's antics cause bodily harm but give rise to a legal argument of defending the home.

The Andy Griffith Show portrays quirky characters in Mayberry, North Carolina, a fictional burg secured by Sheriff Andy Taylor and his cousin, Deputy Barney Fife. It ran for eight seasons from 1960 to 1968 and spawned two spinoffs, *Gomer Pyle U.S.M.C.* and *Mayberry R.F.D.*—in addition to the 1986 reunion TV movie *Return to Mayberry*. An *Andy Griffith* episode focuses on the Christmas season battle between a department store owner and a local moonshiner whose sales cut into the store's profits. Moonshining is against the law, both in Mayberry and real life.

'Tis the season for house decorations and neighbors competing against each other for the most alluring abode in *Deck the Halls*. But what are the potential legal implications of stealing electricity from a neighbor to power an extraordinary display?

Christmas and Crime

The Sopranos highlights the clashes that arise when a New Jersey Mafia boss tries to keep peace within his work family and his real family. A cloud constantly hovers over Tony Soprano: the possibility that one of his underlings could become a witness for the federal government in a prosecution against him for racketeering, murder, and other crimes. During a Christmas season gathering, Tony flashes back to the previous holiday season and deduces the turning point when his associate Salvatore "Big Pussy" Bonpensiero joined the ranks of government informants. The FBI promised witness protection—a cornerstone of federal prosecutions—as part of his deal.

With a beginning that establishes the holiday season, *L.A. Confidential* portrays the seedy underside of Los Angeles in a 1953 setting. A show business tabloid, corrupt cops, prostitution, narcotics and murder combine for a compelling story with locations including the Pacific Electric Building, Crossroads of the World and Boardner's. Definitions of murder and prostitution are deliberated along with the legal problems of Mickey Cohen, a local underworld figure and a major factor in the film.

A variety of television shows depict the New York Police Department. Maybe you prefer the dry humor on *Barney Miller*, the cinematic quality of *Naked City* or the arc of Andy Sipowicz from foul-mouthed alcoholic detective to respected leader of Manhattan's 15th Precinct detective squad on *NYPD Blue*. For two seasons, NBC aired the comedic exploits of a Bronx precinct in *Car 54, Where Are You?* In the episode "Christmas at the 53rd," the cops put on a talent show for the neighborhood, not only exemplifying a police department strengthening bonds with the population that it protects and serves but also offering an opportunity to lay out the reasons, challenges and power of community policing in real-world situations.

Song titles make powerful movie titles. *Stand by Me*, *Pretty Woman*, *My Girl*, *Take This Job and Shove It*, *Sea of Love* and *Can't Buy Me Love* are notable. For the holiday season, *White Christmas* stands out; Irving Berlin's song caps the 1954 movie's climactic scene taking place on Christmas Eve. The issue of resisting arrest plays an important role in the storyline.

The Grinch ranks with Ebenezer Scrooge in *A Christmas Carol* and Henry Potter in *It's a Wonderful Life* as exemplars of anti–Christmas bias, evidenced by stealing presents from the residents of Whoville in CBS's *How the Grinch Stole Christmas!* (1966). Like Scrooge but unlike Potter, the Grinch has a change of heart in this half-hour animated special narrated by Boris Karloff. His dastardly actions open the door for an examination of several criminal violations including burglary, larceny and trespass.

A Christmas Story provides a catharsis for every kid who's ever been bullied when Ralphie Parker unleashes his frustration on Scut Farkus. While there might be a valid argument that Ralphie committed assault, the scenario is examined for a self-defense claim.

Christmas and Copyrights

Love Actually premiered in 2003, two years after the 9/11 attacks. It gave the world a much-needed dose of hope, love and optimism. The song "Love Is All Around" begins the film with a holiday tweak: It's retitled "Christmas Is All Around." Besides being an undercurrent of the various storylines, the song allows a legal analysis of the intricacies involving music publishing rights and recorded songs.

Jack Frost also begins with a song. An amazing rendition of "Frosty the Snowman" by a rhythm and blues band inspires a look at the legal requirements for music publishing rights and live performances.

The Bishop's Wife shows the power of Dudley, an angel guiding a bishop during his travails in financing a new cathedral and allaying the concerns of his biggest benefactor—a widow who demands that her donation for the construction also honor her dead husband. But Dudley discovers that her true love was a poor musician who died young. Dudley plays one of the musician's compositions on the harp and persuades the widow to let the bishop use her donation to help those in need. His performance underscores a look at the complexities involving rights to unpublished works.

Christmas and Government

Parks and Recreation depicts a staff of well-meaning though somewhat eccentric civil servants in a medium-sized Indiana town. Leslie Knope, deputy director of the Parks and Recreation Department, runs for higher office; a Christmas episode featuring campaign gifts leads to the issue of gifts to state government employees.

Michael J. Fox became a star on TV's *Family Ties* playing the role of politically conservative teenager Alex P. Keaton, whose admiration for President Ronald Reagan got a nod in the episode "Miracle in Columbus." It's revealed that he sent jams and jellies to Mr. and Mrs. Reagan for Christmas. While the scene is played for laughs, it also triggers an interesting exploration of the legal implications surrounding gifts to the president of the United States.

Is there a Santa Claus? In *Miracle on 34th Street*, a courtroom scene highlighted by a lawyer emphasizes mail delivery as a foundation of American society and uses the legal authority of the United States Postal Service to prove that his client is "the one and only Santa Claus." The creation, power, and development of the nation's postal service are addressed.

Christmas provides the background for an episode of *Seinfeld* with a storyline in which Elaine dates Ned, a Communist. His political ideology affects Kramer, who works as a department store Santa Claus during the holiday season and takes his newfound knowledge to instruct children. Meanwhile, Elaine's confrontation with a Chinese restaurant worker results in banishment from the restaurant, a status that Ned laments because his father, also a Communist, met with his friends at that restaurant when they were blacklisted. This gives the foundation for chronicling the blacklists of the 1950s generated by investigations, accusations and hearings in Washington, D.C. Senator Joe McCarthy and the House on Un-American Activities Committee spearheaded parallel hearings fueling what came to be known as the Red Scare.

CHRISTMAS AND MONEY

1

Usury (*A Christmas Carol*)

Ebenezer Scrooge has venom that a rattlesnake would envy. But is he a criminal, too?

Film portrayals of Scrooge transforming into a man of tremendous generosity, warmth and sensitivity align with Charles Dickens' *A Christmas Carol*, which implies that the miserly 19th-century Londoner works as a private banker serving customers who cannot get loans elsewhere. His service may require higher rates of interest compared to his competitors.[1]

There are clues regarding Scrooge's profession. Dickens writes, "Once upon a time—of all the good days in the year, on Christmas Eve—old Scrooge sat busy in his counting-house." A "counting-house" is an office where a company conducts its business operations, including bookkeeping and accounting.[2]

Jacob Marley's ghost indicates the banking profession when he warns Scrooge about the impending visits from three spirits—the Ghost of Christmas Past, the Ghost of Christmas Present, the Ghost of Christmas Yet to Come—while expressing remorse for his actions when he was alive: "I cannot rest, I cannot stay, I cannot linger anywhere. My spirit never walked beyond our counting-house—mark me!—in life my spirit never roved beyond the narrow limits of our money-changing hole; and weary journeys lie before me!"[3]

Dickens' use of "money-changing hole" refers to banking operations. It's apparent that Scrooge and Marley conducted a money-lending operation; Scrooge continued the business after his partner's death.

When the Ghost of Christmas Yet to Come visits Scrooge, we see more evidence of banking. The spirit shows Scrooge the nonchalance that others feel toward a certain man's death, not yet revealing that Scrooge is the subject of conversation. Scrooge challenges the spirit to show "any person in the town, who feels emotion caused by this man's death" and the spirit complies by revealing a young married couple in debt:

> At length the long-expected knock was heard. She hurried to the door, and met her husband; a man whose face was care-worn and depressed, though he was

young. There was a remarkable expression in it now; a kind of serious delight of which he felt ashamed, and which he struggled to repress.[4]

Upon learning that their creditor has died, the wife responds with gladness and a touch of regret. Dickens writes, "She was a mild and patient creature if her face spoke truth; but she was thankful in her soul to hear it, and she said so, with clasped hands. She prayed forgiveness the next moment, and was sorry; but the first was the emotion of her heart."

Then she asks her husband about the money that they owe to Scrooge. "To whom will our debt be transferred?"

"I don't know," he responds. "But before that time we shall be ready with the money; and even though we were not, it would be bad fortune indeed to find so merciless a creditor in his successor. We may sleep to-night with light hearts, Caroline!"[5]

Dickens' description of Scrooge implies loans with excessive rates and intractable deadlines. "Usury" is the legal term for the practice of loaning money at rates above those permitted by law. Cornell Law School's Legal Information Institute states, "The three essential elements of usury are: (1) a loan or forbearance of money, (2) an agreement for a return of the money in all events; and (3) an agreement to pay more than the legal rate of interest for its use."[6]

Dickens does not mention, indicate or even hint that Scrooge commits usury but we can infer its commission. Moreover, a similar interpretation of the narrative can be found in Garden City Publishing Company's republished version of *A Christmas Carol* in 1938 with additional elements (illustrations by Everett Shinn and an introduction by Lionel Barrymore).

Familiar as the Scrooge-ish Henry Potter in *It's a Wonderful Life*, Barrymore played Scrooge in *A Christmas Carol* radio specials during the 1930s and 1940s. He viewed Scrooge as a usurious bastard:

> There, in the dank seclusion, is the penurious Scrooge, money-monger, scavenging coppers, jaundiced with the reflections from his gold, a symbol of flinty avarice, gouging deeper, bolstering up his tunnel's walls with usurious gains, spearing his pen into the emaciated bodies that are in need, adjusting a transfusion of the little blood that remains to them to flow into Scrooge's strongbox through the tube of the quill. The incision is scratched with their affixed names on a bond. Now let them bleed![7]

Wearing the cloak of usury as another piece of his Scrooge "costume" during radio performances of *A Christmas Carol*, Barrymore also explained his metamorphosis into Scrooge:

> Once at the stage door (for I am now Scrooge) I pause to compute the interest on a note held by me against a draper. Three years now overdue and no part payments or even a response has come from this man that my loan has saved

from bankruptcy. I will denounce him. I will sell him up. The amount of the principal and interest is staggering. I will have no mercy. He should have foreseen the day of judgment.[8]

Moneylending dates back to the Judeo-Christian foundation of society. Exodus 22:25 states, "If thou lend money to any of My people, even to the poor with thee, thou shalt not be to him as a creditor; neither shall ye lay upon him interest."[9]

But the banking concept rests on an opposing view. Interest on loans is a revenue-generating device for the banking industry. Usury laws cap the interest rate, but that ceiling will vary from state to state. So, what happens when a national bank located in one state issues a credit card with an interest rate differing from the maximum allowed in another state? In 1978, the U.S. Supreme Court answered this question in *Marquette National Bank of Minneapolis vs. First of Omaha Service Corporation* when it issued a unanimous 9–0 decision ruling that the First National Bank of Omaha did not violate federal law when it solicited people from Minnesota.[10]

A bank located in one state can use that state's allowable interest rate in its transactions in other states. The First National Bank of Omaha, according to the Supreme Court, transacted commerce across state lines into Minnesota and within the bounds of the National Bank Act: "The question before us is therefore narrowed to whether Omaha Bank and its BankAmericard program are 'located' in Nebraska and for that reason entitled to charge its Minnesota customers the rate of interest authorized by Nebraska law."[11]

Here, the Supreme Court looked at the Congressional intent behind the National Bank Act and found fodder favoring the Nebraska concern. "Omaha Bank cannot be deprived of this location merely because it is extending credit to residents of a foreign State. Minnesota residents were always free to visit Nebraska and receive loans in that State."

Marquette National Bank of Minneapolis argued that exporting interest rates will "impair the ability of States to enact effective usury laws."[12] While this may be a cause for concern, the Supreme Court saw it as a policy matter for the legislature rather than a legal matter for the judiciary:

> This impairment may, in fact, be accentuated by the ease with which interstate credit is available by mail through the use of modern credit cards. But the protection of state usury laws is an issue of legislative policy, and any plea to alter [the relevant law] to further that end is better addressed to the wisdom of Congress than to the judgment of this Court.[13]

There were no credit cards in Scrooge's time, though he would have likely pursued that business had it existed and consequently enhanced his firm's coffers. However, Dickens' tale underscores the theme that success matters little if it's not used to help those in need; Marley's ghost instructs Scrooge on this point when he expresses remorse for wasted opportunities. Scrooge reminds the apparition of his acumen and achievements: "But you were always a good man of business, Jacob."[14]

Responding with shame, Marley emphasizes the lack of consideration where money overshadowed magnanimity: "Business! Mankind was my business. The common welfare was my business; charity, mercy, forbearance, and benevolence, were, all, my business. The dealings of my trade were but a drop of water in the comprehensive ocean of my business!"[15]

At this early point in *A Christmas Carol*, Scrooge is miserable in the truest sense of the word: able miser. The ablest. He ignores emotions and glorifies money for money's sake. His words are cruel. His actions, heartless. He is vindictive, spiteful and downright nasty. With a glacial heart and an absent soul, Scrooge exemplifies the dismalness of mankind:

> Oh! But he was a tight-fisted hand at the grindstone, Scrooge! a squeezing, wrenching, grasping, scraping, clutching, covetous old sinner! Hard and sharp as flint, from which no steel had ever struck out generous fire; secret, and self-contained, and solitary as an oyster.[16]

Clearly, Scrooge looks at money as the means and the ends of existence. Usurious or close to it, he fulfilled his purpose of lending money to make more money. Niceties, particularly during the holiday season, are easily ignored. When two charity collectors seek Scrooge's donation, the banker dismisses them: "It's not my business. It's enough for a man to understand his own business, and not to interfere with other people's. Mine occupies me constantly. Good afternoon, gentlemen!"[17]

When Scrooge's nephew Freddie invites him to a Christmas party, Scrooge focuses on the lack of material success rather than the friendly gesture: "Merry Christmas! what right have you to be merry? what reason have you to be merry? You're poor enough."[18] When Freddie asks Scrooge not to be cross, Scrooge responds with practicality absent compassion:

> What else can I be when I live in such a world of fools as this Merry Christmas! Out upon merry Christmas. What's Christmas time to you but a time for paying bills without money; a time for finding yourself a year older, and not an hour richer; a time for balancing your books and having every item in 'em through a round dozen of months presented dead against you.[19]

Scrooge's business philosophy interferes with the populist notion of business existing to serve a public need rather than shareholders; but slavish devotion to the bottom line results in a hollow life, the precise point of *A Christmas Carol*. No friends. No substantive emotional connections. Not even fine sustenance to assuage his misery as Scrooge prefers instead to subsist on a menu fit for a pawn—gruel consumed near a weak fire. Affordability is not an issue. Scrooge is miserable. Therefore, he lives miserably. Or vice versa.

Still, Dickens does not provide concrete evidence that Scrooge commits usury or other criminal acts. When the Ghost of Christmas Yet to Come reveals the town's leaders discussing his future passing, Scrooge immediately recognizes them: "He knew these men, also, perfectly. They were men of business: very wealthy, and of great importance. He had made a point always of standing well in their esteem: in a business point of view, that is; strictly in a business point of view."[20]

Apparently, the town's business leaders tolerated Scrooge because of his commerce.

Perhaps they occasionally needed loans from him.

Perhaps they realized that Scrooge's business allowed customers to have money to purchase goods and services.

Perhaps they realized that a strong business attracts other strong businesses.

Ebenezer Scrooge. Guilty of ignorance, lack of compassion and disregard for charity until three ghostly prosecutors made their case against him. After realizing his sins, he received redemption.

2

Bearer Bonds (*Die Hard*)

Hans Gruber would have felt right at home with John Dillinger, Willie Sutton and Jesse James.

In *Die Hard*, Gruber is a robber leading a not-so-merry group of bandits targeting $640 million of negotiable bearer bonds housed in the vault at Nakatomi Corporation's office—Nakatomi Plaza, a skyscraper in Century City, California. They use Nakatomi's Christmas Eve party as a cover, masquerading as terrorists taking hostages until their political demands are met; explosives will cause the FBI to think that they die after detonation. Consequently, agents will not search for Gruber, his gang or the bonds. "When they touch down, we'll blow the roof," explains Gruber. "They'll spend a month sifting through the rubble and by the time they figure out what went wrong, we'll be sitting on a beach earning 20 percent."[1]

Gruber's focus shows financial insight. Legally, the person physically possessing a bearer bond owns it, but the possessor may not necessarily be the person who purchased the bond. Once Gruber and his team steal the bearer bonds, they will be free to sell or trade them without pesky annoyances, for example, identification. Gruber hints at his true intention when he demands the vault code from Nakatomi executive Joseph Takagi.

"You want money? What kind of terrorists are you?"

"Who said we were terrorists?"

Gruber furthers the illusion when he demands the liberation of political prisoners: "The following people are to be released from their captors: In Northern Ireland, the seven members of the New Provo Front. In Canada, the five imprisoned leaders of Liberté de Quebec. In Sri Lanka, the nine members of the Asian Dawn movement."

When a cohort mouths "Asian Dawn" as a question, Gruber replies, "I read about them in *Time* magazine."

Bearer bonds became the focus of a 2002 case with more holes than a colander in the United States Court of Appeals for the Seventh Circuit. In *Marques vs. Federal Reserve Bank of Chicago*, Santiago Marques and Carey Portman claimed that the Federal Reserve Bank of Chicago issued

2. Bearer Bonds (Die Hard)

$25 billion in bearer bonds in 1934 and, in turn, received 1665 metric tons of gold. Marques and Portman wanted redemption of the bonds—as successors to the owners—for face value plus four percent simple interest. The bonds had matured in 1965. Total amount of claim: $100 billion.[2]

Judge Richard Posner, no stranger to outspokenness, wrote the court's decision with his trademark clarity, humor and reasoning:

> The suit is preposterous. There is no record of any such bond issue, and as the national debt of the United States was only $28 billion in 1934, as a year later the entire stock of gold owned by the United States had a value of only $9 billion, and as no securities issue by a U.S. government entity exceeded $100 million before 1940, the claim that in 1934 a federal reserve bank issued bonds that virtually doubled the national debt and added $25 billion in gold to the government's gold holdings can only cause one to laugh.[3]

Posner continued to slice apart the plaintiffs' argument:

> What is more (not that more is needed), although the price at which the government bought gold was fixed at $35 an ounce effective at the beginning of that year, the plaintiffs are claiming that the federal reserve bank bought gold from their predecessors at a price of $467.02 an ounce. The plaintiffs further undermine their case by arguing that there is an international conspiracy to deny the validity of these bonds, a conspiracy pursuant to which the plaintiffs' documents expert, who certified the genuineness of the bonds (in an unsworn and evasive report), has been repeatedly arrested and then released without charges being filed.[4]

Their wacky scheme went awry in the courts with a price tag of embarrassment from Posner's words. Gruber *et al.* used force to obtain Nakatomi's bearer bonds, but that proves to be a costly endeavor paid in blood because of John McClane, an NYPD detective arriving to visit a Nakatomi executive: his estranged wife Holly, who has resumed using her maiden name Gennero. When Gruber and his gang take the employees hostage, McClane evades detection by being in a rest room. Outnumbered, outgunned and maybe even outdated, McClane ultimately defeats the terrorists in a skyscraper thriller based on the 1979 novel *Nothing Lasts Forever* by Roderick Thorp.

A massively successful movie in the summer of 1988, *Die Hard* spawned four sequels. Though Bruce Willis had fame because of his co-starring role in ABC's comedy-drama *Moonlighting* with Cybill Shepherd, he became an international celebrity with *Die Hard*. In Wilmington, Delaware's *Evening Journal*, Harry F. Themal underscored the actor's range:

> [T]he role [of McClane] requires an ability to show emotions and not just expertise with a variety of firepower. What has been largely overlooked after

Willis' TV stardom is his grounding in the theater. He took any acting job he could find, no matter how small, even the chorus and one-liners of a dinner theater. Eventually it led to 100 performances in the New York lead of Sam Shepard's *Fool for Love*.[5]

Timing is everything. *Die Hard* coincided with the popular culture zeitgeist's 1980s tough-guy genre arguably inspired by the aura of President Ronald Reagan—a former film actor turned California governor turned plain-speaking, tough-talking president of the United States. Reagan's image-makers had America believing he bled red, white and blue. Rugged. Patriotic. Strong.

Reagan's star provided a steady light in the Hollywood galaxy from the 1930s to the 1960s, but certainly not a supernova like counterparts Henry Fonda, Clark Gable, Humphrey Bogart and Cary Grant. Often appearing as the second male lead, Reagan used the always-a-best-man-never-a-groom image as fodder for a tale that he often told about the reaction when movie mogul Jack Warner learned of his plan to run for governor of California: "No. Jimmy Stewart for governor. Reagan for best friend."[6]

The fortieth president often embraced the cowboy image as part of his political persona and a reminder of his Hollywood résumé when he wasn't chaperoning a chimp in *Bedtime for Bonzo* or imploring Notre Dame's football coach to win just one for the Gipper in *Knute Rockne, All-American*. The political journey he plotted for himself ended at 1600 Pennsylvania Avenue.

Gruber mocks the Western film genre when he talks to McClane, whose character lineage can be traced to Marshal Will Kane in *High Noon* and other stories where one man defends a group of innocent people against a gang of thieves, rustlers and killers.

Yippee-ki-yay.

3

Contests (*Emmet Otter's Jug-Band Christmas*)

O. Henry's "Gift of the Magi" takes an anthropomorphic turn in the 1977 Canadian television special *Emmet Otter's Jug-Band Christmas*, produced by Jim Henson and based on Russell Hoban's 1971 book. Paul Williams wrote the songs; HBO first aired the special in 1978.[1]

Frogtown Hollow residents Emmet and his mom Alice can't afford Christmas presents with their meager earnings from his odd jobs and her laundry business. Unbeknownst to each other, they enter a talent contest on Christmas Eve in nearby Waterville hoping to win the $50 prize money. Items of importance are sacrificed in their quest. Emmet puts a hole in his mom's washtub so he can play washtub bass in his jug-band; Alice sells the tool chest that Emmet uses for his odd jobs so she can buy material for a dress to wear for her singing performance.

Neither wins. That distinction goes to the River Bottom Nightmare Band, a gang of bullies with a hard rock song. But on the way home, Alice sings with Emmet and his friends. Doc Bullfrog hears the impromptu performance and offers them a job at his restaurant.

Legally, a talent contest is a contest of skill, such as singing or other types of performing, and the winner is determined by a judge or a tribunal. This paradigm occurs in *Emmet Otter's Jug-Band Christmas*: A trio of judges, including Doc Bullfrog, assesses the performers. It's obviously an amateur talent contest emphasized by Waterville mayor Harrison Fox, the master of ceremonies, admonishing Emmet and his friends practicing outside: "You there. Aren't you in this contest? You get in here this minute. You might miss your entrance and we want this show to look professional."

An amateur talent contest is a staple of American culture, with rules varying from jurisdiction to jurisdiction. For example, the 2024 Minnesota State Fair Amateur Talent Contest Entry Rules state:

> All acts are required to use the sound system and sound technician provided by the Minnesota State Fair. The State Fair provides microphones, monitors

and a piano. All other instruments and amplifiers must be provided by [the] act, if needed. The State Fair does not allow microphones supplied by the act.[2]

Emmet and his friends would also need to qualify as amateurs to compete in the Waterville contest. Being a professional performer would negate their entry, but the definition of "professional" may vary. Tennessee's 2024 Dyer County Fair offers these restrictions for the Mid–South Fair Youth Talent Contest:

> A professional entertainer is hereby defined as one who earns more than one-half his/her normal living expenses by performing in any of the categories of competition participating in the Mid-South Fair Youth Talent Contest (i.e., a professional dancer may not compete in the Youth Talent Contest as an amateur singer, musician, etc.).

Further, it states that the "professional" label will apply if the performer is a union member or "has signed a contract with a professional agent or manager who is paid with either salary or commission for services rendered in securing employment in the entertainment field." Also, singing on a record "released for commercial distribution through normal retail outlets" bestows professional status.[3]

The Rice County Fair Talent Show in Minnesota qualifies its definition of "professional" with an exception:

> The contest is open to all amateur entertainers. Professionals are NOT permitted to compete. This includes Union musicians and anyone whose principal source of income is from their talent. Compensation for performing at weddings, etc. does not constitute principal source of income.[4]

The Arkansas State Fair Youth Contest also specifies how a contestant can get paid for performing but still be considered an amateur:

> The purpose of the Arkansas State Fair Youth Talent Contest is to discover, develop, and encourage talent in the youth of Arkansas. It is designed primarily for amateur talent, but any act which qualifies otherwise is eligible even if the act received pay at some time EXCEPT where the person(s) are engaged in the entertainment business or paid instructors of the Arts. Acts that may be considered professional should be brought to the attention of the County/District Fair Manager who will be responsible for notifying the State Youth Talent Director. The State Youth Talent Director will determine the contestant's eligibility. Their decision will be final.[5]

The Northeast Arkansas District Fair's Youth Talent Contest is designed primarily for amateur talent, "but any act which qualifies otherwise is eligible even if the act received pay at some time EXCEPT where the person(s) are actually engaged in the entertainment business or paid instructors of the Arts."[6]

3. *Contests* (Emmet Otter's Jug-Band Christmas)   27

Decorum will be a common topic. It is likely that the behavior of the River Bottom Nightmare Band violates decorum rules in most, if not all, amateur talent contests because the lyrics in its song indicate rebellion, bullying and nastiness. The 2024 Southeast Alaska State Fair states that it is

> a family friendly environment; no explicit content/lyrics are allowed. Any entry that is uncooperative, under the influence of drugs or alcohol, uses profanity, or displays any actions perceived unacceptable by the Fair Event Staff or the competition judges, will be disqualified from the competition and removed from the venue.[7]

The River Bottom Nightmare Band's lack of propriety during the performance is unsurprising. In their first scene, the members mock Kermit the Frog and steal his scarf. They later create chaos in a music store while looking for instruments and frustrating the owner.

Contestants may need to satisfy a residency requirement as talent contests are often used to promote local pride. The Iroquois County Fair Talent Contest Rules state, "Contestants must live in Illinois or students enrolled in an educational/recreational facility in Illinois are also permitted to compete." Further, there's a marital status rule: "All contestants must be single and never married and a resident of Illinois or regularly enrolled in a school located in Illinois."[8]

North Texas Performing Arts has a similar provision in its North Texas' Got Talent extravaganza: "Contestants must reside in the North Texas region (defined for this contest as any zip code north of Waco, Texas)."[9]

Sometimes a talent contest will have separate categories for children, teens and adults. The age requirements for the first two categories may change from contest to contest but there will undoubtedly be a provision for permission from a parent or guardian.

Contest organizers will have other legal concerns including insurance to mitigate financial damages that may arise from a physical injury sustained by a performer or attendee. A good insurance policy will hopefully prevent litigation. Also, if the organizers want to use images of performers in promotional materials concerning the contest, then the performer application will likely have a clause agreeing that the contest organizers have the right to use the names and likenesses of contestants in promotions. This permission is key for the contest to get media coverage in print and video outlets.

There's also the matter of judging. A tribunal respected by the community ensures fairness in evaluating talent, an aura of good will, and a guard against potential claims of wrongdoing such as bribery, favoritism or nepotism. As a precaution, a talent contest may have a provision forbidding relatives of the judges from competing.

The talent contest segment is the climax of *Emmet Otter's Jug-Band Christmas*, highlighted by the music. In a 2017 *Smithsonian* article, folk music teacher Skip Landt homed in on the importance of music to *Emmet Otter*:

> For young kids, early introduction to music is through simple melodies and rhythms, as their sensibilities are not yet developed enough to appreciate more complex forms. Here you have the lives and simple values of the destitute but happy Otter family, two generations living and singing in harmony are contrasted to the rowdy thug-led River Bottom band and their clashing music.[10]

In 2011, Noel Murray's review for the AV Club website noted the story's music:

> Longtime Muppet sympathizer Paul Williams wrote the songs for *Emmet Otter*, and much like his soundtrack for the Brian De Palma horror musical *Phantom of the Paradise*, Williams' *Emmet Otter* songs are such a skilled pastiche of eclectic styles that they sound like they've always existed. Whether Emmet and his Ma are laying down some foreshadowing by singing the hootenanny-ready "Ain't No Hole in the Washtub" or Emmet and his buddies are extolling the virtues of jug-band music in the peppy "Barbeque," Williams' music never sounds out of place. Even when Emmet and Ma are challenged at the talent show by ... the River Bottom Nightmare Band, Williams produces a credible version of Alice Cooper–style shock-rock.[11]

Williams stated, "I've never had songs write themselves as quickly as these songs wrote themselves. And some of the titles are [from] the book. With *Emmet Otter's Jug-Band Christmas*, you have this remarkable tale that has such depth."[12]

4

Private Banking
(*The Beverly Hillbillies*)

In *The Beverly Hillbillies*, Ozark mountaineer Jed Clampett uproots his family after striking oil on his property and receiving $25 million for his land from the OK Oil Company. He packs up a ramshackle jalopy with his daughter Elly May, nephew Jethro Bodine and mother-in-law Daisy Moses aka Granny. Their destination: a city defined by its mansions, millionaires and magnificence—Beverly Hills, California.

CBS premiered *The Beverly Hillbillies* on September 26, 1962, with Buddy Ebsen as Jed; it aired for nine seasons. "I think the basic comment on our show is that the Clampetts are good people, overlooked by the sophisticated element in society," Ebsen said in a 1963 interview. "They believe in honesty, thrift, kindness, and friendship. But in today's sophisticated world, such virtues as thrift have become outmoded."[1]

A representative of the oil company assists the Clampetts by finding a bank in which the $25 million can be deposited; Jed places his fortune with Commerce Bank of Beverly Hills. Milburn Drysdale, bank president, moves the family next door to him in a maneuver to cement his relationship with the well-meaning but simple-minded folks. In addition to the royalties provided by OK Oil's wells, the Clampetts' portfolio grows under Drysdale's leadership, including a movie studio—Mammoth Studios—and other investments.

Drysdale had a keen eye for financial matters. The 1963 episode "The Clampetts Are Overdrawn" informs us that the Clampetts are worth $36,422,000.[2] Granny says the account is worth $68 million in "The Clampett Curse," which aired on January 25, 1967; Drysdale gives a precise figure of $68,415,000 in another scene. It grew further. The Internet Movie Database states that the Clampetts were worth $100 million when CBS aired the last *Beverly Hillbillies* episode in 1971.[3]

Dedication to the blue-chip client is underscored in the first-season episode "Home for Christmas." When the Clampetts pack some belongings

Beverly Hills had several opportunities for banking customers in the 1960s as seen in this photograph of Wilshire Boulevard circa 1960 with four banks clustered near each other (courtesy Los Angeles Public Library/*Los Angeles Herald Examiner* Photo Collection).

and load their jalopy for a trip to spend the holiday season in the Ozarks, Drysdale's assistant hears about it and informs her boss. They misinterpret the situation as the Clampetts moving out for good and taking their money with them; Drysdale is upset and protective. "Why? What could have happened? Who offended them? Whoever it was, I'll have them driven out of Beverly Hills!"[4]

Instead of the family traveling on the road for hundreds of miles, Drysdale arranges a TWA flight; it's just one example of the bank president catering to the needs of his most important client.

The Clampetts' fortune under Drysdale can be classified as a matter of private banking. *Forbes* states that among several roles, a private banker "helps craft a financial strategy and reduces friction when connecting you to additional banking resources." Additionally, the banker (or bankers) responsible for the account must also monitor and analyze the markets, investment risks and economic information to inform the financial strategy. Changes to the investments can be made depending on "major life changes and tumultuous seasons in the market."[5]

4. Private Banking (The Beverly Hillbillies)

The private banker must also need to be cognizant of tax laws as they affect investments, estate planning and charitable donations. However, a private banker is not usually a lawyer or an accountant. A referral may be made but the hiring decision will belong to the customer.

Forbes also points out that the term "private banking" can be misleading if it's used for a service such as a checking account with increased perquisites:

> Eligibility requirements for bona fide private banking vary from bank to bank. But the services are generally reserved for high-net-worth individuals, which, according to the Securities and Exchange Commission means people with at least $750,000 in investable assets.

Money in a checking or savings account would qualify. Also, CDs, stocks, bonds and mutual funds belong in this category. But a bank may have a different benchmark than its competitors regarding the financial threshold. *Forbes* states that "some private banks require investable assets of $5 million or $10 million for account consideration."[6]

In banking parlance, Drysdale would be considered a relationship manager. He's involved in the personal and financial affairs of the Clampett clan, servicing their needs whatever they may be. "A central point of contact, such as a relationship manager, usually acts as a liaison between the customer and the bank and facilitates the customer's use of the bank's financial services and products," explains the Federal Deposit Insurance Corporation.[7]

For a private banker to have a strong relationship with the bank's high net worth customers, effective communication is paramount. Questions need to be asked regarding the customers' goals beyond increasing wealth through investments. A philanthropic customer ought to know about the tax implications of donating cash vs. a stock whose value has risen since its purchase. Further, there's the option of creating a charitable remainder trust where beneficiaries receive dividends from stocks and a designated charity gets the principal when the donor dies.

A private banking customer may want to use money to seed investments in start-up companies, enhance a collection of highly valued items such as paintings, or provide family members with enough money to ensure that the wealth can be protected through several generations. Whatever the desire, the private banker's advice depends on constant communication with the customer because goals, needs and economic factors will change.

Bankers don't work for free, though. Charging a percentage of the assets managed is one option, but the banker may additionally charge a commission for investments made. There's also a promotional benefit: A private banker may ask an existing customer to provide a reference to a prospective customer.

A bank must satisfy several requirements regarding an account of this nature; a due diligence program protects the customers. For the Clampetts, Drysdale needs to know "the identity of all nominal and beneficial owners" of the account, plus fulfill his obligation to manage the assets under his authority. The Code of Federal Regulations stipulates,

> Review the activity of the account to ensure that it is consistent with the information obtained about the client's source of funds, and with the stated purpose and expected use of the account, as needed to guard against money laundering, and to report, in accordance with applicable law and regulation, any known or suspected money laundering or suspicious activity conducted to, from, or through a private banking account.[8]

Drysdale and his colleagues would also need to follow the mandates of recordkeeping outlined in Title 12 of the United States Code. Assuming that Commerce Bank of Beverly Hills belongs to the classification of "insured depository institutions," it is subject to maintaining

> a microfilm or other reproduction of each check, draft, or similar instrument drawn on it and presented to it for payment; and a record of each check, draft, or similar instrument received by it for deposit or collection, together with an identification of the party for whose account it is to be deposited.[9]

Customers with the level of wealth that allows them private banking status will likely get exclusive benefits, including a higher interest on a savings account or certificate of deposit. The Wells Fargo website explains that its Private Bank CD has certain requirements:

> The Private Bank CD requires a $500,000 minimum opening deposit and a minimum of $500,000 in money new to Wells Fargo. Funds new to Wells Fargo must be from sources outside of Wells Fargo Bank, N.A., or its affiliates. Maximum deposit allowed per client in one or multiple The Private Bank CDs is $25,000,000. Only consumer and consumer trust entities are eligible.[10]

With a banker of Drysdale's stature, there's a weighty consideration to keep him employed at Commerce Bank of Beverly Hills: If he leaves for another financial institution, it's likely that his clients will follow with their accounts. One example happened in 2024, when Merrill Lynch hired a top private banker from JPMorgan Chase in Los Angeles. L. Brandt Daniel had been in the banking industry for more than 20 years; his tenure with JPMorgan Chase dated back to 2015.

An article in advisorhub.com explained the importance of bankers at Daniel's level to their employers and mentioned his list of clients worth $4.3 billion in 2020, citing a *Barron's* article. However, the advisorhub.com piece also claims that the figure "had more than doubled" since that time and cited two unnamed sources. It continued:

> Bankers, who are paid a combination of salary and bonus, fit with the firm's strategy to cross-sell wealthy customers on banking, estate planning and other services beyond their investments. They also bring a Rolodex of ultra-wealthy customers, although transferring assets is more challenging given garden leave restrictions and customers' close ties to the parent bank.[11]

Further, the article explains that J.P. Morgan Private Bank managed assets worth more than $970 billion. The figure for Merrill Lynch—part of Bank of America—was $3.2 trillion. Either figure would have brought tears of joy to the eyes of Milburn Drysdale.[12]

CBS canceled *The Beverly Hillbillies* in 1971 along with the other rural comedies *Green Acres*, *Petticoat Junction* and *Mayberry R.F.D.* It can be presumed from the 1981 TV movie *Return of the Beverly Hillbillies* that Drysdale effectively spearheaded Jed Clampett's estate planning by coalescing a team to provide top-notch advice in the legal and tax arenas. Jed moved back to his cabin in the Ozarks after bestowing gargantuan financial gifts to Jethro and Elly May. Drysdale's former assistant Jane Hathaway (aka Miss Jane) now works for the federal government and visits the Clampett patriarch to get a sample of Granny's moonshine, aka White Lightning, because she thinks it can be a viable alternative fuel and help solve the energy crisis. Drysdale is neither mentioned nor seen.[13]

When Jed asks Miss Jane if she saw Jethro and Elly May, she responds affirmatively and mentions Jed's "generosity." This refers to a financial gift, which allowed Jethro to become a successful producer at Mammoth. Because of her love for animals, Elly May opened a zoo; it's logical to presume that she used part of her bounty to fund this venture. Granny has died, so a thesis can be made that Jed sold the Beverly Hills mansion after her death, gifted most— or all—of his fortune to his daughter and nephew, and returned to the Ozarks where he is content to pass the time hunting and fishing.

On May 24, 1993, CBS aired the one-hour special *The Legend of the Beverly Hillbillies*. Filmed in a mockumentary style, it reveals that Drysdale embezzled most of the Clampett fortune. Jed Clampett holds no grudge. Miss Hathaway received witness protection for her testimony to put the banker in prison. But after Jed is finished being interviewed by a reporter, he puts a stick in the ground and oil comes to the surface, indicating another potential windfall.[14]

In a promotional interview, Ebsen talked about the series' cancellation—beginning by saying that he didn't know if this was a true story:

> Bill Paley used to be the head of CBS, and Mrs. Bill Paley used to go to the Colony Restaurant in New York. There was a certain amount of cattiness among

their friends. She walked in one day and one of her friends said, "Here comes the wife of the owner of the hillbilly network." Shortly after that, they began canceling all of them.[15]

During the 1993 holiday season, a movie version of *The Beverly Hillbillies* starring Jim Varney and Dabney Coleman increased Jed Clampett's payout from the oil to $1 billion. Ebsen makes a cameo appearance as his other famous TV character, private investigator Barnaby Jones. (CBS aired *Barnaby Jones* from 1973 to 1980.[16])

5

Offer (*Cheers*)

A bar can be a safe haven where one can find a warm welcome. From 1982 to 1993, NBC aired *Cheers*, a prime-time sitcom depicting a Boston watering hole with the same name as the series and a friendly atmosphere, immediately apparent from the theme song: "Where Everybody Knows Your Name." An ample part of the show's charm emerged from the constant flow of eccentric guests entering the domain owned by former Red Sox relief pitcher Sam "Mayday" Malone.

One such guest was Eric Finch in the episode "The Spy Who Came In for a Cold One," which takes place during the Christmas season. The first shot is a closeup of the wreath on the back of the bar's entrance door; Cheers regular Norm Peterson mentions a holiday trip to Maine with his wife.[1]

Initially claiming to be a spy, Finch fascinates Norm, waitress Carla Tortelli, and Cheers' resident know-it-all Cliff Clavin, but then he suffers a debunking of his persona. Diane Chambers, the bar's highly educated and sometimes snobby waitress, sees through the Englishman's veneer, then wilts when he claims to be a poet. Disappointment follows when she telephones a professor to read him one of Finch's passages only to find out that it's been plagiarized.

For the *coup de grâce*, Finch thanks Sam and the gang for allowing him to entertain himself at their expense and offers to buy the bar. Thinking it's just another trick, Sam jokingly says that his price is $1 million. Then he raises it to $2 million. Finch agrees. Crestfallen from being duped, Diane intervenes and rips up Finch's check.

And that's when the wheels fall off the wagon for the Cheers group. Finch's chauffeur enters and informs the masquerader that his plane is ready at the airport. It turns out that Finch is wealthy. Really wealthy. Sam lets Diane off the hook when she apologizes for preventing him from receiving a windfall. He would never sell Cheers.

Was Finch's offer valid? Most certainly. In his offer for Cheers, he presented something of value or "consideration" in legal terms. Cornell Law

School's Legal Information Institute defines "offer" as: "part of contract negotiations where a party agrees to do or not do something in exchange for consideration. An offer must be stated and delivered in a way that would lead a reasonable person to expect a binding contract to arise from its acceptance."[2]

In Massachusetts, the definition of offer and acceptance reads in part: "Unless otherwise unambiguously indicated by the language or circumstances, an offer to make a contract shall be construed as inviting acceptance in any manner and by any medium reasonable in the circumstances."[3]

Had Diane curbed her anger and waited a few seconds, it would have been reasonable, if not obvious, to conclude that Finch had the means for a valid offer to buy the bar. There's nothing ambiguous about Finch's intention because signing the check qualifies as an affirmative act conveying his intent to purchase Cheers, though it's clear that his offer is more for frivolity than finance. Finch finds the patrons pleasant and amusing. Therefore, it's a realistic presumption that he neither needs nor wants to add Cheers to his portfolio other than as a place to hang out and possibly tell newcomers some tall tales for his own enjoyment.

Sam might have a valid argument to enforce the offer because he did not authorize Diane to make financial decisions regarding the bar nor did she have the expertise to value it; Finch could have simply given Sam another check for $2 million.

But the check might not be sufficient by itself. A contract would be needed to formalize the offer, Sam's acceptance and the terms. A commercial real estate purchase agreement will include the names of the parties and their mailing addresses in addition to a legal description of Cheers including the address, any improvements that Sam has made, and information about fixtures. In addition, the purchase price will be noted. Finch's offer appears to be all cash, which an agreement would specify and formalize as well as give the buyer the right to inspect the property or have his representatives (such as electricians and plumbers) do it.

Because Finch placed an offer on a bar, he would likely want to know about potential problems involving drainage in addition to disclosures about outstanding debt to service providers and outstanding tabs by the bar patrons. Revelations of legal and financial vulnerabilities could cause a buyer to walk away from the deal.

In the episode "Bad Neighbor Sam," we learn that John Allen Hill—the owner of Melville's, the restaurant upstairs from Cheers—claims ownership of the bar area housing the pool room. But let's assume that the Cheers property and Melville's property are completely separate entities for the sake of a legal discussion; Finch would be prudent to ask if

5. *Offer* (Cheers)

Cheers has any outstanding liens or other encumbrances before buying the property.[4]

The Massachusetts Association of Realtors provides a form for a contract to purchase real estate on its website. The clause on inspections reads:

> The buyer's obligations under this agreement are subject to the right to obtain inspection(s) of the Premises or any aspect thereof, including, but not limited to, home, pest, radon, lead paint, energy usage/efficiency, septic/sewer, water quality, and water drainage by consultant(s) regularly in the business of conducting said inspections, of Buyer's own choosing, and at Buyer's sole cost by [date TBA]. If the results are not satisfactory to Buyer, in Buyer's sole discretion, Buyer shall have the right to give written notice received by the Seller or Seller's agent by 5:00 p.m. on the calendar day after the date set forth above, terminating this agreement. Upon receipt of such notice this agreement shall be void and all monies deposited by the Buyer shall be returned. Failure to provide timely notice of termination shall constitute a waiver. In the event that the Buyer does not exercise the right to have such inspection(s) or to so terminate, the Seller and the listing broker are each released from claims relating to the condition of the Premises that the Buyer or the Buyer's consultants could reasonably have discovered.[5]

The Massachusetts Legislature requires that the parties need to be on board with a purchase agreement before it's recorded, so Sam and Finch would need to take action beyond the acceptance of the check. "No agreement for the purchase and sale of real estate or any extension thereof shall be received for record in any registry of deeds unless such agreement or extension thereof is acknowledged by the parties agreeing to sell such real estate or one of them."[6]

Let's assume that Diane hadn't ripped up the check. Sam would need a reasonable time to consider Finch's offer before accepting, refusing or countering. But the circumstances will dictate what is reasonable. In the 1876 case *Minnesota Linseed Oil Co. vs. Collier White Lead Company*, the analysis concerned an offer by telegraph. The circuit court considered that the parties must either have an understanding or should have an understanding, which will inform reasonableness. Citing from *Farsons on Contracts* in its ruling, the court explained,

> Applying this rule, it seems clear that the intention of the plaintiff, in making the offer by telegraph, to sell an article which fluctuates so much in price, must have been upon the understanding that the acceptance, if at all, should be immediate, and as soon after the receipt of the offer as would give a fair opportunity for consideration.[7]

But if Finch had waived his rights to inspection in favor of an immediate decision by Sam, then an argument can be made that the trade-off was reasonable. Finch would take the risks of unknown defects in the title and property itself plus any debts while Sam would risk not knowing if he could get a better offer for Cheers from Finch through negotiation, or from another buyer.

Sam might also have a cause of action against Diane for interference with prospective contractual relations. Tearing up the check after Finch's offer was a conscious act stemming from her disappointment and a presumed desire to protect Sam from a man whom she considered to be a charlatan. However, she did not have all the facts plus she had neither explicit nor implicit permission to participate in the business dynamic between Finch and Sam.

The *William Mitchell Law Review* article "Interference with Contract in the Competitive Marketplace" (1989) explains that the tort of interference with contracts had been expanded since its origins in ancient Roman law and the subsequent necessity of physical force or threat to back up a claim. Hiring employees from competitors was also a component. According to the article, the tort in the U.S. "extends far beyond the old enticement-of-servant action which was the basis of Lumley vs. Gye. The tort of interference with contract now encompasses virtually every type of contract and economic relationship and the violence requirement no longer exists."[8]

Recent scholarship argues that the offer-acceptance model is outdated, which would render Finch's overt act unnecessary or extraneous to cementing a deal for Sam's bar. The 2015 *California Law Review* article "Offer and Acceptance in Modern Contract Law: A Needless Concept" considers a classical situation involving an offer and acceptance that are "salient" but overshadowed by other acts leading to a valid contract:

> [T]he parties might contemporaneously sign a common document, shake hands, use a series of increasingly certain verbal cues to indicate that they believe themselves to be bound, or allow a third party or computer technology to match them firmly with one another. Moreover, even in cases that may fit factually into the classical offer-and-acceptance paradigm, the model tends to obscure the substantive and interpretive questions that underlie contract formation.[9]

It's an interesting theory, but the offer-acceptance model remains a cornerstone of contract law.

Finch's attempt to buy Cheers is not the only time that Sam received an offer. He later sold Cheers to the Lillian Corporation and left Boston to sail around the world, but returned when the sailboat sank. He worked as an employee and finally got the opportunity to buy Cheers for one dollar when he alerted the company's executives to fraud committed by their colleague Robin Colcord. Sam got some leeway on the price after failing to have a dollar on him or get that amount from anyone in the bar. Final purchase price: 85 cents.[10]

5. *Offer* (Cheers)

NBC premiered *Cheers* on September 30, 1982, in the Thursday night lineup. Although *Cheers* ranked near the bottom of the Nielsen ratings, NBC programming chief Brandon Tartikoff kept the show on the air. Ratings be damned! *Cheers* became a cornerstone of NBC's success in the 1980s, lasting 11 seasons and winning 28 Prime Time Emmys.

When the 90-minute finale aired on May 20, 1993, millions of America's TV viewers tuned in to see Sam leave the bar to marry Diane, with whom he'd reconnected after six years, only to return without getting hitched. Norm explains that Sam always comes back to his true love. At first, Sam doesn't know the identity of the woman, then he realizes that Norm meant Cheers.

A front-page story in the *Boston Globe* on the day before the finale's broadcast highlights the importance of Boston as the setting for the show:

> The choice of Boston, the Mecca and Medina of fun-seeking undergraduates, was deliberate. Not only could the city's obsession with sports and politics provide script material, but downtown Boston is a neighborhood in itself. *Cheers* is an urban concept, unimaginable in a sunbelt or suburban demographic.[11]

Boston icons solidified the verisimilitude. Speaker of the House of Representatives Tip O'Neill, Senator John Kerry, Governor Michael Dukakis, Ethel Kennedy, Red Sox slugger Wade Boggs, ex–Red Sox pitcher Luis Tiant and Celtics star Kevin McHale appeared on the show. Robert Urich made a cameo in a 1988 episode, coinciding with the 1985–88 run of his Boston-set show *Spenser: For Hire* on ABC.[12]

Cheers' roster of guest stars include actors and actresses who later soared to fame on TV in other roles: Julia Duffy (*Newhart*), Michael Richards (*Seinfeld*), Lisa Kudrow (*Friends*), Fred Dryer (*Hunter*), Leah Remini (*The Kings of Queens*) and Markie Post and Harry Anderson (*Night Court*).[13]

6

Bank Runs, Larceny (*It's a Wonderful Life*)

Bailey Brothers Building & Loan is a bedrock of Bedford Falls in the 1946 Christmas film *It's a Wonderful Life*.[1]

Peter and Billy Bailey started this enterprise in upstate New York at the turn of the 20th century. George and Harry are Peter's sons; Billy has no children. Harry is four years younger than George, who works full time for his father and uncle after graduating from Bedford Falls High School.

At dinner in the Bailey home on the evening of Harry's graduation party, held at the school in 1928, George reminds his father of a plan for the family business: Harry will begin working for Peter while George goes to college. When he graduates, it will be Harry's turn. George complains of "hoarding pennies like a miser" to afford college after most of his friends have already completed their higher education; he goes to Harry's party and gets surprised by the beauty of Mary Hatch, sister of his friend Marty. George and Mary dance together, fall into the swimming pool beneath the gym floor, and enjoy a nice walk afterward, which is when Billy finds them and imparts tragic news: Peter has suffered a stroke (that later proves to be fatal).

With the family in mourning and the future of Bailey Brothers Building & Loan in jeopardy, there is a meeting of the board of directors. Henry F. Potter—presumably the largest depositor in the local bank and a businessman with tentacles reaching into just about every nook and cranny of Bedford Falls except the Bailey firm—criticizes the methods that the Baileys use to determine a borrower's financial fitness. He recommends that its assets be turned over to the receiver. It's implied that the bank has lent a substantial amount of money to the building and loan, so Potter's plan would effectively terminate its operations. George gives a passionate defense of his father and points out the benefit of the family's business for Bedford Falls: "This town needs this measly one-horse institution if only to have someplace where people can come without crawling to Potter!"

6. Bank Runs, Larceny (It's a Wonderful Life)   41

George's monologue persuades the board to continue operating based on one condition: George succeeds his father as its chief executive. Initially dismissive, George acquiesces when he learns that the board will go with Potter's idea if he declines the job. He gives his younger brother the money that he had saved, and gets another emotional wallop when Harry comes home after graduating college with a bride and a job in his father-in-law's company.

Rather than handing over the reins of Bailey Brothers Building & Loan so he can see the world as he always dreamed of doing, George glumly stays in Bedford Falls and continues helping his fellow townspeople buy homes. Encouraged by his mother, he visits Mary; they begin a romance that leads to marriage.

It's logical to infer that the nuptials take place in the last half of 1932 or the first half of 1933. As Ernie the cab driver is taking George and Mary away—probably to the train station to begin their honeymoon—he notices a mob of people. "Don't look now but there's something funny going on over there at the bank, George. I've never really seen one but that's got all the earmarks of being a run."

The scene reflects the harsh reality that bloodied America's banking industry during the Great Depression when depositors "ran" to withdraw their money from banks, prompted by fears of a collapse. If a bank didn't have enough cash in reserves to cover the withdrawals, it went under. Depositors flooded the offices of Bailey Brothers Building & Loan to get their money, frustrating George and putting the institution in a perilous situation. Moreover, Potter takes control of the bank by assuring its executives that he'll keep his deposits there if it closes for a week; if the Bailey firm dissolves, Potter will have a financial monopoly.

Mary suggests using their wedding gifts totaling $2000 to keep the business afloat until the panic subsides; George agrees because of his concern regarding the company's financial stability. Their wedding bounty scheme works with two dollars to spare, giving Bedford Falls a buffer against Potter.

Bank runs made a vicious impact in the Great Depression with around 9000 banks ceasing operations and depositors losing assets amounting to approximately $7 billion. There was no such thing as "too big to fail."[2]

The Bank of United States had a dominant position as the fourth biggest bank in the country. Its collapse not only proved the vulnerability of banking Goliaths but also lit the fuse that decimated a wide array of financial institutions. On December 11, 1930, *The New York Times* reported that a false rumor caused a panic in a Bronx branch; this triggered runs at other branches. Police estimated a range of between 20,000 and 25,000 people in the vicinity but noted that "most of them [were] curious spectators." A bank executive provided an estimate of "about $2,000,000" withdrawn by customers numbering between 2500 and 3000 at the first run.[3]

A day later, Bank of United States stopped operating its 60 branches and turned over its business to New York State's Banking Department; deposits totaled "approximately $160,000,000." The Federal Reserve Bank of New York joined the bank's executives in a meeting that went to four a.m. Consequently, the bank issued a resolution acknowledging rumors leading to "abnormal withdrawals of deposits" and a fear that this trend would continue if the bank stayed open.

Suspending operations affected customers across the board, but the ones without deep pockets suffered the most. Other banks formed a Clearing House to assist them. "Of these $160,000,000 deposits, more than one-half, it was learned, represent 'thrift' deposits, the small savings of comparatively poor people," reported the *Times*. "Bankers who attempted to prevent the closing of the bank were deeply concerned to prevent hardship to these small depositors. It was for this reason that the Clearing House banks offered to lend to the depositors."[4]

Bank of United States had been a force in the finance industry since 1913, funded initially with $100,000. There were 59 branches in four of New York City's five boroughs: 30 in Manhattan, 11 in the Bronx, 17 in Brooklyn and one in Queens. Expansion was in the air in the late 1920s. The bank merged with Central Mercantile Bank and Trust Company in addition to Cosmopolitan Bank in 1928. Mergers with Colonial Bank and Municipal Bank and Trust Company followed in 1929.[5]

A hiatus known as a "bank holiday" dictated at different times by different states took place across the country in the 1930s, allowing customers' concerns to cool off much like Potter's scheme with the Bedford Falls bank. But the combination of the 1929 Wall Street crash and subsequent closures like Bank of United States required a demonstrable solution for America's banking industry to restore confidence, stability and sustenance.

In 1930 and 1931, bank closures devastated the finance industry. When customers lost confidence in the banks that remained, they kept their money at home and created a tangible problem because banks generate revenue by lending money to be paid back with interest. Less money means fewer loans. Plus, banks sat on the money in preexisting accounts.

Gary Richardson of the Federal Reserve Bank of Richmond served as the Federal Reserve System historian from 2012 to 2016. He labels the customers' behavior as hoarding and the banks' actions as accumulating in an article for the Federal Reserve History website explaining a terrifying consequence:

Together, hoarding and accumulating reduced the supply of money, particularly the amount of money in checking accounts, which at the time were the principal means of payment for goods and services. As the stock of money declined, the prices of goods necessarily followed. Deflation harmed the economy in many ways. Deflation forced banks, firms, and debtors into bankruptcy; distorted economic decision-making; reduced consumption; and increased unemployment.[6]

Philadelphia suffered tremendously, losing 30 of 89 banks and trust companies between July 1930 and March 1933. In addition, George Bailey's real-life peers followed with failures of "hundreds of the city's building and loan associations" in the same period; deposits plummeted by 23 percent in a stark symbol of the dour mood across the country.[7]

Franklin D. Roosevelt became America's 32nd president on March 4, 1933, and declared a bank holiday beginning on March 6. Though he projected it to last four days, Roosevelt expanded the period; banks began reopening on March 13.[8]

The evening before the reopening, Roosevelt held his first "fireside chat" on the radio; this tactic of communicating directly with the public proved to be a signature of his administration. He explained how the banking system works regarding deposits, much like George Bailey did during the run on Bailey Brothers Building & Loan. Roosevelt stated,

> [L]et me state the simple fact that when you deposit money in a bank the bank does not put the money into a safe deposit vault. It invests your money in many different forms of credit—bonds, commercial paper, mortgages and many other kinds of loans. In other words, the bank puts your money to work to keep the wheels of industry and of agriculture turning around. A comparatively small part of the money you put into the bank is kept in currency—an amount which in normal times is wholly sufficient to cover the cash needs of the average citizen. In other words, the total amount of all the currency in the country is only a small fraction of the total deposits in all of the banks.[9]

Three months later, Roosevelt signed the Banking Act of 1933 to create the Federal Deposit Insurance Corporation. A temporary plan and a permanent plan were set to begin on January 1, 1934, and July 1, 1934, respectively, with the U.S. Treasury and the dozen Federal Reserve Banks providing capital for the FDIC—$150 million and each bank getting capital stock.

"The temporary plan of deposit insurance initially limited protection to $2500 for each depositor," explains the FDIC on its website. "Banks admitted to insurance under the temporary plan were to be assessed an amount equal to one-half of 1 percent of insurable deposits. One-half of the assessment was payable at once; the rest was payable upon call by the FDIC."[10]

A plan encompassed in the Banking Act of 1935 eclipsed the initial permanent plan. Roosevelt signed it into law on August 23, 1935, establishing an umbrella of safety for each depositor up to $5000 and assuring that "approximately 98 percent of depositors in U.S. banks would be fully covered." Bailey Brothers Building & Loan would have fallen under this protection because the FDIC covers state savings associations, which includes "any building and loan association." This would be welcome news not only to the Baileys but also their customers, from the brash one who demanded $242 of the $2000 to the meek one who asked for $17.50 during the run.[11]

Another financial crisis hits Bailey Brothers Building & Loan on December 24, 1945. Proud of Harry for receiving a Congressional Medal of Honor for his heroic exploits as a Navy pilot in World War II, Billy goes to the bank to deposit $8000 in cash; encounters the wheelchair-bound Potter holding a newspaper; and grabs it to show his nephew's story on the front page. With a full heart and absent mind, Billy places his envelope with $8000 in the newspaper and folds it; Potter snatches back the newspaper. When Billy goes to the teller, he realizes that he no longer has the money and cannot remember where he lost custody; Billy's faulty memory is a running theme throughout the movie. Potter keeps the cash and eyes Billy's movements in the bank lobby to see if he'll recall. He doesn't.

Is Potter vulnerable to a charge of larceny? He neither knows the envelope is in the newspaper when he grabs it from Billy nor takes the money intentionally. However, a Bedford Falls prosecutor would not be affected when applying the concept of "lost property." Larceny encompasses

> a wrongful taking, obtaining or withholding of another's property by acquiring lost property. A person acquires lost property when he exercises control over property of another which he knows to have been lost or mislaid, or to have been delivered under a mistake as to the identity of the recipient or the nature or amount of the property, without taking reasonable measures to return such property to the owner.[12]

Potter knows the real status but keeps the money, thus a larceny charge is appropriate. If he were found to have the stash of cash in his office or home, he could claim a logical though ultimately flimsy defense that he's a busy man with many holdings, so $8000 came from many sources but remains insignificant compared to his bottom line. It would be perjury but there's no evidence in the story that he lies for his own gain. Hard-nosed? Yes. Unethical? That depends on how you define the term.

He's committed to accumulating wealth, sometimes at the expense of his Bedford Falls neighbors. During the run on Bailey Brothers Building & Loan, George uses the term "slums" to describe Potter's properties and points out to one customer: "Joe, you lived in one of his houses, didn't you? Well, have you forgotten? Have you forgotten what he charged you for that broken-down shack?"

George also explains that Potter controls the bus line and the department stores, plus the bank because of his scheme during the run. Had Potter withdrawn his money, it most certainly would have collapsed. But on December 24, 1945, a much different scenario would likely arise for the richest man in Bedford Falls if he's discovered to be larcenous. Billy intended to deposit the eight grand, so the bank is also a victim of Potter's actions. It's reasonable to believe the bank's executives would urge prosecution.

The missing money could result in the collapse of Bailey Brothers Building & Loan. Through Mary's urging, the townspeople come to the rescue and pour into the Bailey home with money, apparently unaware of the circumstances. Mary only told them that George was in trouble; they responded. Additionally, George's childhood friend Sam Wainwright, now a successful businessman, okayed the wiring of funds up to $25,000 once he learned about the plight from Mr. Gower, the town druggist and George's former boss; George worked at the drugstore when he was a kid.

Although Sam's munificence is impressive, it may be a reward for George's insight. On the night that George went to visit Mary, Sam called her and asked to speak to George once he found out his old friend was there. He recalled with great enthusiasm a conversation that took place years before, when George mentioned an article describing the manufacture of plastics from soybeans.

Excited by this prospect, Sam's father has targeted a factory outside Rochester for this operation until George reminds him that the tool and machinery works in Bedford Falls is available to the Wainwright patriarch "for a song" plus labor because "half the town was thrown out of work when they closed down."

When America entered World War II, Sam inflated his accounts further with government contracts because of the plastic needed for planes. His fortune resulted from George's advice. Whether the IRS would classify the $25,000 transfer as an investment, income, gift, reward or loan with no interest depends on how Sam and George describe the infusion.

The financial health of Bailey Brothers Building & Loan thanks to the Christmas Eve bounty gives rise to a reasonable forecast: George *et al.* would have benefited from the post–World War II expansion of suburbia by issuing loans to developers, contractors and homebuyers not only in the environs of Bedford Falls but also in other areas of the Empire State such as Elmira, Syracuse, Rochester, Binghamton and Albany.

While the American economy enjoyed prosperity and suffered

recessions, the FDIC raised the limit on its coverage seven times. These actions would have been welcome news to the Bedford Falls depositors because the likely growth of their accounts in the post–World War II economy would require a commensurate increase in the financial safety net.[13]

FDIC limits on coverage

1933	$2500
1934	$5000
1950	$10,000
1966	$15,000
1969	$20,000
1974	$40,000
1980	$100,000
2010	$250,000

7

Military Funerals
(*The West Wing*)

The West Wing made government work look compelling rather than mundane.

Aaron Sorkin's one-hour drama aired on NBC from 1999 to 2006, overflowing with good-natured people among the senior staff of the fictional Jed Bartlet presidency. A former New Hampshire Congressman and governor, Bartlet is a Democrat with Franklin D. Roosevelt's idealism, Harry Truman's folksiness, John F. Kennedy's inspiration and Bill Clinton's ability to connect with voters on an emotional level.

Nominated for 95 Emmy Awards, *The West Wing* won 26 in its seven-year run and received high praise from critics when it debuted during Clinton's second term, when he was burdened by a sex scandal. In the *Daily News* (New York), David Bianculli wrote,

> Instead of going for the sort of sordid absurdities churned out by the real White House occupants of late, Sorkin pulls back and gives us a fictitious chief executive ... driven more by politics than sexual urges. In tonight's pilot, the most embarrassing thing the President does is ride his bicycle into a tree and, as it turns out, there's a reason even for that.[1]

Pittsburgh Post-Gazette TV critic Rob Owen noted NBC's summer promotion before the fall premiere. "And guess what? It lives up to the hype. *The West Wing* is an intriguing behind-the-scenes drama with moments of dewy-eyed idealism." Political columnist Richard Reeves observed:

> [T]he producers got more right than wrong. The action was a little too frenetic, with choreographed young actors popping in, out and through narrow hallways, but the dialogue caught the wonder and bumbling innocence—and the fatigue—of young people having more power than they would in the real world outside guarded gates.[2]

In the first-season Christmas episode "In Excelsis Deo," communications director Toby Ziegler is called to the scene of a homeless man's death because the police found his business card in the man's jacket pocket; Toby had given the coat to charity. After some probing, Toby learns that the man was a Marine veteran of the Korean War; his brother is also homeless. Leveraging the president's name, Toby ensures that the deceased man gets military funeral honors.

Images of the White House staff gathering to hear a children's choir singing "The Little Drummer Boy" set against the burial ceremony (including the three volleys of shots fired by seven riflemen at Arlington National Cemetery) exemplifies how impactful television can be. Sorkin won an Emmy for the episode.

Veteran character actor Richard Schiff, who played Toby, brought an impressive roster of guest spots on TV: *Brooklyn South*, *The Practice*, *NYPD Blue*, *Chicago Hope*, *ER*, *Murder One*, *Love & War*, *Ally McBeal* and *Murphy Brown*. His previous film credits included *Major League II*, *City Hall*, *Grace of My Heart*, *Volcano* and *Deep Impact*.

More than 20 years after the airing of "In Excelsis Deo," Schiff explained the evolution of Toby and how this episode proved to be a turning point though the original idea differed from the final product:

> It had Toby getting only reluctantly involved. It totally misunderstood him. So [Sorkin] and I sat down and spent three weeks rewriting it. Fortunately, we had the luxury of that time, and we made it work. ...This episode defined the character of Toby for the next six years. And it was important for the show itself.[3]

In a 2013 interview with Washington, D.C., radio host Diane Rehm, Schiff revealed the intricacies in producing the episode:

> You know, I just drove on the way here by the Korean War Memorial and just remembered shooting that whole sequence in the Mall, finding the veteran on the bench and the kiosk, and then shooting that little sequence in the memorial, which apparently is illegal. So we were doing some guerilla filmmaking back then, sneaking shots in the memorial.[4]

On the podcast *West Wing Weekly*, co-hosted by show alumnus Josh Malina, Schiff further explained the development of the story and Sorkin's original intent to have Rob Lowe's character, deputy communications director Sam Seaborn, be the focal point. The rewrite for Toby was not to Schiff's liking.

> I was looking for stuff underneath. And I think [Sorkin] recognized that. And then he wrote something very simple, it's really only four or five scenes, this episode, that I'm in. But that was from the correct perspective, I think. And that's how it evolved into becoming, I think, one of fans' favorite episodes. It doesn't just come out of someone's brain and then it's brilliant. These things have to happen, where someone has a visceral reaction to something that might not be right, and then people go, "Well, [expletive deleted], that makes

sense," and then adjust it. And then it's better than you could have even imagined it would have been from the beginning.[5]

Toby's arrangement of the military funeral relies on using the president's name, though it's an unnecessary tactic. Public Law 106–65 states, "The Secretary of Defense shall ensure that, upon request, a funeral honors detail is provided for the funeral of any veteran." Further, it offers guidance concerning the detail's composition: "At least two members of the funeral honors detail for a veteran's funeral shall be members of the armed forces, at least one of whom shall be a member of the armed force of which the veteran was a member."[6]

In the scene where Toby explains the situation to President Bartlet, he mentions that the veteran was a Marine with the second of the seventh. Presumably, this refers to the Second Battalion, Seventh Marines, part of the First Marine Division. Today, the Seventh Regiment is based at Marine Corps Air Ground Combat Center in Twentynine Palms, California. According to the Marines website,

> The 1st, 5th and 7th Marine Regiments each consist of one headquarters company and four infantry battalions, with one battalion deployed outside the continental United States at all times. The infantry battalions are the basic tactical units the regiment uses to accomplish its mission of locating, closing with and destroying the enemy by fire and maneuver.[7]

It can be inferred that Toby's passion for giving the veteran a rightful, patriotic ceremony is sourced in the terrifying action that the soldier saw during his Korean War service. For example, a sequence described in the U.S. Marines compendium *A Brief History of the 7th Marines* involves the Second Battalion fighting the North Korean Army and trying to capture "a vital hill" after five attempts failed. Led by Corporal Lee H. Phillips, the Marines took the hill:

> A furious counterattack followed. Greatly outnumbered, Corporal Phillips rallied his men and stopped the enemy with grenades and rifle fire. The enemy counterattacked again. With only two other Marines left, the thrust was repulsed. The 20-year-old Georgian in spite of heavy enemy fire emerged victorious and uninjured. Fate eventually caught up with him for he died in combat less than 4 weeks later.[8]

Seven rifles are fired in the "In Excelsis Deo" funeral scene, which adds realism to the story. The U.S. Navy's website describes the purpose of the Firing Party, a group of seven riflemen who perform this ritual at Arlington National Cemetery's naval funerals:

> A burst of volume and energy during an otherwise somber and quiet ceremony, this historic salute delivers a powerful emotional charge to all who attend. The Firing Party endeavors to execute this salute in three separate and

Arlington National Cemetery conducts between 24 and 27 funeral services each weekday, according to the cemetery's website. There are no funeral services on the weekend (Arlington National Cemetery).

clean volleys of seven rifles firing at the same exact moment, as though three cannon rounds were fired.

It is an honor to be selected for the Firing Party, which presents a tremendous responsibility for precision, teamwork and concentration. Further, the Navy describes the incredible attention to detail required for this maneuver that punctuates the funeral ceremony:

> The sound of a single rifle firing late is unmistakable and to the riflemen of the Ceremonial Guard Firing Party, unacceptable. The Firing Party trains daily and relentlessly in order to synchronize their movements. One rhythmic motion of seven index fingers on seven separate triggers is the product of the numerous motions performed immediately prior to the salute and the countless hours of training endured in order for each member to be eligible to perform as a rifleman in the Firing Party.[9]

Protocol dictates that an American flag be presented to the deceased veteran's next of kin. But if there is none found, or if nobody in that category claims it, there is an alternative. A request can be made by "a friend or associate of the deceased veteran."[10]

When the flag is presented by a military service member, words of appreciation are uttered. In 2012, the Defense Department created a template that must be followed:

7. Military Funerals (The West Wing)

On behalf of the president of the United States, (the United States Army; the United States Marine Corps; the United States Navy; the United States Air Force, or the United States Coast Guard), and a grateful nation, please accept this flag as a symbol of our appreciation for your loved one's honorable and faithful service.[11]

In addition, "Taps" is played. The ritual dates back to 1891 but it became codified for military funerals by the National Defense Authorization Act in the fiscal year of 2000. While a live bugler certainly adds a sense of drama, a facsimile is permissible either by a recording played on an audio system or a "ceremonial bugle," described as "an electronic device that fits directly inside the bell portion of a bugle."[12]

Military service members comprise a community of pride. They are selfless. Giving your fellow servicemen or servicewomen a proper sendoff is an honor not only for the deceased but for the participants in the ceremony. In a 2022 interview, Captain Joseph Biggie emphasized this unique piece of Americana and revealed how the ceremony affects his job with the 412th Civil Affairs Battalion (Airborne) in Columbus, Ohio, where he leads an Army Reserve funeral honors team:

> This job is important to me because every single one of us has dedicated time to our country knowing that when it's time for us to pass away, the legacy of service we've created for our families and country, as well as our bodily remains, are taken care of by our respective branch of service. When I pass on, I would want the same respect given to my widow and my family. I make sure that everyone on my team has that same dignity, honor and respect that a family deserves to be given when we do a service.[13]

Toby's dedication to honoring a deceased veteran is backed by the law but also his moral duty. Though dismayed at the initial nonchalance of the police regarding the death before realizing that the deceased served his country, Toby takes action to give the veteran a rightful and legal burial ceremony instead of complaining about the plight of the homeless.

Respect for the military is seen again in *The West Wing* when Sam investigates a claim that a woman's grandfather was a Russian spy working at a high level in the U.S. government in the 1940s. Initially skeptical, Sam learns that the man committed espionage and takes great offense at the idea of a civil servant betraying his country. Using a phrase from Lincoln's Gettysburg Address to underscore his fury, Sam exclaims to a colleague:

> It was high treason, and it mattered a great deal! This country is an idea, and one that's lit the world for two centuries, and treason against that idea is not just a crime against the living! This ground holds the graves of people who died for it, who gave what Lincoln called the last full measure of devotion. Of fidelity.[14]

Amen.

8

The Geneva Convention, Copyright Infringement (*Stalag 17*)

All is not as it appears to be in the 1953 film *Stalag 17* starring William Holden.[1] This film was based on the same-name Broadway play written by Donald Bevan and Edmund Trzcinsky, who based the story on their experiences as prisoners of war in World War II.

Stalag 17 is set in a POW camp near the Danube River just a few days before Christmas 1944. Germans rule with iron fists and they have a secret weapon: a spy masquerading as an American prisoner, who reports to the German overseers about the prisoners' escape attempts and other forbidden actions.

There are 75 men in Barracks 4, where J.J. Sefton is a smooth-talking, fast-thinking operator dealing with the camp's guards for trinkets and luxuries, such as time and access to visit with Russian women nearby. His condescension inspires distrust among his fellow prisoners, who think that Sefton revealed information about a recent escape attempt by two soldiers (killed by guards as they fled).

Lt. James Dunbar and Sergeant Bagradian are captured and assimilated into Sefton's barracks. Bagradian praises Dunbar, who blew up a German munitions train by lighting a cigarette and putting it inside a book of matches as a time-delayed incendiary device. Stalag 17's commander, Oberst von Scherbach, interrogates Dunbar but has no proof regarding the explosion; part of the interrogation involves denying sleep.

Meanwhile, the tension between Sefton and the other prisoners increases when a guard confiscates their hidden radio; they believe Sefton squealed about its location in the barracks and beat him as a punishment. Hoffy, the head of Barracks 4, engineers a scheme that creates mass confusion when the camp's guards are about to transfer Dunbar to the SS officers who will accompany him to another site, presumably for more

8. The Geneva Convention, Copyright Infringement (Stalag 17)

questioning (possibly complemented by torture). An improvised smoke bomb allows the prisoners to create a chaotic situation, and Hoffy ushers Dunbar to a hiding spot—the water tower.

Sefton discovers that the spy in Barracks 4 is Price, the security chief who claims to be from Cleveland. Through a fast quiz about the date and time of the Pearl Harbor attack, it's revealed that Price was having dinner when Japanese pilots assaulted the U.S. Navy. Sefton points out that it was lunch time in Cleveland but dinner time in Berlin; he deduces that Price grew up in Cleveland, then went to Germany when the war began so he could help the Fatherland. Sefton's fellow prisoners are convinced.

Once the barracks scourge, Sefton leverages his newfound respect to get a green light for the film's climax: getting Dunbar out of the water tower, using wire cutters to create an opening in the barbed wire fence, and escaping from the camp. The prisoners create a distraction by tying tin cups to Price and throwing him into the compound; he draws spotlights and gunshots from the camp's guards. The scheme is successful. Price is killed; Sefton and Dunbar escape.

There was only one successful escape from the real Stalag 17-B. It happened at the beginning of 1945 thanks to a flight engineer named Ned Handy, once dragged to a shed by a guard who assaulted him. "In January 1945, he swapped identities with Frank Grey, an American POW wanted by the Gestapo for prior escapes, and helped Grey slip away," wrote Eric Ethier in the magazine *America in World War II*. "Grey ultimately reached Yugoslavia, where anti–Nazi partisans assisted him."[2]

Stalag 17 director Billy Wilder talked with fellow director Cameron Crowe about the movie for *Vanity Fair* in 1999 and noted the rescue of Dunbar punctuating Sefton's arc: villain, hero, then something in between. "And he only does it because the mother of the lieutenant who is captured is a rich woman, and he's gonna get $10,000. *He's no hero*, he's a black-market dealer—a good character, and wonderfully played by Holden."[3]

New York Times film critic Bosley Crowther also lauded Holden's portrayal, which earned the Academy Award for Best Actor:

> [A]s a consequence of this character, there emerges something in this film that considerably underscores the drama. It is a cynical sort of display of effectiveness in a group dilemma of a selfish philosophy and approach. It isn't pretty, but it is realistic—another comment on the shabbiness of war. It goes with a certain hollow jesting about the Geneva conventions and the Red Cross.[4]

Crowther's mention of the Red Cross and Geneva Convention refers to scenes involving a Red Cross inspector ensuring that the prisoners are treated humanely. The Geneva Convention originated in 1864 thanks to the International Committee of the Red Cross coordinating participation by several governments. "This treaty obliged armies to care for wounded soldiers, whatever side they were on, and introduced a unified emblem for the medical services: a red cross on a white background," explains the committee. There were updates to the convention in 1906, 1929 and 1949.[5]

Inspection of Barracks 4 reveals that the prisoners will be fed a meal of bean soup with a ham hock. But the ham hock is not in the pot. This moment indicates that the preparation of the prisoners' food does not reach the baseline required by the Geneva Convention, which states, "The food ration of prisoners of war shall be equal in quantity and quality to that of troops at base camps."[6]

Guards distribute new, clean blankets to project an image that the prisoners are being treated well. Hoffy notes, "Yeah, yeah. We know. We had 'em last year. Five minutes after the Geneva man was gone, the blankets were gone." This action may violate another convention rule: "Clothing, underwear and footwear shall be supplied to prisoners of war by the detaining Power. The regular replacement and repair of such articles shall be assured."[7]

Denying sleep to Dunbar is arguably a tactic that violates the Geneva Convention. The section about capture of prisoners states in part,

> No coercion may be used on prisoners to secure information relative to the condition of their army or country. Prisoners who refuse to answer may not be threatened, insulted, or exposed to unpleasant or disadvantageous treatment of any kind whatever.[8]

During the inspection, the men of Barracks 4 are silent about their treatment by the stalag's leaders and guards, but Hoffy mentions that Dunbar has been taken from the barracks and offers appreciation if the inspector would look into it. Claiming that Dunbar is not a prisoner but a saboteur because of the train explosion, von Scherbach maintains that the inspector is out of his jurisdiction. Dunbar denies making a time bomb and mentions that he got searched by Stalag 17's guards. "And the way you search your prisoners, it does sound rather unlikely," states the inspector.

It's a standoff ending with von Scherbach ignoring the Geneva Convention inspector's warning that a war crimes commission will be created after hostilities cease; Dunbar remains in the custody of von Scherbach.

There were other instances of abuse amounting to coercion in *Stalag 17*. When Dunbar goes missing, the audience learns from the narration provided by Cookie—Sefton's sidekick—that von Scherbach used tear gas in all the barracks to try and smoke out Dunbar; additionally, he ordered every prisoner to stand for six hours until Dunbar's location was revealed. Until Hoffy okayed Sefton to be Dunbar's liberator, only he knew that Dunbar hid in the water tower.

8. The Geneva Convention, Copyright Infringement (Stalag 17)   55

The inspector's forecast was correct. Three weeks after Vice President Harry S. Truman ascended to the presidency in 1945, he appointed Justice Robert S. Jackson to oversee prosecution of war crimes for the United States through Executive Order 9547. Jackson and his fellow prosecutors tried 199 defendants in what became known as the Nuremberg Trials. Their efforts resulted in 161 convictions and 37 death sentences.[9]

A scene showing the prisoners getting letters from home tracks with the Geneva Convention rule on mail:

> Letters and consignments of money or valuables, as well as parcels by post intended for prisoners of war or dispatched by them, either directly, or by the mediation of the information bureaus provided for in Article 77, shall be exempt from all postal duties in the countries of origin and destination, as well as in the countries they pass through.[10]

Article 77 governs the authority and responsibility of an information bureau, including receiving details concerning capture of the prisoners, "allowing it quickly to advise the families concerned, and informing it of the official addresses to which families may write to prisoners."[11]

The Malmedy Massacre is an example of Germany breaking the Geneva Convention's rules. On December 17, 1944, SS troops slaughtered more than 70 American prisoners of war near Malmedy, Belgium; they violated Article 2 of the convention's General Provisions section:

> Prisoners of war are in the power of the hostile Power, but not of the individuals or corps who have captured them. They must at all times be humanely treated and protected, particularly against acts of violence, insults and public curiosity. Measures of reprisal against them are prohibited.[12]

Historian Fred Borch III points out that a court convened by the U.S. military conducted a trial of 74 Germans, resulting in 73 guilty verdicts for the Malmedy violence. Sentences: 43 hanging deaths, 22 life terms in prison, and eight terms varying between 10 and 20 years. "However, no one was actually put to death, and by Christmas 1956, all the convicted men had been released from prison." Further, Borch notes that the prosecution had nearly 100 written sworn statements connecting the SS officers to the slaughters, plus eyewitness accounts from Belgian and German civilians. "The testimony, especially of the German witnesses, was designed to prove that the killing of the American POWs and Belgian civilians was premeditated because it had been part of a conspiracy or common design."[13]

There was another horrific example of German military conduct on January 31, 1945. Evacuating Stalag III-C because of the Russian army's imminent encroachment led to prisoners being killed in the crossfire between Russian and German soldiers on a day with vicious winter weather. The American Graves Registration Command researched the incident; according to the National World War II Museum,

> AGRC teams did determine that 22 American POWs were killed and almost 50 were wounded in the incident; the actual number might be higher. For decades after the war, several of the deceased remained categorized as "unrecoverable" as their remains could not be located despite prodigious work undertaken by AGRC in the immediate postwar years.[14]

American soldiers in World War II had a manual—*Rules of Land Warfare*—which begins with an explanation about the boundaries within which wars are fought:

> Among civilized nations the conduct of war is regulated by certain well-established rules known as the rules or laws of war. These rules cover and regulate warfare both on land and sea. Those which pertain particularly to war on land are called the rules of land warfare.[15]

In the Pacific Theater, Japanese treatment of American prisoners of war also reached brutal levels in direct contravention of accepted rules. The Truman Library Institute reveals,

> While no nation, Allied or Axis, ended the war with a spotless record, Japanese troops gained notoriety for their cruelty toward prisoners. Early in the war, Japan had pledged to follow the protocols of the 1929 Geneva Convention—which forbade mistreatment of POWs—but Japanese leaders violated this agreement, encouraging their soldiers to brutalize enemy captives. Japanese troops used some POWs for bayonet practice, tortured and starved others, and forced many to perform hard labor. Nearly one-third of American POWs held by the Japanese died in captivity.[16]

Hostilities in Europe ceased when Germany formally surrendered on May 8, 1945. Japan surrendered on August 15, and the formalities took place aboard the USS *Missouri* in Tokyo Bay on September 2. World War II was the last military conflict where the U.S. Congress declared war, a legal authority stemming from Article I, Section 8, of the Constitution: "The Congress shall have Power to ... declare War, grant letters of Marque and Reprisal, and make Rules concerning Captures on Land and Water."[17]

On December 7, 1941, the Japanese attack on Pearl Harbor led the U.S. to declare war on Japan on December 8 at the urging of President Franklin Roosevelt; the House of Representatives voted 388–1 while the Senate had a unanimous vote of 82–0. Three days later, Germany and Italy declared war on the U.S.; Roosevelt asked Congress to respond with a declaration of war against Germany because of its belligerent behavior including submarines attacking merchant ships and a declaration against Italy. "Never before has there been a greater challenge to life, liberty and civilization," the president wrote in his message.[18]

8. The Geneva Convention, Copyright Infringement (Stalag 17) 57

The House of Representatives affirmed with a 393–0 vote complemented by the Senate's 88–0 vote regarding Germany; unanimous decisions happened with the declaration of war against Italy on the same day with 399–0 and 90–0 tallies. However, Roosevelt had issued a "shoot-on-sight" order for the Navy in early September, three months before the Pearl Harbor attack. The USS *Greer*, a destroyer ship, followed the German submarine U-652 near Iceland and the Germans attacked; *Greer*'s captain responded by ordering the release of depth charges which damaged U-652. The Navy says that Roosevelt's order commanded it "to attack any ship threatening U.S. shipping or foreign shipping under escort."[19]

Stalag 17 stands out among films set during World War II with a terrific display of the claustrophobic atmosphere in a POW camp and the necessary camaraderie to combat it. In addition to the Geneva Convention, it prompts examination of another legal issue: copyright infringement and *Hogan's Heroes*.

Airing on CBS from 1965 to 1971, *Hogan's Heroes* revolves around the Allied prisoners led by Colonel Robert Hogan in Stalag 13. Escapes are common through an "emergency tunnel" but only to fulfill assignments of sabotage they receive from London on a radio system while outsmarting the prison's commandant Wilhelm Klink and a guard, Sergeant Schultz. Hogan and his men also use their barracks as a way station to funnel escaped prisoners to freedom with false documents, currency, German uniforms and other accoutrements.

Bevan and Trczinski sued CBS for copyright infringement, claiming that *Hogan's Heroes* matched the story and characters of the play. Ten years after *Stalag 17* hit movie theaters, they started to develop a TV show and pitched it to CBS, which did not pursue it further but bought the pilot for *Hogan's Heroes* from Bing Crosby Productions at the end of 1964.

There were similarities between *Stalag 17* and *Hogan's Heroes*. Among them: Both were set in a World War II prisoner of war camp; had a guard named Schultz as a main character, and featured escape attempts. In 1971, District Court Judge Harold Tyler in the Southern District of New York failed to find a highly significant overlapping of the two works:

> Contrary to plaintiffs' assertions, *Hogan's Heroes* is virtually empty of the grim, heroic content predominant in *Stalag 17*. The *Hogan's* series is unabashed slapstick; the suspense created revolves around *how* the prisoners will succeed in outwitting the Germans, and not *whether* they will do so and survive, as in the play. Although there are comic interludes in *Stalag 17*, they serve only to heighten and relieve the grim and desperate themes.

Further, the judge found striking differences between both Schultz characters. The Schultz from *Stalag 17* was stern while the *Hogan's Heroes* version was inept, likable and naïve. Regarding the comparison of Sefton to Hogan, it's true that both were fast thinkers. But Sefton was an outcast; Hogan was a leader.[20]

In 1989, a former prisoner of the real Stalag 17 compared the movie and *Hogan's Heroes* with his experience: "We certainly didn't have the freedom you see on the [TV] show but it did depict the spirit we all had. That's what kept us alive. We were just a bunch of young defiant Americans and I never doubted that I would be liberated."[21]

9

Falsifying Military Records (M*A*S*H)

Dr. Benjamin Franklin "Hawkeye" Pierce and his fellow staff members of Mobile Army Surgical Hospital #4077 treated all sorts of patients during the Korean War on *M*A*S*H*, which aired on CBS from 1972 to 1983.

Captain Arnold Chandler thought he was Jesus Christ. USO singer Marina Ryan underwent an appendectomy. Former champion prizefighter "Gentleman Joe" Cavanaugh suffered a stroke during a goodwill tour. Private David Sheridan, a classical pianist, lost effective use of his right hand for his profession; Dr. Charles Emerson Winchester III, a classical music aficionado, persuaded him to follow the path of Paul Wittgenstein, a concert pianist who commissioned music for the left hand after his right hand was amputated during World War I.[1]

The 4077th also treated one of their own—Corporal Radar O'Reilly, assistant to the commanding officer, first Lieutenant Colonel Henry Blake and then Colonel Sherman T. Potter. When Radar laments being a virgin, Hawkeye urges him to take action—go to Seoul, find a woman at the Pink Pagoda, and complete the sexual rite of passage.

After Radar's Jeep is attacked on the trek, the corporal is in a group of wounded soldiers arriving for triage and treatment, which stuns Hawkeye with an emotional force equivalent to a howitzer and triggers epic guilt for the talented, wisecracking surgeon. He later gets drunk and leaves the operating room with a hangover, destroying the naïve, Iowa-bred soldier's idol worship of Hawkeye though the two tentatively mend their friendship.[2]

Private Wendell is a 15-year-old who enlisted with phony papers to prove his bravery to a girl back home; Hawkeye reveals Wendell's secret to the 4077th head nurse, Major Margaret Houlihan, as the first step toward sending him home. In the same episode, Hawkeye's friend Tommy Gillis is working on a book called *You Never Hear the Bullet*. During combat,

Tommy is wounded and then brought to the 4077th but Hawkeye is unable to save his friend.[3]

Hawkeye and fellow surgeon B.J. Hunnicutt join with Margaret one Christmas to treat an American soldier with a head wound courtesy of a sniper in the episode "Death Takes a Holiday." His prognosis is grave; saving his life is impossible. Margaret discovers a photo with an inscription: "To the best husband and daddy in the world. Come home soon. We love you. Scott, Jeannie, and Lynn." B.J. encourages his colleagues to keep the solider alive until midnight, so the family won't have to think of Christmas as the day he died.[4]

They come close. The soldier dies a little before 11:30 p.m., prompting Hawkeye to move the hour hand past 12:00 a.m. "Time of death. 12:05. December 26." B.J. and Margaret concur along with Father Mulcahy, who administers the last rites. "Christmas should be thought of as a day of birth," says the 4077th priest, whose responsibilities as a military chaplain include overseeing last rites for the soldier. Although Father Mulcahy is not a licensed counselor under any legal definition, his role as the camp chaplain includes counseling regarding personal issues for the hospital staff in addition to offering religious and moral insight, overseeing religious services and hearing confessions.[5]

Margaret says, "Falsify a record. That'll be a first for me." Their intent is noble but perhaps also criminal. Article 107 of the Uniform Code of Military Justice states:

> Any person subject to this chapter who, with intent to deceive, signs any false record, return, regulation, order, or other official document, knowing it to be false, or makes any other false official statement knowing it to be false, shall be punished as a court-martial may direct.[6]

United States vs. Spicer states that Article 107 applies

> to statements affecting military functions, a phrase derived from Supreme Court case law, and which encompasses matters within the jurisdiction of the military departments and services. This includes statements based on the standpoint of the speaker, where either the speaker is acting in the line of duty or the statements directly relate to the speaker's official military duties, and statements based on the position of the hearer, when the hearer is either a military member carrying out a military duty or the hearer is a civilian necessarily performing a military function when the statement is made.[7]

Hawkeye, Margaret and B.J. are clearly acting in their official capacity as medical personnel for the U.S. Army because they're tending to the soldier's wounds by relying on their training, experience and instinct. It's within their responsibility to assess whether life functions have ceased.

Falsification of a medical document at a military hospital falls under the UCMJ umbrella, so an investigation could begin if the information leaks beyond the four members of the 4077th staff in the room and Colonel Potter, who knew about their plan. It's not clear at the end of the episode if he knew about the change in the time of death.

A "regular Army" veteran doctor who went by the book, Potter sided with doctors when needless paperwork or policy jeopardized a soldier's health; it's doubtful that he would squeal on his staff if he had knowledge. There's an example of Potter's rule-breaking in the episode "Mr. and Mrs. Who": When the staff members discuss patients suffering from Korean Hemorrhagic Fever in the Post Operative Ward, they are concerned by a mortality rate hovering between 10 and 20 percent. Among the symptoms are high urinary output, high sodium output and loss of appetite.

Regarding sodium intake for these patients, Potter underscores the Army's ban on saline. But a patient, Corporal Shaw, faces a gloomy scenario unless the doctors take a new approach. Potter contravenes the Army's rule and goes with a plan developed by Hawkeye and B.J. Reasoning that Shaw will die if they adhere to the directive, they provide isotonic saline with less than 1 percent saline rather than the usual 5 percent; this will equal the saline amount in blood plasma.[8]

There are other legal issues connected to "Death Takes a Holiday." For example, the soldier's family would receive financial benefits from the Insurance Act of 1951, which aimed to help America's military personnel involved in the Korean War. The U.S. Department of Veterans Affairs says, "During this period, all service members on active duty were covered by $10,000 of free insurance under a program known as Servicemen's Indemnity."[9]

Additionally, the department has a program called Aid and Attendance to help widows of servicemembers killed during the Korean War. To qualify, the deceased soldier must have at least 90 days of active duty but only one day during the period of June 27, 1950, to January 31, 1955. Combat service is not required but the discharge status matters. General, honorable or family hardship are valid for the widow to get benefits; a dishonorable discharge is invalid.

There are marital restrictions as well. Marriage for less than a year and a child; marriage to another veteran who also qualifies for a military service pension, and remarriage on or after January 1, 1971, with termination (through death or divorce) before November 1 are all qualifying circumstances. But the widow needs to consult with the VA to find out if she meets the requirements regarding income and assets. American Veterans Aid explains, "Aid and Attendance is a VA pension for veterans or spouses who need the help of another individual to perform daily living activities (ADLs). It is estimated that nearly half of Americans age 65 and over will need help performing ADLs, and eventually enter a care facility."

ADL activities include assistance with dressing, toileting, eating and long-term care at home or in a facility described as assisted living, skilled nursing or independent living.[10]

Although the actions in "Death Takes a Holiday" are rather benign, falsifying military records is a serious charge that can result in prosecution and a dishonorable discharge. Two examples are prominent. In 2015, federal prosecutors issued an indictment with 50 counts concerning a Department of Veterans Affairs employee at Charlie Norwood VA Medical Center in Augusta, Georgia. They alleged that Cathedral Henderson falsified patients' medical records by claiming that "services have been completed or patient refused services."

The VA emphasized the tremendous concern regarding patient care and wide-ranging impact of the actions alleged. "Alterations of medical records and false statements in these records needlessly expose patients to harm and also undermine the integrity of VA data relied upon by VA decision-makers, who oversee and manage operations," said Quentin G. Aucoin, assistant inspector general for investigations.[11]

Henderson's trial resulted in convictions for violating Title 18, Section 1035(a)(1) and (2), of the United States Code:

> Whoever, in any matter involving a health care benefit program, knowingly and willfully falsifies, conceals, or covers up by any trick, scheme, or device a material fact; or makes any materially false, fictitious, or fraudulent statements or representations, or makes or uses any materially false writing or document knowing the same to contain any materially false, fictitious, or fraudulent statement or entry, in connection with the delivery of or payment for health care benefits, items, or services, shall be fined under this title or imprisoned not more than 5 years, or both.[12]

The U.S. Court of Appeals for the Eleventh Circuit affirmed the district court's finding of guilt on 50 counts. Henderson motioned for a reduced sentence based on Federal Rule of Criminal Procedure 35, but the appellate court noted that it lacked jurisdiction for this issue.

Further, the court explained that even if it had jurisdiction, Henderson fell short of any substantive argument that the district court blundered in the analysis underlining its ruling that his actions created a risk of death or serious bodily injury:

> The Government presented myriad evidence that the false entries in CPRS could have delayed and influenced patient care. Even a delay in order to follow up on the ambiguous consult language could have caused death or serious bodily injury. The Government did not need to show actual evidence of death or serious bodily injury; the enhancement "focuses on the defendant's disregard of risk, rather than on the result."[13]

9. Falsifying Military Records (M*A*S*H)

In 2023, a Rhode Island woman received a federal prison sentence of nearly six years for what the U.S. Attorney's Office described as a "massive fraud scheme by falsely masquerading as a Purple Heart and Bronze Star decorated United States Marine who claimed to have been wounded by an IED in Iraq and to have developed service-related cancer."

She got more than $250,000 from charitable donations and veterans benefits. With a Marine uniform complemented by the Purple Heart and Bronze Star (all purchased on the Internet), she yanked at heartstrings. This not only resulted in a tangible financial boost but also perquisites such as gym memberships, gift cards and physical therapy.[14]

In "Death Takes a Holiday," an effort to postpone a patient's death past Christmas is gallant, not greedy. There's no glory in it for the medical staff, just the notion that they did a noble thing in a horrible situation for a family that they'll never meet. It's an example of *M*A*S*H* showcasing the mental, emotional and physical anguish that doctors and nurses endured in treating battle-wounded soldiers through the Korean War. America's involvement in the Korean War began soon after North Korea's military invaded South Korea on June 25, 1950, but there wasn't a formal declaration of war; its official title was a "police action."

On June 27, President Harry S. Truman issued a statement explaining the hostility and his response regarding the United Nations Security Council resolution calling for the retreat of North Korea's soldiers to the 38th parallel:

> The Security Council called upon all members of the United Nations to render every assistance to the United Nations in the execution of this resolution. In these circumstances I have ordered United States air and sea forces to give the Korean Government troops cover and support.[15]

The U.S. Constitution vests the president with certain powers regarding the military. Article II states in part: "The President shall be Commander in Chief of the Army and Navy of the United States, and of the Militia of the several States, when called into the actual Service of the United States."[16]

But Truman's decision to place American forces alongside those from other nations raised ire in some quarters of Capitol Hill. In 1951, Senator Karl Mundt of South Dakota spoke on the Senate floor about the controversial decision, describing the cause of America's involvement as "a curious extralegal presidential device." It created concern not only for the present situation but also future scenarios where presidents could act unilaterally. Mundt said,

> This is a warning sign which clearly demonstrates what can happen in this closely knit and tempestuous world if we are to accept as permanent and

standing operating procedure the dictum that the president can rightfully involve this country in a shooting war to which we are not committed by treaty obligations, which is of major size and of long endurance, and on which he has neither consulted with Congress nor asked it to declare war in accordance with our ancient and honorable constitutional procedures.[17]

On July 27, 1953, hostilities ceased with the signing of the Armistice Agreement for the Restoration of the South Korean State. Consequences included the withdrawal of military forces and equipment from an area (dubbed the Demilitarized Zone) which separated North and South Korea. American involvement totaled 1.8 million men and women; deaths numbered more than 36,500.[18]

President Dwight Eisenhower, who had defeated Truman in the 1952 election, gave a televised address on July 26 with one section dedicated to the victims both on the battlefield and the home front, like the ones in the photo in "Death Takes a Holiday." Eisenhower said,

> With special feelings of sorrow—and of solemn gratitude—we think of those who were called upon to lay down their lives in that far-off land to prove once again that only courage and sacrifice can keep freedom alive upon the earth. To the widows and orphans of this war, and to those veterans who bear disabling wounds, America renews tonight her pledge of lasting devotion and care.[19]

Maine native Richard Hornberger chronicled his experiences serving as a surgeon in Mobile Army Surgical Hospital #8055 during the Korean War and based the character of Hawkeye on himself for the novel *MASH*, published under his pen name Richard Hooker. The novel inspired 20th Century–Fox to produce the movie version and add asterisks. *M*A*S*H* premiered in 1970.

Fox's television version premiered in 1972 on CBS with Alan Alda as Hawkeye, who often talked about being drafted into the Army's medical service. It stemmed from reality. On September 1, 1950, Congress sent a bill regarding the drafting of medical personnel to President Truman. The Selective Service had authority for overseeing the draft; the bill's status amounted to an amendment of the Selective Service Act.[20]

On October 6, the president authorized drafting doctors, dentists and veterinarians who hadn't reached the age of 50, served for 21 months on active duty, and weren't currently in the armed forces or reserves. He said that these medical professionals "are urgently needed for service in the armed services of the United States." The *New York Times* reported that "more than 2300 medical professionals registered on October 16 at their respective Selective Service locations, including the agency's headquarters in the Empire State Building."[21]

9. Falsifying Military Records (M*A*S*H)

Hornberger was one of the drafted doctors who was sent to Korea. His novel captured the medical challenges in treating wounded soldiers with one passage summarizing a massive number of patients arriving at the 4077th in a two-week stretch. He called it "The Deluge":

> For a full two weeks the wounded would come and keep coming, and for a full two weeks every surgeon and every nurse and every corpsman, as the shifts overlapped, would work from twelve to fourteen to sixteen hours a day, every day, and sometimes some of them would work twenty out of the twenty-four. It could have been chaos, and it almost was. They came in by helicopter and they came in by ambulance—arteries, lungs, bowels, bladders, livers, spleens, kidneys, larynxes, pharynxes, bones, stomachs.[22]

When the soldier in "Death Takes a Holiday" expires, B.J. calls for adrenaline in an attempt to revive him; Hawkeye intervenes ("No. It's over. Let him rest"). In a way, it's a reflection of something that Lieutenant Colonel Henry Blake—the former commanding officer of the 4077th—told Hawkeye after Tommy Gillis died: "Look, all I know is what they taught me at command school. There are certain rules about a war. And rule number one is, young men die. And rule number two is, doctors can't change rule number one."[23]

10

Draft Dodging
(*All in the Family*)

All in the Family combined current events with humor, pathos and drama. Based on the BBC sitcom *Till Death Do Us Part* and developed by Norman Lear, the series aired on CBS from 1971 to 1979 and revolved around Archie Bunker, a World War II veteran and prototype of a middle-aged, conservative, blue-collar worker troubled by the political and social changes in the 1970s.

Nothing is taboo for discussion in the Bunker house at 704 Hauser Street in Queens, New York, where Archie often collides with his liberal son-in-law, Mike Stivic, regarding hot-button issues: civil rights, affirmative action, antisemitism, women's liberation, religion, gun control, crime, President Nixon's Watergate scandal, the Vietnam War and more.

The 1976 episode "The Draft Dodger" focuses on the controversial topic of American men refusing to serve in the military during the Vietnam War and avoiding the draft by going to Canada. It aired on Christmas Day. Though the topic is clear from the title, its resolution has an amazing twist. Mike and his wife Gloria—Archie's daughter—have invited their friend David to the Bunker house for Christmas dinner. Another guest is Archie's friend Pinky.

When David reveals that he dodged the draft, Archie gets agitated and raises his voice as he exclaims that harboring David could make them accessories to a crime and get them arrested. Pinky feels a different way. A Gold Star father who lost his son in Vietnam, Pinky does not take sides, bears no ill will toward David, and explains that his son Steve opposed the war but fought in it and died. In turn, Pinky suggests that if Steve were alive, he'd want to have Christmas dinner with David at the table. Archie is put in his place without getting put down. Archie's wife, Edith, offers her solace when he leaves the table; she says that Archie should come back to dinner, but he responds that he needs to think about what just happened before rejoining the group.[1]

10. Draft Dodging (All in the Family)

David violated the Selective Training and Service Act, which became a law in 1940 and allowed the U.S. military to draft 2.2 million American men during the Vietnam War. The available pool totaled 27 million. Technically, it was a peacetime draft because the U.S. did not declare war against North Vietnam. Though a viable source of soldiers for the military, it only provided 25 percent of the service members in combat; volunteers comprised the remainder. Young men like David had legal options with conditions. You could defer if you were a college student or a father. Some men joined the National Guard to avoid going to Southeast Asia.[2]

An exact figure is not discernible, but a 2018 article on politico.com states that "an estimated 50,000 draft dodgers chose to settle permanently in Canada."[3]

In 1970, President Richard Nixon underscored his desire to end the draft—albeit gradually—after considering a report from the Commission on an All-Volunteer Armed Force led by former Secretary of Defense Thomas S. Gates. Nixon's missive to Congress read in part:

> First, the draft cannot be ended all at once. It must be phased out, so that we can be certain of maintaining our defense strength at every step. Second, existing induction authority expires on July 1, 1971, and I expect that it will be necessary for the next Congress to extend this authority. And third, as we move away from reliance on the draft, we must make provisions to establish a standby draft system that can be used in case of emergency.[4]

In late September 1971, Nixon signed a bill adding two years to the draft with a condition: freezing a military pay increase of $2.4 billion slated for October 1 until a month and a half later. It also ended student deferments for men who matriculated in the fall of 1971.[5]

Secretary of Defense Melvin Laird took a step closer to scaling down America's military involvement in the Vietnam War on January 24, 1973, when he announced the suspension of "virtually all personnel movements to Vietnam." Three days later, Laird made another announcement when the Paris Peace Accords were signed: "The use of the draft has ended."[6]

There was a caveat. America's draft structure stood in case the nation encountered "an emergency" but Congress authorized a measure to be used first: men who served in the Reserves and the National Guard.[7]

Nixon resigned the presidency on August 9, 1974; his vice-president Gerald Ford succeeded him. On September 16, Ford announced that draft evaders and military deserters during the Vietnam War could reconcile with the government provided they meet certain conditions:

> In furtherance of our national commitment to justice and mercy these young Americans should have the chance to contribute a share to the rebuilding of peace among ourselves and with all nations. They should be allowed the

opportunity to earn return to their country, their communities, and their families, upon their agreement to a period of alternate service in the national interest, together with an acknowledgment of their allegiance to the country and its Constitution.[8]

After the Paris Peace Accords, it's estimated that approximately 5000 Americans stayed in South Vietnam including diplomats based in the American embassy in Saigon, the capital. As the North Vietnamese Army increasingly encroached, the two largest South Vietnamese cities fell. Da Nang went first; Saigon followed on April 30, 1975.

American diplomats tried to get South Vietnamese people to a safe egress at the embassy and transport them by helicopter, an epic task considering about 10,000 people sought to escape. Thanks to the pilots working for 19 consecutive hours, 7000 succeeded; among them were 5500 South Vietnam natives. Wolfgang J. Lehmann, the embassy deputy chief of mission, said,

> We could see the lights of the North Vietnamese convoys approaching the city.... The chopper was packed with the rest of the staff and remaining civilian guards ... and it was utterly silent except for the rotors of the engine. I don't think I said a word on the way out and I don't think anybody else did. The prevailing emotion was tremendous sadness.[9]

Saigon's fall ended a painful period in America's history resulting in more than 58,000 deaths of American service members. This journey began on August 7, 1964, with the Gulf of Tonkin Resolution. Three days earlier, President Lyndon Johnson gave a televised address explaining the recent attacks on American naval ships in the Gulf of Tonkin, close to North Vietnam. Johnson asked Congress to endorse his decision to take military action by sending planes to the area. The joint resolution stated that Congress approved and supported the determination of the president "to take all necessary measures to repel any armed attack against the forces of the United States and to prevent any further aggression."[10]

Had the Bunkers hosted David the following Christmas, there would have been no legal reason for Archie's worry about potential arrests. President Jimmy Carter pardoned the draft dodgers on January 21, 1977, a day after his inauguration. Using his constitutional authority in Article II, Section 2, he issued a proclamation that declared a full, complete and unconditional pardon to "all persons who may have committed any offense between August 4, 1964, and March 28, 1973, in violation of the Military Selective Service Act or any rule or regulation promulgated thereunder."

Additionally, the pardon covered anyone convicted of *any* offense connected with the Act during that time window. However, the pardon applied to civilians, not deserters already wearing a uniform or service members convicted for breaking a military law. Further, persons convicted of offenses involving "force or violence" connected to the Act could not avail themselves of the pardon.[11]

According to *The Washington Post*, the Justice Department indicated that Carter's pardon "would cover about 2600 draft dodgers still under indictment, about 9000 who were convicted or pleaded guilty and who could have their records erased and about 1200 who were under investigation."[12]

Democratic Senators Ted Kennedy and George McGovern—the party's 1972 presidential nominee—used the word "compassionate" in their assessment of Carter's action. Senator Barry Goldwater, the 1964 Republican presidential nominee, had a different take, calling Carter's decision "the most disgraceful thing that a president has ever done," and predicting that it would "utterly destroy the effectiveness of any draft should we feel the need to go back to a selective service." Republican Senator Jake Garn concurred: "First day in office as President and he pardons people who were disloyal to their country, who were not willing to serve it."[13]

References to Vietnam in prime time TV predated *All in the Family*, tracing back to the early 1960s. *Route 66* starred Glenn Corbett as Linc Case; he debuted in the 1963 episode "Fifty Miles from Home," which mentions his military service in the Vietnam War. Linc later discovers that his former Army platoon leader has a severely impacted mental acuity because of injuries sustained in combat. Linc's friend Tod Stiles underscores that the former soldier has the mind of an eight-year-old.[14]

In "Herman the Rookie," a 1965 episode of *The Munsters*, Herman Munster destroys a baseball field during a tryout for the Los Angeles Dodgers. For example, his strength causes a batted ball to knock over the scoreboard. Dodgers coach Leo Durocher observes, "I don't know whether to sign him with the Dodgers or send him to Vietnam."[15]

The Vietnam War provided a valuable source of story fodder for TV writers in the 1970s and 1980s. Three of *Magnum, P.I.*'s main characters served in the war, as did Detective Stan "Wojo" Wojciehowicz (*Barney Miller*), J.R. Ewing (*Dallas*) and Lt. Dan "Hondo" Harrelson (*S.W.A.T.*).

A standout *All in the Family* episode, "The Draft Dodger" elevated storytelling on television beyond the banal sitcoms of the 1960s. Renny Temple, who played David, recalls, "It was an unusual audition because I got the call and went to CBS and sat down with the director, Paul Bogart. Highly irregular." He continued:

> Most auditions have many actors try out for a part and do so in a room filled with the "judges": casting agents, producers, writers and the like. I sat literally across from Bogart, alone, in a small office. When I read the sides, the episode was called "The Deserter." They later thought it was too strong for

the character to be AWOL from active duty. That it would turn off too many people.

The "Draft Dodger" character was softer; more appealing. Paul liked the way I read the part and called the other producers in and said, "I think we have our draft dodger." An actor never hears those words from the powers that be. It's a phone call from an agent days later to tell you that you have the part. But the producers were very casual about it. Not me. This was my very first television show!

Kind of blown away as the week went on. Rehearsals, in those days, sometimes had shows swapping sets for lack of studio space. We were actually rehearsing in an empty room with the layout of the real set taped on the floor; a room with just chairs and tables. I came in and said hi to everybody, and I couldn't believe I was working on the most popular show on television.

Rob Reiner and Carroll O'Connor, on breaks, would mark up their scripts, writing notes. When I asked Rob why, he told me that their live audience was mainly Orange County conservatives and they really liked Archie, so Rob and Carroll were altering the script to have Archie avoid getting applause at the wrong places. I found that amazing.

As sitcoms do, they shot twice in front of two audiences and later edited them together into one "performance." In both shootings, however, there was one moment where I was terrified—when Archie, figuring out who David is, looks across the dinner table and asks me if I'm a draft dodger. And then the camera cuts to me. I thought I was gonna die! When a genuine actor like Carroll O'Connor, as Archie, looks at you with seething hate, you feel it right down to the leather in your shoes. These actors were really good at what they did.

There's another moment in the show when Archie walks away from the table to figure out what he's going to do in this predicament, and Edith, his wife, follows him, begging for him to rejoin the Christmas family dinner. Archie says he can't, and Edith replies, "Please Archie, do it ... for me." He turns and looks at her, and you see the entire loving Bunker relationship in the two, three silent seconds they share, before Archie grudgingly gives in. A magic moment of two indelible characters. It was the perfect blend of tragedy and comedy.[16]

11

Humanitarian Missions
(*Operation Christmas Drop*)

Military operations secure freedom.

Comprised of British and American forces invading the beaches of Normandy, France, on June 6, 1944 (otherwise known as D-Day), Operation Overlord gave the Allies a major step toward breaking the German military's grip on Europe in World War II. Targeting beaches nicknamed Utah, Omaha, Sword, Juno and Gold with paratroopers complemented by soldiers using Higgins boats, this mission also had a heartbreaking cost: More than 4400 lives were lost.[1]

Operation Rolling Thunder took place during the Vietnam War over three and a half years from February 1965 to October 1968 under the auspices of the Air Force and Navy, consisting of bombing North Vietnam but proving ultimately unsuccessful because of shifting priorities. According to the Air Force Historical Support Division, the Johnson administration

> imposed strict limits on the targets that could be attacked, for China and the Soviet Union were seen as defenders of Communism who might intervene if the North Vietnamese faced defeat. Consequently, the administration tried to punish the North without provoking the two nations believed to be its protectors. In the view of the Air Force leadership, the campaign had no clear-cut objective nor did its authors have any real estimate of the cost of lives and aircraft.[2]

President George H.W. Bush's administration executed Operation Desert Storm, the name given to the 1991 Gulf War campaign that drove Iraqi forces to abandon their invasion of Kuwait. In 2003, Baghdad fell in Operation Iraqi Freedom; it launched after the United Nations Security Council ruled that Iraq violated Resolution 1441, which required disarmament encompassing "a currently accurate, full, and complete declaration of all aspects of its programs to develop chemical, biological, and nuclear weapons, ballistic missiles, and other delivery systems." The operation continued until 2011, resulting in the deaths of nearly 4500 American service members. Many others returned home with severe mental and physical injuries.[3]

But not all military operations involve ammunition, weapons and surveillance. A longstanding humanitarian mission began during the waning days of the Truman administration in 1952: Operation Christmas Drop. It's the subject of the 2020 Netflix TV movie *Operation Christmas Drop*, filmed on location at Andersen Air Force Base and other sites in Guam.[4] According to the base's website,

> The tradition began during the Christmas season in 1952 when a B-29 Superfortress aircrew saw islanders waving at them from the island of Kapingamarangi, 3500 miles southwest of Hawaii. In the spirit of Christmas the aircrew dropped a bundle of supplies attached to a parachute to the islanders below, giving the operation its name. Today, air drop operations include more than 50 islands throughout the Pacific.[5]

Andersen Air Force Base notes that Operation Christmas Drop's deliveries may include food, supplies, educational materials and toys "to islanders throughout the Federated States of Micronesia, and Republic of Palau. These islands are some of the most remote locations on the globe spanning a distance nearly as broad as the continental U.S."[6]

Operation Christmas Drop, the Department of Defense's longest running humanitarian airlift operation, began in 1952. Headquartered at Andersen Air Force Base in Guam, crews drop bundles of supplies via parachutes to more than 50 Pacific islands (Andersen Air Force Base, Department of Defense).

11. Humanitarian Missions (Operation Christmas Drop)

The *Operation Christmas Drop* storyline places the program in jeopardy due to the Base Realignment and Closure Commission headed by Congresswoman Bradford (Virginia Madsen). With hopes of shutting the operation down, she sends her legislative aide, Erica Miller, to investigate on site a week before Christmas. There's immediate friction between Erica and Captain Andrew Jantz, who takes the holiday mission very seriously.

The captain's superior officer is already aware that Capitol Hill is targeting the base for realignment or closure. "But, sir, we're the most strategically important location in the South Pacific," argues Jantz. It doesn't matter; Washington lawmakers have the final say over the military's budget. Moreover, a recent *Indianapolis Post* online article frames the operation as frivolous rather than necessary, which gives the Congresswoman's office more impetus to shut down the base. Instead of assigning a public affairs officer, Jantz's boss wants to keep the visit as informal as possible and tasks the captain to chaperone Erica because he has "mad people skills."

In dialogue serving as exposition for the audience, Captain Jantz tells the D.C. visitor about Andersen's background:

> This base is home to the 36th Wing in the 734th Air Mobility Squadron. Bombers and heavy transport as well as fighter groups like these F-15s here rotate through on a regular basis. We have operations all around the island. See, despite the impression that the article gave, there is no slack here. Everybody is busy with very serious work.

Predictably though entertainingly, romance blossoms between the captain and Erica, whom he initially describes as "the most high-maintenance, condescending pencil-pusher I've ever met." Scenic shots have a lushness revealing Guam's beauty of greenery, beaches and sea life.

When the Congresswoman pays a surprise visit, Captain Jantz tries to explain the value of the base to its biggest political threat: "[T]he mission of this base is to provide a U.S.–based war fighting platform, as well as a rapid response humanitarian relief program worldwide."

But Congresswoman Bradford isn't the only problem. A typhoon is bearing down on the region. When the typhoon is downgraded to a tropical storm, the base's staff pull together to keep the tradition of Operation Christmas Drop thriving. Erica stays to help, defying an order from the Congresswoman to return to D.C. and urging her to live up to the promise of her first campaign: make the world a better place.

Bradford accedes and flies with the staff; her outlook changes from hard-nosed to good-hearted when she sees the joy that Operation Christmas Drop brings to the islanders. "That was what Christmas should look like," she says upon returning to the base. A postscript notes that 50,000 pounds of supplies are delivered to 56 islands in an area more than 1.8 million square nautical miles through Operation Christmas Drop. These bundles help 22,000 islanders.

Critic Richard Roeper wrote that the movie's location shots give it "a genuinely cinematic style [and] a feature-film look on a relatively restrained budget."[7]

Operation Christmas Drop is under the Department of Defense's Denton Humanitarian Assistance Program, which receives its authority from Title 10, Section 402, of the United States Code. It states in part:

> [The] Secretary of Defense may transport to any country, without charge, supplies which have been furnished by a nongovernmental source and which are intended for humanitarian assistance. Such supplies may be transported only on a space available basis."

However, there are requirements: consistency with U.S. foreign policy, suitability and usability of the products, legitimate humanitarian need, usage for humanitarian purposes and viable distribution.[8]

United States Transportation Command—USTRANSCOM—manages the transportation effort, which begins with an application filed online with the Overseas Humanitarian Assistance Shared Information System of the Defense Security Cooperation Agency.[9] Overseeing the entire hierarchy is the Humanitarian Assistance Program of the Department of Defense, which has other avenues of benevolence across the globe for Partner Nations. It is explained on the department's Defense Security Cooperation Agency website. For example, the Humanitarian Mine Program aims to demine "landmines, explosive remnants of war (ERW), and the hazardous effects of unexploded ordinance (UXO)."[10]

The department's Excess Property Program gives "non-lethal property" classified as tangible items, not land. "Property may include vehicles, equipment, supplies, and other non-lethal items that have been declared excess by DoD."[11]

Transportation will come under the Humanitarian Assistance Transportation Programs, which allows goods to be conveyed in two ways, either "on a space-available basis in DoD assets or on a funded basis in DoD–contracted shipping carriers."[12]

Perhaps the most visible program is Foreign Disaster Relief, which occurs because the Department of Defense has assets such as surveillance, communication technology and specialized vehicles that can be implemented effectively to deal with the aftermath of hurricanes, earthquakes and floods. "Typical DoD support includes logistics, transportation, delivery of relief supplies, aerial reconnaissance, and search and rescue operations."

11. Humanitarian Missions (Operation Christmas Drop)

But there's a certain amount of red tape to be conquered before funds are deployed and operations commence in disaster response situations abroad:

> The Department of State (DOS) submits a request to the DoD Executive Secretary requesting DoD support for FDR. The Secretary of Defense (SecDef) provides an authorization memo and subsequent tasking of the affected Combatant Command (CCMD).[13]

The U.S. military's humanitarian efforts in a disaster extend to the Selected Reserve and Individual Ready Reserve for helping civilians manage disaster response under the power granted by Title 10, Section 12304, of the United States Code, which gives the president authority to order reserve members "to provide assistance to either the Federal Government or a State in time of a serious natural or manmade disaster, accident, or catastrophe."[14]

Potential areas in a domestic emergency range from search and rescue—or extraction—to potable water to public information. Whether it's a natural disaster, attack or accident, members will leverage their expertise and training. The Army Reserve website states,

> For example, Army Reserve aircraft rapidly transport patients to critical-care facilities, and deliver critical personnel, supplies, equipment into affected areas. In the homeland, the Army Reserve is fully integrated into the standing Department of Defense task force postured for response to Chemical, Biological, Radiological and Nuclear (CBRN) events.[15]

Operation Christmas Drop is a notable part of the massive humanitarian aid distributed by the United States; these missions become a bit complex when a country has unreasonable restrictions on its borders being crossed. Earthquakes in Syria and Turkey during 2023 caused a tremendous amount of damage requiring aid but Syria's rules prevented it from getting to the citizens in dire need. An online article for the Lieber Institute for Law & Land Warfare at West Point notes the importance of International Humanitarian Law: "A preliminary rule, based on sovereignty, is that a State has the primary obligation to meet the needs of the population within its territory or under its control."

The same article highlights the tangible complications even if humanitarian aid gets a legal blessing such as a United Nations resolution authorizing the distribution. A nation ruled by a governmental structure uninterested in human rights may endanger the lives of aid workers in jeopardy when armed criminals have either an implicit or explicit green light to raid vehicles for the aid packages.[16]

While critics like the movie's Congresswoman Bradford may look at

Operation Christmas Drop as a wasteful though benevolent use of military resources, it has benefits that extend beyond illustrating American goodwill. Since the operation requires coordination, communication and commitment between several nations, it helps the nation's military troubleshoot potential problems that may arise in other joint actions. Japan, Canada, Australia, the Philippines and the Republic of Korea combine with the United States in this effort, emphasized by U.S. Pacific Air Forces for its value in international relationships: "This multinational endeavor underscores the commitment to regional security and humanitarian cooperation in the Indo-Pacific."[17]

Of course, there's the satisfaction that service members get from their participation. In 2023, the holiday operation lasted six days and covered 1.8 million miles as it dropped packages by air to 58 islands. More than 42,000 islanders benefited. Air Force Operation Christmas Drop Mission Commander and pilot Major Zach "Badger" Overbey said, "Operationally, my favorite part is seeing everyone's faces when they come back after doing their first real drop. They see the aid they're giving the islanders and the difference they're making."[18]

12

Civil Negligence
(*The Man Who Came to Dinner*)

The Christmas season brings families and friends together. But every circle usually has one visitor whose presence (because of bloodline, custom or courtesy) is an unwelcome burden. Hosts must endure the person being loud, condescending or generally obnoxious with no avenue of amelioration except to quietly count the minutes until that person's exit is imminent.

In the 1942 film *The Man Who Came to Dinner*, the troublesome guest of the Stanley clan in Mesalia, Ohio, is Sheridan Whiteside (Monty Woolley), a nationally known author, radio commentator and culture lecturer. He visits this burg of the Buckeye State an hour's drive from Cleveland to make an appearance at the Mesalia Opera House on December 9. His fee—$1500 per lecture. The family's house at 39 Norton Street is one of his stops during his Mesalia visit, accorded the honor because the Stanleys are leading citizens; Ernest Stanley is a ball bearings manufacturer and Daisy Stanley is president of the Women's Club.[1]

Whiteside slips on an icy patch on the front steps, suffering an injury. The commentator described as the "idol of the airways [sic]" must cancel the lecture and recuperate at the Stanley abode. His celebrity status makes the injury international news. Telegrams, visitors and gifts—including an octopus from a famous naturalist—overwhelm the once quiet household. Whiteside's circle includes Great Britain's prime minister, Winston Churchill, who calls to offer his good wishes.

Confined to a wheelchair in the Stanley home "for at least another ten days" according to his doctor's orders, Whiteside threatens to sue Mr. Stanley for $150,000; he suffers the banality of this Midwestern family as they suffer his haughtiness. Injury does not negate his self-importance one iota, evidenced by his commandeering the home—which he calls "a moldy mortuary"—like a general invading enemy territory. He has no regard for the Stanleys and their household evidenced by declaring exclusive use of the house's living room, library and telephone so he can continue to work plus a room for his loyal assistant of ten years, Maggie Cutler. Further, his demands include peacefulness until he wakes up at noon.

Whiteside's worldliness creates an upside for the Stanley children on the verge of adulthood as inspiration abounds from the commentator. Richard wants to be a photographer and see the world rather than settle for a quiet though pedestrian life; Whiteside embraces Richard's talent. June wants to marry her beau, Sandy. But it's complicated. Sandy works at the ball bearings factory and urges his fellow employees to form a union; Mr. Stanley sees this action as a threat to his bottom line.

Meanwhile, Maggie has tired of the fancy life filled with caviar, champagne and celebrities. Whiteside views her as indispensable; romance threatens his paradigm. When she falls for local reporter Bert Jefferson and expresses her willingness to stay with him in Mesalia, Whiteside lures a famous actress—Lorraine Sheldon—to seduce the scribe, who has written a play that might be a great opportunity for the actress.

However, Whiteside has another dilemma when his doctor reveals that he's been looking at the wrong X-rays. Whiteside can walk; there's no injury keeping him in the wheelchair. But he must stay confined to complete the charade. So the commentator makes a deal: He'll read the doctor's lengthy memoir about 40 years of medical practice and offer a critique if the doctor will stay silent about his true condition.

Christmas gifts arrive for Whiteside from Churchill, Deanna Durbin, Gypsy Rose Lee, W. Somerset Maugham and other notables. Another contribution representing the animal kingdom comes from the great explorer Admiral Richard Byrd: four penguins. It's a momentous occasion when Whiteside delivers his Christmas Eve radio broadcast, an event of national appeal. On Christmas Day, after discovering that Mr. Stanley's sister murdered their parents with an axe decades ago, Whiteside uses it as leverage. If Mr. Stanley agrees to let his offspring follow their passions, Whiteside shall keep the secret. Otherwise, there will be publicity, and shame will follow. The Stanley patriarch acquiesces.

Whiteside's nurse quits, having reached her limit dealing with the demanding patient. "If Florence Nightingale had ever nursed you, she would have married Jack the Ripper instead of founding the Red Cross," she exclaims. But Sarah and John, the family's cook and butler, are fond of Whiteside and immediately accept his offer to work for them in New York City after ten years of service to the Stanleys.

The famed commentator has also changed his mind about Maggie and takes care of the competition for Bert's affections by trapping Lorraine

12. Civil Negligence (The Man Who Came to Dinner)

in a sarcophagus sent by an Egyptian VIP. Banjo, an entertainer friend who has visited Whiteside during his healing, spirits it out of the house and promises that he'll release Lorraine after he gets it on a plane, which he does. Whiteside never reads the doctor's memoir.

In addition to the octopus and penguins, Whiteside also receives a baby seal and other animal gifts; he leaves them with the Stanleys during his exit. All's well that ends well until he slips on the front steps upon leaving for New York City and vows to sue for $250,000. It looks like he will recuperate in the Stanley house again.

Whiteside ignited chaos during his holiday season recuperation, so Mr. Stanley is justified in his frustration resulting from the guest's demeanor highlighted by gruffness, sarcasm and arrogance. But he and his wife might also be legally culpable for the civil tort of negligence as the homeowners. It is a generally accepted principle that negligence claims rest on a foursome of factors: duty, breach, causation, damage.

Certainly, the Stanleys had a duty to keep their front steps free of obstacles and dangers for visitors. The 1951 Ohio case *Scheibel vs. Lipton* ignored the recognized categorization of visitors like Whiteside as licensees—people who are invited to the premises for social rather than business reasons and thus owed a lesser duty of care:

> If a social guest is to be classified in Ohio as a licensee and is, therefore, entitled only to the protection of a licensee in accordance with the duties owed to a licensee as such duties are defined by Ohio decisions, then the duty owed to him by the host would be very meager.[2]

But did they breach their duty? Other people accompanied Whiteside with no problem getting up the steps. Whiteside may argue that the duty even extended to warning him and other visitors of a possible hazardous situation but that's a difficult argument to make because no one else was injured.

If Whiteside argues successfully that a breach occurred, there needs to be a connection to his injury. Here, causation is present. Clearly, the ice caused Whiteside's slip and fall. He would then have the more difficult task of proving that he incurred damages. Under Ohio law, "economic loss" is defined broadly and includes this description: "All wages, salaries, or other compensation lost as a result of an injury, death, or loss to person or property that is a subject of a tort action, including wages, salaries, or other compensation lost as of the date of a judgment and future expected lost earnings."[3]

There doesn't appear to be much, if any, financial impact regarding Whiteside's vocation as one of America's leading thinkers, critics and lecturers. Live appearances can be rescheduled; his Christmas Eve broadcast is neither delayed nor cancelled. Whiteside's standing as a leading cultural commentator remains intact.

Medical costs may be an easier avenue in arguing for damages. The "economic law" clause states:

> All expenditures for medical care or treatment, rehabilitation services, or other care, treatment, services, products, or accommodations incurred as a result of an injury, death, or loss to person that is a subject of a tort action, including expenditures for those purposes that were incurred as of the date of a judgment and expenditures for those purposes that, in the determination of the trier of fact, will be incurred in the future because of the injury, whether paid by the injured person or by another person on behalf of the injured person.[4]

Assuming that the prongs of duty, breach, causation and damages are met, the Stanleys would likely be found liable for Whiteside's medical costs. But to what end? The costs must be reasonable, not excessive. For example, Whiteside had a private nurse doting on him until she quit because of stress, but a judge may deem her service to have been unnecessary if her duties amounted to being an assistant more than a caregiver.

During the pre-trial phase of discovery, the Stanleys' attorney would likely ask for a full accounting of Whiteside's medical expenditures, potentially including the doctor's visits to the Stanley home; salary for the private nurse; prescription medication, and X-rays. To determine if Whiteside is being frivolous in his attempt to recoup medical costs, a comparison will be made with other local providers of the same services to see what they charge.

Whiteside shouldn't celebrate too quickly if the judge rules in his favor. Or even at all. The Stanleys have a valid claim against him for the wear and tear on the house caused by his shenanigans, assuming they could prove a tangible financial impact. Emotional distress resulting from the tumult that destroys the home's quietude might be a stronger argument resting on a basic question. Whiteside's success has presumably resulted in financial security, so why didn't he rent a hotel suite to accommodate his needs rather than inconvenience the Stanleys?

Also, Whiteside could face an argument of contributory negligence. Nobody else had a problem ascending the stairs, so a legal proceeding would involve questioning Whiteside's behavior. He was engaged in conversation as he climbed the steps, but did this distract him? Did he pay attention to the weather conditions? What was his mood? Was he in good shape?

If his actions don't supersede those of the Stanleys, he will have a valid legal argument for a negligence claim though a court will factor his contribution into the analysis and rule accordingly on the damages owed. The Ohio Revised Code states,

12. Civil Negligence (The Man Who Came to Dinner)

The contributory fault of a person does not bar the person as plaintiff from recovering damages that have directly and proximately resulted from the tortious conduct of one or more other persons, if the contributory fault of the plaintiff was not greater than the combined tortious conduct of all other persons from whom the plaintiff seeks recovery in this action and of all other persons from whom the plaintiff does not seek recovery in this action.[5]

The Schiebel case provided a similar scenario involving a lawn with a depression described as "from two to three feet in width and from eight to twelve inches in depth," which the plaintiff claimed caused "a severe injury to his foot and ankle" when he stepped in it. A paved walk extended from the front door to the driveway, which the court considered to be "a suitable and customary approach" sufficient for the plaintiff to traverse even though a walkway directly to the street might have been easier.

Consequently, the homeowners were justified in leaving the depression because otherwise they'd have to ensure the lawn is completely level by fixing every hole and mound. The court wrote,

If a host must so police his front yard must he, at sundown each day, gather up all wagons, scooters, croquet balls and other toys or be charged with negligence by a guest who might trip over one of them? We do not believe that a social guest can reasonably demand such care be taken by the host.[6]

Had Whiteside's slip occurred in front of a brownstone on the Upper West Side of Manhattan owned by someone in his world such as a university president, millionaire businessman or famous author, there probably would have been no threatened lawsuit. Whiteside's anger stems from being a man of letters stuck in a Midwestern location that can be described as quaint though antiquated for his tastes, therein providing the conflict and the comedy.

Written by George S. Kaufman and Moss Hart, the play *The Man Who Came to Dinner* premiered in 1939 at the Plymouth Theatre in Boston and opened at the Music Box Theatre later that year. In his rave review, *New York Times* critic Brooks Atkinson called it "the funniest comedy of this season, and … likely to remain so long after the competition has grown stiffer." Woolley's efforts gained Atkinson's approval: "Having a sense of humor of his own, Mr. Woolley plays the part in the grand manner with dignity and knavery."[7]

For the 1942 film, Woolley reprised his stage role and received similar plaudits. Herbert L. Monk of the *St. Louis Globe-Democrat* opined, "In the actor's hands, Whiteside becomes a character so utterly vile, so completely unprincipled in his relations with others, even those closest to him, that he is, strangely enough, amusing."[8]

Woolley and the supporting cast (including Ann Sheridan, Bette Davis and Jimmy Durante) offer a version that "sets a high mark in comedy for the Hollywood humorists to shoot at in 1942," wrote Kaspar Monahan in the *Pittsburgh Press*. "And I doubt that they'll equal it, let alone top it."[9]

Davis in the role of Maggie "[is] very convincing in her sufferings," wrote Ardis Smith in the *Buffalo Evening News*. He also lauded Sheridan's portrayal of Lorraine, calling her "a fierce little farceuse."[10]

Torts lawyers will see potential legal storylines between the laughs caused by the fish-out-of-water premise in the movie adaptation penned by twin brothers Julius J. Epstein and Philip G. Epstein. Whiteside's strength and vulnerability in a negligence claim will have their legal minds digesting the best possible arguments for a lawsuit and the likely counterarguments that they will need to overcome.

13

Subletting
(*The Apartment*)

C.C. "Bud" Baxter is a cog in the enormous, enticing and byzantine world of corporate America represented in *The Apartment*. But he is a valuable cog to his superiors at Consolidated Life of New York.[1]

Jack Lemmon stars as Baxter in this 1960 film that received ten Oscar nominations and won five: Best Art Direction (Black-and-White), Best Director, Best Film Editing, Best Picture and Best Story and Screenplay. Billy Wilder directed and co-wrote the screenplay with I.A.L. Diamond.

Baxter works on the 19th floor in the Ordinary Policy Department, Premium Accounting Division, Section W, Desk Number 861. His usefulness at this Goliath in the insurance industry—described by Baxter as one of the top five companies in the country, though he doesn't specify if that classification is restricted to insurance companies—stems from an asset beyond insight, analysis or work ethic. Baxter's apartment at 51 West 67th Street in Manhattan—half a block from Central Park—is a safe place for secret trysts between Consolidated's executives and their mistresses.

In exchange, Baxter receives promises of stellar performance reports and promotions—which he gets—but there's little, if any, regard for his personal life. One example is an executive calling Baxter at 11 p.m. to use the apartment because he's picked up a blonde who looks like Marilyn Monroe. Baxter has worked at Consolidated for nearly four years and his take-home pay is $94.70 weekly, so a boost in his bank account is welcome even if it means staying late at the office for an hour or two on the nights that he allows use of the apartment.

Consolidated Life is based at 2 Broadway, a skyscraper that opened in 1959. It authorizes a modern look for the film. The office atmosphere is loose, to say the least. At the company's boisterous Christmas party, there are makeout sessions in the 19th floor bullpen, a foyer and even Baxter's office, leading the audience to believe that more extensive bacchanalian activities are taking place off screen. Baxter does not participate. He has eyes for Fran Kubelik, the elevator operator, who, unbeknownst to him, is being bedded in his apartment by Jeff Sheldrake, Consolidated's director of personnel. Shirley MacLaine plays Fran; Fred MacMurray plays Sheldrake.

When Sheldrake gives Baxter tickets for *The Music Man*, the underling asks Fran to accompany him; she agrees. But after meeting with Sheldrake first and succumbing to his hollow promises, she ditches Baxter. During the party, Fran learns from Sheldrake's loose-lipped secretary that the executive has seduced a string of women who work at Consolidated. Burdened by the news of being one arrow in his quiver of sexual conquests, a devastated Fran goes to the apartment and meets with Sheldrake; it doesn't go well. Sheldrake leaves. Meanwhile, Baxter has drowned his sorrows in liquor over Fran's coupling and picked up a married woman whose husband is in jail in Havana; he's a jockey who doped horses.

Upon returning to the apartment and discovering Fran unconscious from overdosing on Seconal, he tells the barfly to leave. Fran later returns to Sheldrake when he reveals his availability; Mrs. Sheldrake threw him out of the house after the secretary disclosed his affairs. Baxter gets a promotion to the assistant director of personnel position with perquisites including the adjacent office to Sheldrake's, key to the executive washroom, access to the executive dining room and an expense account. On December 31, Baxter refuses Sheldrake's request for the apartment key and says that the boss won't be taking any more women to the apartment, especially Fran. He quits.

Later that night, while at a bar celebrating New Year's Eve, Sheldrake tells Fran what happened. He is puzzled more than angry about Baxter's words and actions. Delighted that Baxter has regained full use of the abode and his integrity, Fran leaves Sheldrake and bolts from the bar when the lights go out and everyone sings "Auld Lang Syne." She arrives at Baxter's apartment to usher in the New Year, ending the movie on a high note of a viable romance.

Variety opined:

> The dialogue, and its execution, are frank. There is no hiding that full-fledged lovemaking is going on in these quarters. To Wilder's striking credit, the picture has atmosphere, it creates a feeling about people, and, along the way, it makes a few pertinent comments about big businessmen and their infidelities.[2]

Baxter's actions regarding the use of his apartment may technically be considered subletting. The legal solutions and technology division of Thomson Reuters offers a definition of "sublease": "A lease by a lessee to a third party, conveying some or all of the leased property for a shorter term than that of the lessee, who retains a reversion in the lease."[3]

13. Subletting (The Apartment)

There's no exchange of money as there would be in a classic sublease situation, but Baxter receives compensation that can be tangibly measured by an elevation in salary. To square matters legally, he would need to consult an attorney to work out the particulars.

The right to sublease depends on the dwelling having at least four residential units, which appears to be the case in the brownstone where Baxter resides; tenants in public housing would be excluded from subleasing. The New York City Bar Association website states:

> If your landlord agrees in writing, you can lease your apartment to another person. If you will be returning to live in your apartment after the other person leaves, this is called a sublease. If you would like to sublease your apartment, you must first tell your landlord that you want to do this. You must make the request in writing and send it by certified mail, return receipt requested. You must include in your written request certain information about yourself and the subtenant which is required by law.[4]

Unless the landlord has a reasonable argument to refuse to permit a sublease, Baxter is in the clear. But he must provide basic information such as the sublessee's identity, the length of time that the sublease will be in effect, and the address. He will also need to supply the reason for the request, which may be trickier. He might state that his apartment ensures privacy needed by Consolidated executives to handle certain confidential business matters, though it is unlikely that this argument will survive a rigorous investigation.

If Baxter does satisfy the information requirement, that's not his only hurdle. According to the New York City Rent Guidelines Board website,

> The landlord has ten days to ask for additional information which you must provide so long as the request is not unduly burdensome. If the landlord fails to respond to the sublet request within 30 days, then a failure to respond is deemed consent. If the landlord unreasonably withholds consent the tenant may proceed with the sublet.[5]

New York law states: "Such consent shall not be unreasonably withheld." Additionally, Baxter's sharing the apartment does not absolve him of obligations toward the landlord; rent must be paid on time and other conditions in the lease must be met. "If the landlord consents, the premises may be sublet in accordance with the request, but the tenant thereunder shall nevertheless remain liable for the performance of tenant's obligations under said lease," mandates the law.[6]

Although Baxter's actions may be unseemly to most people, he should be legally okay. After all, he's allowing the Consolidated executives the chance to use the apartment without certifying exactly what's transpiring there. He cannot verify the behavior unless he's present. Moreover, there's the intent behind Section 226-B. A 1981 article in *Fordham Urban Law Journal* emphasizes,

> Although the statute purports to give tenants the right to sublease it does *not* give that right without landlord consent. Section 226-b, however, was not intended to limit a tenant's common law right to sublet. The common law right to sublet is available to a tenant where the lease contains no subletting provision or where the landlord expressly covenants not to unreasonably withhold consent to a sublease. In this instance, a tenant's remedies are to: (1) sublease the apartment in spite of the landlord's refusal; or (2) sue for a declaratory judgment to determine whether consent has been unreasonably withheld and either obtain specific performance or recover damages.[7]

If Baxter and the executives agree to memorialize their arrangement with a contract, then he will want to make sure that certain items are spelled out clearly with no room for ambiguity, doubletalk or vagueness from the Consolidated bosses. Baxter's increase in salary, holiday bonus, performance bonuses and new job title with commensurate responsibilities will be paramount concerns for the rising executive to explain in detail. Also, Baxter will probably want to set a time limit for the apartment usage and reasonable boundaries of availability to prevent him from being kicked out late at night, like the incident with the Marilyn Monroe lookalike.

If Baxter is concerned about his neighbors or landlord discovering the arrangement, his attorneys can insert a clause stating that the sublessee agrees to limit the sound of voices to a conversational level. Music must also be played at a reasonable volume. Further, a clause about the arrangement being confidential will serve both parties well.

There's also the subject of insurance. The executives will want Baxter to confirm that the apartment is covered by insurance; Baxter will comply because if someone is injured in the apartment, he may be on the hook for damages. If an injury takes place in a common area such as a walkway or corridor, the landlord's insurance company would be contacted. In addition, Baxter must provide that his place is habitable even for a short stay, otherwise known as the "warranty of habitability" for real estate lawyers.

Even if he has his legal ducks in a row for subletting and insurance, there are other considerations for Baxter to cease selling use of his residence as part of a scheme to climb the corporate ladder. Let's suppose that a Consolidated executive takes his secretary to the apartment and one of their sexual encounters results in a pregnancy. In the 1960s, abortion was illegal. If she sues the executive and the company for costs incurred during the pregnancy and birth plus the costs to raise the child, Baxter could be called as a witness if a suit is not settled. His participation would be part of the public record.

13. Subletting (The Apartment)

Further, if she sues for harassment or sexual assault because of the executive's power over her job, Baxter might not only be classified as a witness but also as a defendant. Baxter allowed the executive to use his apartment, so a creative plaintiff's lawyer may claim that he engaged in a conspiracy with the executive to coerce sexual activity with the secretary by supplying a site that virtually guaranteed privacy. If the secretary's reputation is harmed, that will likely be factored into the damages sought.

A claim of harassment may arise if the executive promises the secretary—or another female underling—a promotion with increased salary in exchange for sex either in explicit or implicit terms. If it's not realized and she sues the executive and Consolidated, a similar paradigm will arise regarding Baxter being added to the suit. He allowed use of his apartment in exchange for compensation, so he would be seen by a plaintiff's lawyer as being part of an overall design by the executive to make promises with no intention of delivering. If there's a criminal prosecution, the D.A.'s office could label him an accessory.

Baxter's reputation is on the line as well. Sheldrake is married, so Baxter would likely be called as a witness for Mrs. Sheldrake in a divorce proceeding. It's a good bet that the circumstances of his promotion and perquisites at Consolidated will be part of his testimony, thereby pummeling his character at water coolers across the company and its peers, resulting in massive, almost unrecoverable, damage to his name. Mrs. Sheldrake's lawyers will want to hear from Mr. Sheldrake, Baxter and the personnel officers about the particulars of his promotions and perquisites.

There's a potential scenario that could lead to eviction of Baxter. If a neighbor tells the landlord that men and women are coming into Baxter's apartment during the day and evening when he's not present, the landlord would be within his or her rights to make an inquiry, presuming there's no agreement to sublease. A major concern will be potential damage to the image of the building as a place where polite people respect decorum.

Consequently, a barrage of questions will arise. Who are these people using Baxter's apartment? How much time are they spending in the apartment? What is the reason? Is Baxter getting paid and if so, how much? How long has it been going on?

The analysis regarding Baxter's exploitation of his apartment amounting to a sublease requires creative thinking, but it's a journey that reveals an area of property law fraught with pitfalls for New Yorkers. If a renter is going to sublease an apartment, then a contract needs to be drafted to protect that renter from a sublessee's negligence, ignorance or less than honorable intent regarding payment, usage and behavior.

14

Defense of Home
(*Home Alone*)

Macauley Culkin represents every kid's greatest fantasy and deepest fear in *Home Alone*, the 1990 holiday blockbuster that vaulted Culkin to household name status for his performance as Kevin McAllister.[1]

The McAllister house at 671 Lincoln Boulevard in Winnetka, Illinois, is chaotic with 15 people preparing for a trip to celebrate Christmas in Paris: Kevin plus his parents, brothers, sisters, cousins, aunt and uncle. Between the bullying by his older brother Buzz and the prospect of sleeping in a bed with his bedwetting cousin, Kevin is despondent, angry and spiteful. He wishes that he didn't have a family.

The next morning, he gets his wish when the entire McAllister clan oversleeps; Kevin's parents wake up at noon instead of eight a.m. After corralling everyone, they have 45 minutes to get to O'Hare International Airport for their flight. Spending the night in a bed in the attic, Kevin oversleeps as well. When a member of the clan lines up her peers to count them, she believes a nosy neighbor is Kevin because his back is to her.

Kevin wakes up to an empty house after the family departs. He relishes the solitude. Initially, at least. He eats junk food, watches a gangster movie called *Angels with Filthy Souls*, and rides a toboggan down the stairs and out through the front doorway. A severe wind has caused a huge tree branch to knock out the phone lines, so Kevin's parents have no way to contact him. A call to the local police station amounts to nothing because Kevin either doesn't answer the door or doesn't hear the cop knocking when he comes to investigate.

When Kevin recognizes the driver of a plumbing and heating van as the police officer who stopped by the McAllister abode on the night before the trip, he realizes that the man is really an impostor, indeed a thief with an accomplice. Harry and Marv (Joe Pesci and Daniel Stern) have targeted five houses on the street after learning that the families are vacationing. Marv has a signature gimmick: leaving the water running when they rob

14. Defense of Home (Home Alone)

a house so they can be known as the Wet Bandits. Harry calls the McAllister house "the silver tuna" for its allure. Kevin later confronts the gravity of the situation and makes a declaration to himself: "This is my house. I have to defend it."

What follows is a battle between the thieves and Kevin, who utilizes the items in his home to fortify his defense. Among his weapons: toy cars, water that will turn to ice on the front walk and stairs in the back, a BB gun and ornaments. Kevin shoots Harry in the crotch through a space in a door that appears to be for a dog. Marv sticks his head through it and Kevin employs his marksmanship again with a shot to the head.

Harry slips on the icy front walk and falls on his back; Marv slips down the outside steps. When Marv pulls on a cord to turn on the light, he finds it's attached to an iron that smacks him on the head. A hot coil hung on the front doorknob inside the house transfers heat to the outside, thereby burning Harry's hand when he tries to open the door. Kevin tars the steps to the basement, which causes Marv to lose his shoes and puncture a foot when he steps on a nail strategically placed by the McAllister lad.

Harry tries to go into the house, but a string attached to the door turns on a blowtorch that ignites his hat and burns the top of his head. Marv climbs through a window and steps on glass ornaments with his bare feet. Both thieves slip on toy cars. When they chase Kevin up the main stairway and threaten him, they both get hit in the face with a paint can. Ultimately, the Wet Bandits are arrested.

Were Kevin's actions justified? In Illinois, the relevant statute reads in part:

> A person is justified in the use of force against another when and to the extent that he reasonably believes that such conduct is necessary to prevent or terminate such other's unlawful entry into or attack upon a dwelling. However, he is justified in the use of force which is intended or likely to cause death or great bodily harm only if: (1) The entry is made or attempted in a violent, riotous, or tumultuous manner, and he reasonably believes that such force is necessary to prevent an assault upon, or offer of personal violence to, him or another then in the dwelling, or (2) He reasonably believes that such force is necessary to prevent the commission of a felony in the dwelling.[2]

It is a solid argument that Kevin had a reasonable belief regarding his actions as necessary to protect the McAllister home. Harry and Marv trespassed; used a crowbar to try and enter the house intending to steal, and issued verbal threats of "personal violence." Those actions satisfy the "violent, riotous, or tumultuous manner."

Any Illinois juror would applaud Kevin's actions; Harry and Marv threatened his safety. It's obvious that the Wet Bandits would have injured

Kevin and restricted him so he couldn't run to get help, perhaps tying him up. He heard the thieves' intimidating language, plus there's potential testimony pointing out that Harry impersonated a police officer to learn the holiday vacation schedules of homeowners. Kevin faced a dire situation when they finally caught him at a vacationing neighbor's home and hung him on a hook after he tried to escape, only to be saved by a kindly neighbor who knocked out the thieves with a shovel.

Kevin had forethought in planning his escape. He called the police to report a burglary at a neighbor's house and claimed to be the homeowner, rightfully believing that the Wet Bandits would follow him to that house but didn't count on Harry and Marv catching him before the police arrived. After the climactic rescue of Kevin, the police arrested the thieves on multiple charges; this house had the water running and led them to deduce that the culpability for other burglaries with this signature falls upon Harry and Marv. On Christmas morning, Kevin's mom returns after a harrowing experience trying to get a flight and reconciles with her son. His father and siblings arrive a few minutes later, surprising them.

What if the Wet Bandits pursue a civil claim against Kevin McAllister—and his parents as the house's legal owners—for injuries sustained during their invasion? It would be as welcome as wearing a Packers jersey in the bleachers at Soldier Field for a game against the Bears. The statute would allow Kevin to avoid being penalized in civil court if his actions are held to be justifiable by prosecutors. It reads in part:

> In no case shall any act involving the use of force justified under this Section give rise to any claim or liability brought by or on behalf of any person acting within the definition of "aggressor" set forth in Section 7-4 of this Article, or the estate, spouse, or other family member of such a person, against the person or estate of the person using such justified force, unless the use of force involves willful or wanton misconduct.[3]

Certainly, the Wet Bandits each satisfy the definition of "aggressor" in Section 7-4 without the availability of exceptions allowing them to use force if they believed they were "in imminent danger of death or great bodily harm" or withdrew from the fray "in good faith." The statute defines an aggressor as someone who

> is attempting to commit, committing, or escaping after the commission of a forcible felony; or initially provokes the use of force against himself, with the intent to use such force as an excuse to inflict bodily harm upon the assailant; or otherwise initially provokes the use of force against himself.[4]

Harry and Marv are textbook examples. They committed the felony of burglary and provoked Kevin to use force as a defensive measure. There's

14. Defense of Home (Home Alone)

not a judge in the Land of Lincoln who would allow the Wet Bandits to seek financial redress for their injuries.

Kevin's actions stem from the common law principle called the Castle Doctrine. Sir Edward Coke ruled on it in Semayne's Case, a 1604 case in England that has become a foundation for defense attorneys:

> That the house of every one is to him as his Castle and Fortress as well for defence against injury and violence, as for his repose; and although the life of man is precious and favoured in law; so that although a man kill another in his defence, or kill one per infortuntun' (by misfortune), without any intent, yet it is felony, and in such case he shall forfeit his goods and chattels, for the great regard which the law hath of a mans [sic] life; But if theeves [sic] come to a mans house to rob him, or murder, and the owner or his servants kill any of the theeves in defence of himself and his house, it is no felony, and he shall lose nothing.[5]

Illinois is not alone. The Castle Doctrine has influenced legal flexibility for defending abodes throughout several jurisdictions. The National Conference of State Legislatures notes that at least 23 states "provide civil immunity under certain self-defense circumstances."[6]

The Castle Doctrine has been codified and expanded to the principle of "stand your ground," a viable defense in more than 30 states. Kevin used a BB gun, but Stand Your Ground may extend the right of defense to firearm use and remove the legal requirement of homeowners having a duty to retreat when faced with a dangerous person seeking to do harm, depending on the jurisdiction. A 2023 article on the Rockefeller Institute of Government website notes the impact of the Stand Your Ground defense in Florida, a leading state on the issue when it became a Sunshine State law in 2005:

> An exhaustive study of Florida's law through 2014 found that the law's chief beneficiaries were "those with records of crime and violence." Nearly 60 percent of those making self-defense claims when a person was killed had been arrested at least once before, one-third had been accused of violent crimes or drug offenses in the past, and over one-third had illegally carried guns in the past or had threatened others with guns. In 79 percent, the assailant could have retreated to avoid the confrontation. In 70 percent of the cases, the person killed was unarmed. In all, stand-your-ground claims succeeded 67 percent of the time.[7]

But would Kevin or other defenders of homes need an expansion of the Castle Doctrine? The Association of Prosecuting Attorneys doesn't think so. It has a caveat regarding the potential impact on future matters:

> Prosecutors, as upholders of justice and the integrity within our criminal justice system, retain a special role within the community through which confidence in our criminal justice system and public safety are maintained. The

expansion of the Castle Doctrine may have unintended consequences and inhibits the ability of law enforcement and prosecutors to fully hold violent criminals accountable for their acts.[8]

The APA adds that the right of self-defense and the right to defend one's home against invasion "are well established in Common Law. The proper use of prosecutorial discretion ensures that justified acts of homicide are not prosecuted. For these reasons, expansions of the Castle Doctrine are unnecessary."[9]

Home Alone likely had defense attorneys pontificating on the legality of Kevin's actions. It struck a chord of good feeling with audiences, grossing nearly $286 million against tough competition, including *Rocky V*, *Three Men and a Little Lady*, *The Rescuers Down Under* and *Ghost*.[10]

Some critics offered unfavorable reviews despite the emotionally impactful ending when the family returns early from their trip capped by a hug between Kevin and his mom (Catherine O'Hara). Joe DeChick of the *Cincinnati Enquirer* began his critique with a biting sentence: "*Home Alone* is all gimmick and little execution." In his two-star review for Syracuse's *Post-Standard*, Doug Brode pointed to the lack of believability in John Hughes' script and Chris Columbus' direction: "Hughes and Columbus try to get us to accept and believe all of this in scenes that just won't play, no matter how hard the game cast tries."[11]

Roger Ebert praised Culkin as the saving grace in a movie that he found unbelievable; he didn't like the storyline involving the burglars, which prompted most of the audience laughter. "The plot is so implausible that it makes it hard for us to really care about the plight of the kid."[12]

Jeffrey Westhoff's review had a similar vibe and singled out Pesci and Stern, whose cluelessness led to tremendous scenes of slapstick. "Because John Hughes' script doesn't flesh out these characters, they never form a convincing team."[13]

If the naysayers were surprised by the film's success anchored by an underdog facing off against two opponents of greater size, the screenwriter wasn't. "We weren't on anybody's list of upcoming films for the holiday, not even in the longshot dark-horse column," said Hughes, who also wrote and directed *The Breakfast Club*, *Pretty in Pink*, *Some Kind of Wonderful* and *Ferris Bueller's Day Off*. "But I felt that the concept, the idea of a kid taking care of himself, was the most important thing."[14]

15

Moonshining
(*The Andy Griffith Show*)

The Andy Griffith Show gave us the fictional burg of Mayberry, North Carolina, a bucolic community based on Griffith's hometown—Mount Airy. Stories revolved around life lessons during the CBS series' eight-year span (1960 to 1968).

An early episode set the folksy tone that became the show's hallmark. When car trouble strands a businessman in Mayberry, the townspeople's slow and easy approach to life frustrates him but he acclimates to the easygoing ways of strangers who welcome him as they would kin.[1]

Sheriff Andy Taylor, Griffith's character, has stature, integrity and respect, allowing him to resolve disputes without a gun. In the episode "Christmas Story," department store owner Ben Weaver wants moonshiner Sam behind bars, no matter that the culprit made his home brew—a type of whisky—for consumption rather than distribution; no matter that he has a family, and no matter that it's the day before Christmas.

The grumpy, craggy and obstinate capitalist has a point, though. He claims that "half the county" makes their own alcohol, which decreases sales of spirits in his store and others. Andy's gentler, kinder way of law enforcement has no effect; Weaver threatens to report Andy to the state authorities if he doesn't lock up Sam. Further, the Mayberry merchant won't even allow Sam to be jailed on December 26 so he can spend the holiday with his family.

Andy gets creative: He also arrests Sam's wife, two sons and daughter so they can celebrate Christmas together in the jail cell. His legal basis: They're accessories because they knew about the moonshining. Weaver has a change of heart when he sees that the family's holiday spirit persists behind bars; he steals a bench that's public property to get arrested and join the crowd. But the sheriff shows his generosity by refusing to put him in jail. So Weaver parks in front of a fire hydrant and tears up Deputy Sheriff Barney Fife's ticket. That's for naught, as well; Ellie, the town

TV Land sponsored this statue paying homage to Andy Griffith and Ron Howard in the opening credits of *The Andy Griffith Show*. The statue was dedicated in Raleigh, North Carolina, in 2003. A year later, Griffith's hometown of Mount Airy, North Carolina, received its own statue, also sponsored by TV Land. Stuart Williamson is the sculptor. Photograph by Donald Burgess Tilley, Jr. (courtesy Commemorative Landscapes of North Carolina, https://docsouth.unc.edu/commland/).

pharmacist, pays the $2 fine. When Weaver empties a garbage can in the street, Andy figures out his ploy. Together, they go to the store and bring back presents for everyone. Andy is forced to let Sam go home because there's no more evidence: Weaver drank the moonshine!²

While Sheriff Taylor might have a friendly and flexible way of enforcing the law against what he deems to be minor offenses, Sam would have a formidable challenge in the modern world, particularly at the federal level.

15. Moonshining (The Andy Griffith Show)

The Alcohol and Tobacco Tax and Trade Bureau relies on Title 26, Section 5601, of the United States Code in its enforcement against the manufacture of "distilled spirits at any place other than a TTB-qualified distilled spirits plant." Potential violations with criminal penalties are outlined on the TTB website, resulting in a potential sentence of up to five years in prison and a fine of up to $10,000 per violation.[3]

- 5601(a)(1)—Possession of an unregistered still.
- 5601(a)(2)—Engaging in business as a distiller without filing an application and receiving notice of registration.
- 5601(a)(6)—Distilling on a prohibited premises. (Under 26 U.S.C. 5178[a][1][B], a distilled spirits plant may not be located in a residence or in sheds, yards, or enclosures connected to a residence.)
- 5601(a)(7)—Unlawful production or use of material fit for production of distilled spirits.
- 5601(a)(8)—Unlawful production of distilled spirits.
- 5601(a)(11)—Purchase, receipt, and/or processing of distilled spirits when the person who does so knows or has reasonable grounds to believe that Federal excise tax has not been paid on the spirits.
- 5601(a)(12)—Removal or concealment of distilled spirits on which tax has not been paid.

Clearly, Sam violates 5601(a)(1), 5601(a)(6) and 5601(a)(8). He needs a still to produce the moonshine at home. Although it's stated that Sam produced his concoction for consumption rather than distribution, there may be others in Mayberry with visions of selling their products. Without a tax, they will be in violation of Section 5602 with a potential punishment of up to five years in prison and a $10,000 fine.[4]

Sam did himself a favor by limiting his production and consumption of alcohol to his homestead, otherwise Ben Weaver could have taken his grievances even further by contacting the Bureau of Alcohol, Tobacco, Firearms and Explosives. The ATF's website defines the purpose of enforcement:

> to target, identify, and dismantle criminal enterprises with ties to violent crime, that traffic illicit liquor or contraband tobacco in interstate commerce; seize and deny their access to assets and funds; and prevent their encroachment into the legitimate alcohol or tobacco industry.[5]

North Carolina's laws do not exempt a moonshiner from the law if homemade alcohol is consumed at home. But wine and malt beverages, such as beer, will be exempt depending on how the product is used. Section 18B-306 allows,

An individual may make, possess, and transport wines and malt beverages for the individual's own use, the use of the individual's family and guests, or the use at organized affairs, exhibitions, or competitions. For purposes of this section, the term 'organized affairs, exhibitions, or competitions' includes homemaker's contests, tastings, and judgings.

But the state law forbids the alcohol from being "sold or offered for sale."[6]

Sam's foray into moonshine follows a longstanding tradition in North Carolina, which claims to be the site where the term "moonshine" began. North Carolina's official website attributes its success to "ample water resources as well as grain and a variety of products for the production of alcohol." In addition, a "robust rail system" made the state an efficient place for moonshiners to distribute their wares. Prohibition from 1919 to 1933 amplified the need for distillers, complemented later by the improvement in automobile technology that led to the creation of a sport. "The production of illegal whiskey was also connected to the rise of stock car racing, as many moonshiners would use their modified cars to outrun law enforcement on the back roads."[7]

In 2021, a North Carolina distiller named Roger "Buck" Nance, who worked in North Wilkesboro at a licensed moonshine distillery (Copper Barrel), faced accusations of making more than 9000 gallons of untaxed liquor for an illegal still during a two-year period. Along with four other men, he was charged in a scheme that included tax evasion amounting to approximately $100,000 in lost tax revenue combined at the state and federal levels. Other charges: conspiracy to defraud the United States, aiding and abetting, unlawful production of distilled spirits and possession of an unregistered still.[8]

The five men pleaded guilty and received their sentences in June 2022. Nance got two years of probation but needed to stay at home for one year subject to electronic monitoring. One man received a six-month prison sentence plus three years of "supervised release" with six months at home. Two other men each got two years of probation plus the stay-at-home requirement for six months. The fifth man accepted probation for a year.[9]

It was reported that $186,000 escaped tax collection in North Carolina, Virginia and the federal government because of their actions, which prompted another part of the punishment: $23,619 from each defendant for federal taxes.[10]

The South is a reservoir of lore and fact handed down from generation to generation, so it's possible that Sam, Ben and Andy would have heard about a massive case in federal court involving moonshine from the neighboring state of Virginia and covering a conspiracy spanning September 1928 to February 1935.

Prosecutors and defense attorneys sparred in a federal district

15. Moonshining (The Andy Griffith Show)

courtroom for over ten weeks; 400 witnesses testified. Jurors took two days to render their decision regarding the fate of 23 defendants and issued their verdict on July 1, 1935. Guilty: 20. Acquittal: 3. The *Roanoke Times* reported,

> Specifically the indictment charged the defendants with operation of unregistered distilleries, carrying on the business of a distiller, wholesaler and retailer of liquors without a license or having given bond, removing and concealing, and aiding and abetting in the removal and concealment.

The newspaper described the feeling in the sweltering courtroom when the clerk announced the verdict:

> Hardly a sound was audible save for a gasp of surprise or relief here and there.... The wife of one defendant wept silently, dabbing a handkerchief to her eyes, but the wives and women relatives of other defendants remained stoical and apparently as unmoved as those who had just been convicted.[11]

The three acquittals were for Virginia prosecutor Charles Carter Lee and two deputy sheriffs. Lee utilized powerful character witnesses—two justices on the state's Supreme Court of Appeals, a Roanoke judge and a state circuit court judge. Certainly, the judges before whom he tried cases could testify about his professionalism. After the verdict, Lee pointed to the motive of certain witnesses as questionable. "I was entirely clear of all such charges, which were founded in political prejudice, and anger on the part of criminals whom I had prosecuted, in their attempt to get vengeance."[12]

Sam would have applauded a 2024 decision by a federal judge in Texas, who overturned a ban dating back to the 19th century regarding at-home distilling. In *Hobby Distillers Association vs. Alcohol and Tobacco Tax and Trade Bureau*, the Plaintiff was an organization with "approximately 1300 members nationwide." There were also four individual plaintiffs. Judge Mark Pittman expressed concern about a threat made by the Tax and Trade Bureau via letter: "Though this letter does not make it *certain* that Plaintiffs' [sic] will be prosecuted, it certainly makes it credible."[13]

In a footnote, the judge further discusses the letter and the scenario of government overreach in this instance:

> As a matter of principle, this Court is distressed at an impropriety contained in TTB's letter. Regardless of the reader's level of comfort with the federal government receiving purchase data and using that data to "forewarn" ne'er-do-well citizens about potential criminal liability, this Court is highly disturbed that the letter attempts to threaten a "$500,000 fine" when the statutory maximum is $10,000.[14]

The judge cited the 1958 Supreme Court case *Trop vs. Dulles* for the Constitution's importance. "The provisions of the Constitution are not time-worn adages or hollow shibboleths … they are the rules of government."[15] He added,

> And Plaintiffs have met their burden to demonstrate that a currently enforced statute has no constitutional backing. In other words, they've shown that Congress and the TTB have not been playing by the rules of government. And the judicial responsibility to "enforce the paramount commands of the Constitution" is not removed simply because an agency has been playing by the wrong rules for a long time.[16]

Regarding governmental concerns about the loss of tax revenue, Judge Pittman balanced the community interest against overreach through government fiat. "While prohibiting the possession of an at-home still meant to distill beverage alcohol might be *convenient* to protect tax revenue on spirits, it is not a sufficiently clear corollary to the positive power of laying and collecting taxes."[17]

Like Sam's moonshine in *The Andy Griffith Show*, concoctions made by members of the Hobby Distillers Association may be more potent than liquor purchased in stores. It will look different, plus there are health considerations because a legitimate distiller will make whisky under sanitary requirements mandated by law. Walton's Distillery in Jacksonville, North Carolina, explains that aging is a key factor:

> When whisky comes out of the still, it's so clear it looks like water. Moonshiners bottle it and sell it just like that. Commercial alcohols have an amber or golden color to them—this is because they are aged for years in charred oak barrels. The aging process gives them color and mellows the harsh taste. There's no such mellowing with moonshine, which is why it has such "kick."

There's also the issue of moonshine's ingredients. Legitimate alcohol producers have a greater variety, which leads to more choices for the consumer. According to Walton's website:

> Moonshine made from grain, like corn or rye, is whisky. But alcohol can be made from many different ingredients. During Prohibition, profit-hungry moonshiners started using white sugar instead of corn meal, producing a cheaper product that was technically rum, not whisky. Fruits could also be used instead of grains—today, moonshiners in Appalachian states still manufacture apple brandy.[18]

Along with the Christmas episode of *The Andy Griffith Show*, moonshining can be seen or referenced in the films *Moonrunners, Greased Lightning, White Lightning, Walking Tall* and *Thunder Road* as well as the TV shows *M*A*S*H, The Waltons, The Dukes of Hazzard* and *The Beverly Hillbillies.*

16

Theft of Electricity
(*Deck the Halls*)

A man's home is his castle.

It provides a source of tremendous pride and pleasure, both as a residence and a reflection of passion. A sports fan may adorn a room with memorabilia, pennants, jerseys, autographed photos, artwork, movie posters and a large-screen television. A gardener may give neighbors the vegetables that he harvests in his backyard while proclaiming their superiority over supermarket produce. A fan of midcentury modern furniture may fill his living room with vintage couches, chairs, and tables purchased from an estate sale.

In the 2006 comedy film *Deck the Halls*, salesman Buddy Hall's (Danny DeVito) passion is Christmas decorations. Boredom with his success in sales (cars, carpets, copiers, futons) causes restlessness and, in turn, several moves for his wife and two teenage daughters. Their latest stop is Cloverdale, a small town in western Massachusetts where everyone seems to know everyone else. The Halls move into their new house on the evening of December 1, across the street from the Finches.[1]

Dr. Steven Finch (Matthew Broderick), Cloverdale's leading optometrist, fancies himself to be the community's expert on Christmas. Steve's wife calls him "intense," but he responds that he's "just extremely organized." Broderick recalled a different experience as a kid in Manhattan during the Christmas season. "When I was growing up, it was hanging lights on the fire escape," said the actor, who had also starred in *Ferris Bueller's Day Off*, *WarGames*, *Biloxi Blues*, *The Cable Guy*, *Glory* and *The Producers*.[2]

Being the Christmas connoisseur of Cloverdale fuels Steve's ego but he has another reason for absorbing himself in the holiday season. Like his portrayer, Steve didn't really have a traditional Christmas. Because his father was in the Air Force, their family moved around a lot (like the Halls). When Buddy targets his energy into creating a grand display of

Christmas lights, Steve feels threatened by the attention, awe and respect that friends and strangers alike bestow upon his new neighbor. In addition to the lights, Buddy creates a manger with live animals including a camel and cow, plus a huge sled complemented by horses with fake antlers, and music synchronized to the lights.

A news reporter comes to the house for an interview, giving Buddy an opportunity to share his mission. "And I'm not gonna stop until I have the biggest and brightest light display in the world. I really want my house to be seen from space. Outer space." To accomplish this goal, Buddy steals electricity from Steve's house by using an extension cord and covering it with snow; Steve later discovers his subterfuge. Given Buddy's celebrity status caused by the display, an arrest for stealing electricity could be a realistic consequence.

The Commonwealth of Massachusetts addresses this action in Section 127A of the General Laws:

> Whoever unlawfully and intentionally injures or destroys, or suffers to be injured or destroyed, any meter, pipe, conduit, wire, line, pole, lamp or other apparatus belonging to a corporation, including municipal corporations which own municipal lighting plants engaged in the manufacture or sale of electricity or gas or to any person,
>
> or unlawfully and intentionally prevents an electric or gas meter from duly registering the quantity of electricity or gas supplied,
>
> or in any way interferes with its proper action or just registration,
>
> or, without the consent of such corporation or person, unlawfully and intentionally diverts or suffers to be diverted any electric current from any wire or gas from any pipe of such corporation or person,
>
> or otherwise unlawfully and intentionally uses or causes to be used, without the consent of such corporation or person, any electricity or gas manufactured or distributed by such corporation, or charged to such person
>
> shall be liable to such corporation or person for triple the amount of damages sustained thereby or one thousand dollars whichever is greater.
>
> Damages shall include the value of the electricity or gas used and the cost of equipment repair and replacement. Any damages assessed under the provisions of this section in excess of the actual damages sustained by the corporation or person manufacturing, distributing or selling such electricity or gas shall be paid to the commonwealth; provided, however, that if a municipal lighting plant brings an action pursuant to this section such damages in excess of the actual damages shall be paid to such municipal lighting plant.[3]

Applying the statute's first consent provision to Buddy's actions leads to a conclusion that a case for prosecution is logical and viable because Buddy did not have consent to siphon electricity from Steve's house. Therefore, his act of diverting the electricity may be described as unlawful and intentional. Also, it's reasonable to presume that Steve pays a

16. Theft of Electricity (Deck the Halls)

utility company for his electricity rather than generating it himself, so the requirement of the meter, pipe, etc., belonging to a corporation will likely be met.

Then there's the issue of damages. It's rational to conclude that Buddy's display would exceed $1000 because of its massive size and scope. As a comparison, look at Bob Martel's commitment to decorations of his home in Hamilton, New Jersey, also known as Martel's Christmas Wonderland. A 2022 article underscored the challenge, attraction and appeal of Martel's display that had a 36-year history at the time of the article's publication and noted the immense numbers involved: "100 blow-up decorations, more than 500 molded figures and about 60,000 lights."

Cost: Martel estimated an electric bill of $1800 in December, which decreased to $400 because of LED lights. His creativity resulted in winning a major bounty in 2020: the $50,000 prize on ABC's *The Great Christmas Light Fight*.[4]

Buddy might argue that he got carried away during a moment of weakness but stealing electricity is an act with terrific gravity, causing companies to be adamantine about identifying and punishing thieves. Oncor, the largest energy delivery company in Texas, notes the impact: "In an average month, Oncor investigates 2400 cases of suspected theft. Industry experts estimate that $6 billion of electricity is stolen each year in the U.S."

Oncor and its brethren in the utility spectrum have strategies for investigating, finding and squashing the pilfering thanks to employees with deep knowledge of the complex issues surrounding electricity theft. "They're experts at detecting the quirks in meter data that can point to someone drawing off electricity for free or tricking a meter into an incorrect reading."[5]

An arrest would probably draw media attention. The Christmas angle adds to the allure of the story, though electricity theft has been a storyline for every season. In 2018, the Carter County (Tennessee) Sheriff's Office arrested an Elizabethton man for stealing electricity from a neighbor with an extension cord, causing her to suffer a $150 increase in her electric bill. The *Elizabethton Star* reported that the woman did not give permission; there was another charge of resisting a stop-arrest.[6]

In 2023, an Oklahoma City man faced accusations of using an extension cord to steal electricity from two neighbors in a condominium complex served by Oklahoma Gas & Electric. A 75-year-old woman living on Social Security claims she caught the culprit "at least three times." The alleged theft incurred her ire. "Who do they think they are to steal from us? And if they don't understand that, they really need to get good with God. And I'd have to think they better pray hard for their own soul, because they're losing it."[7]

In 2018, a feature article on the Everything Lubbock website warned that homeowners can be vulnerable because thieves will either tamper with their electricity meters or steal them. Lubbock Power and Light advised that stealing electricity could bring the attention of police and prosecutors with legal consequences to follow. Company executive Matt Rose said,

> If any individual was to come into your backyard and do something to your meter, there would [be] various different offenses that would occur there. One would be attempted [theft] or theft of electricity. Another would be destruction of utility and city property, and potentially it would be destruction to the homeowner.[8]

Lee County Electric Cooperative (LCEC), a non-profit electricity distribution cooperative with more than 250,000 members in Southwest Florida, battles electricity pirates with the same steadfastness as its counterparts owned by municipalities and investors. It's an industry-wide problem, emphasized by this organization that began in 1940:

> LCEC remains vigilant in its efforts to identify and stop meter cheaters through a program that utilizes automated meter-reading technology, business intelligence reporting and field investigations to detect theft, reduce losses and prevent injury to those who choose to steal electricity.[9]

It doesn't only happen with neighbors. In 2024, police arrested three people in Harris County, Texas, for stealing almost $3000 of electricity when they "diverted power from an electrical pole by connecting wiring to the pole and running the connection into one of the suspects' homes."[10]

Thieves can be shrewd. But a California energy bandit couldn't outwit Pacific Gas & Electric forever. In 2021, the California Court of Appeal for the Third District upheld a restitution hearing decision by the trial court ordering payment of $219,035.32 to PG&E for the financial damages caused when he bypassed the circuitry.

The company's investigators had calculated the final tally by following the provision outlined in the California Penal Code, which states that if a victim suffers economic loss as a result of the defendant's conduct,

> the court shall require that the defendant make restitution to the victim or victims in an amount established by court order, based on the amount of loss claimed by the victim or victims or any other showing to the court. If the amount of loss cannot be ascertained at the time of sentencing, the restitution order shall include a provision that the amount shall be determined at the direction of the court. The court shall order full restitution.[11]

PG&E's theft investigator looked at the damages and based his decision on factors including "the cost of the electricity at the time of the theft over the period [it was] believed defendant was stealing electricity, based on reasonable assumptions on usage patterns and the equipment's manufactured dates." The court ruled that the figure satisfied the "rational method" requirement established in a line of California cases.[12]

Utility companies have added a weapon in monitoring electricity usage thanks to technological progress. CenterPoint Energy is an example with more than 2.4 million Smart Meters across Houston. "Smart Meters are designed to send alerts when they're tampered with. Technology is helpful, but the eyes and ears of our customers remain essential for deterring theft and keeping energy costs low."[13]

Electricity theft is analyzed on a case-by-case basis. Duke Energy notes that not all thieves have malice, greed and defiance. "Often, the work is emotionally draining as investigators meet people who are stealing because they are single parents or recently lost their job. The company is not interested in punishing people, but wants to reclaim revenue and correct unsafe situations."[14]

A thief's shame, if it exists at all, might not be limited to a courtroom. In 2023, a Ring doorbell camera captured a man stealing electricity from his neighbor in Rockford, Illinois. The video went viral on TikTok.[15]

Electricity thieves also create a safety risk. Safe Electricity, a non-profit organization formed in 1952, warns about the dangers of stealing electricity including the potential for draining power and injuring linemen:

> The power line could become overloaded with electric energy, which could harm your electronics and appliances designed to receive a certain steady amount of electricity. Electricity theft makes power service less reliable and lower quality for paying customers. Electricity thieves may also unknowingly feed energy back into the power line. This is dangerous for lineworkers, who may assume the power line they are working on is deenergized.[16]

Buddy's actions in *Deck the Halls* are hazardous. Besides a demonstrable financial impact that Steve and the utility would be able to prove, there's the potential danger of a fire if Buddy overloads the power grid through the wires and his auxiliary generator.

At the end of the movie, Buddy achieves his goal of making his Christmas lights spectacle visible from a space satellite. But his zealotry could have the lawyers of his electricity provider adding a couple of words to the lyrics in Mariah Carey's holiday standard: "All I want for Christmas is you in court."

17

Burglary
(*How the Grinch Stole Christmas!*)

In 1966, TV had a banner year. *Batman, Star Trek, That Girl, The Monkees* and *Mission: Impossible* premiered. *Green Acres* and *Hogan's Heroes* completed their first of six seasons in prime time. Set during Ulysses S. Grant's presidency, *The Wild Wild West* also finished its rookie season capitalizing on the popular spy genre of the 1960s. Charles Schulz debuted *It's the Great Pumpkin, Charlie Brown*, his second animated special featuring characters from the *Peanuts* comic strip.

On December 18, another icon graced TV screens for the first time: *How the Grinch Stole Christmas!* Narrated by Boris Karloff and based on the 1957 book of the same name by Dr. Seuss (the pen name of Theodor Geisel), it depicts the transformation of a character who acts upon his dastardly intentions and then has a change of heart.[1]

Visual quality exceeded the accepted norms in TV animation. The *Los Angeles Times* reported,

> Approximately 25,000 individual drawings have been made in animating *How the Grinch Stole Christmas!*, instead of the 2000 or so done for the average half-hour *Flintstones* [or] *Huckleberry Hound* cartoon. Original music has been composed by Albert Hague (Dr. Seuss did the lyrics) and it is performed by a 34-piece orchestra with a 12-voice choir."[2]

Geisel's initial reluctance to put the book in the hands of Hollywood had nothing to do with compensation as he received a healthy income from royalties on his constantly expanding portfolio of work, which included *And to Think That I Saw It on Mulberry Street, Gerald McBoing Boing, The Cat in the Hat* and *Green Eggs and Ham*. Geisel sought to protect the integrity of the work if used for another medium.

Chuck Jones, the legendary producer of Warner Brothers' *Looney Tunes* cartoons, knew Geisel from their military service during World War

17. Burglary (How the Grinch Stole Christmas!)

II when they produced training films for the Army. Geisel trusted him. "I wanted creative control over what happened to my characters," said the author. "And most of the offers just were that: offers of a lot of money and kindly stay home and let us tend to the TV business. With Chuck, I knew I could work actively with him on the Grinch."[3]

How did he know? Jones could point to his massive volume of stories with Bugs Bunny, Daffy Duck, Porky Pig *et al.* to exemplify his value, but there was an added layer of complexity. Geisel served as both writer and artist for his books; Jones needed to earn Geisel's confidence that he could interpret the Grinch story in animated form while maintaining a compelling narrative. "[Geisel] was afraid nobody else could draw his characters; he illustrates his own books," said Jones. "He can draw a different Grinch for every page if he likes. But with animation you have to be more precise. So I proved to him that I could do his characters in a way that would please him. And also asked him to be co-producer with me."[4]

It worked. Plus, Geisel raved about the talent that Karloff brought to the tale: "Karloff's marvelous voice range has the effect of a musical instrument. He runs the scale from the raspy, spiteful character of the Grinch to ingenuous little Cindy Lou, representing all that is most heart-warming in a child's idea of Christmas."[5]

Grinch had some fans among the critics. Donald Freeman of the *Daily Breeze*, a newspaper serving the South Bay region of Los Angeles, lauded the expansion of the Grinch from a literary platform to television: "Deliciously entertaining, fresh and inventive and aglow with a special Seussian warmth.... The result—and I can conceive of no stronger praise—had the Dr. Seuss imprint throughout."[6]

Variety gave a rousing endorsement as well. "Animation excellently captured the spirit [of] Seuss' fictional characters and had enough farcical sight gags so the kiddies geared to standard cartoon fare wouldn't feel left out. Boris Karloff's narrative was right on the mood."[7]

At first, the Grinch does not merely express disgust at the joy in Whoville during the Christmas season; ruination of the holiday becomes his mission. He aims for pure, emotional devastation by stealing the Christmas presents of Whoville's residents during the night, anticipating a consequent depression for them and elation for himself. But when he hears singing from Whoville after the loss of gifts, he realizes that the spirit of Christmas sustains them. He rushes to return the gifts and receives a welcome to be part of Whoville's celebration, including the honor of carving the "roast beast" for the community's dinner.

It's a heartwarming story. But Grinch's acts clearly violate the law even though he remedies his actions and the citizens of Whoville do not seem to mind the theft. Using New York as a template for a strict legal analysis, the Grinch engaged in criminal behavior, specifically, burglary, larceny and trespass.

The Grinch committed burglary when he snuck in the houses in the middle of the night to steal the gifts. Cindy Lou Who could be called as a witness because she saw him; his lie about the gifts being broken and taking them home for repairs amplifies the argument for burglary. In New York, burglary in the third degree occurs "when that person knowingly enters unlawfully in a building with intent to commit a crime therein."[8]

Larceny is evident as well. The Grinch took the gifts from the house and headed toward his home before changing his mind and heart about Whoville. "A person steals property and commits larceny when, with intent to deprive another of property or to appropriate the same to himself or to a third person, he wrongfully takes, obtains or withholds such property from an owner thereof."[9]

Prosecutors in Whoville would need to determine the value of the property stolen for the appropriate level of larceny. If it exceeds $1000, then the Grinch faces a charge of grand larceny in the fourth degree.[10] A value exceeding $3000 leads to a third degree charge.[11] If it's more than $50,000, then the charge is grand larceny in the second degree.[12] An increase to more than $1,000,000 escalates the theft to grand larceny in the first degree.[13]

Prosecutors may use the fair market value of the presents, which should be an easy task comprised of asking the victims for receipts. Alternatively, the stores that sold the gifts can provide prices and records. If the Grinch wanted to sell the stolen property—or dismantle a product and sell the parts individually—on the black market and get a higher price, then the prosecutors might want to analogize the 1974 case of *People vs. Colasanti*, which dealt with the theft of prescription drugs used for medical experiments with no charge to hospitals or doctors. The Court of Appeals for the State of New York stated, "Under some circumstances, courts have found that the underworld value of contraband may be used in determining value for the purposes of a larceny or criminal possession statute."[14]

Trespass would be another charge, for sure. The Grinch went into the houses without permission in the middle of the night. "A person is guilty of trespass when he knowingly enters or remains unlawfully in or upon premises."[15]

If the Grinch's home is over the border separating Whoville's state from another state, federal law may be triggered. Under the National Stolen Property Act, the Grinch faces a charge of transporting stolen goods if a financial barrier is met: "Whoever transports, transmits, or transfers in interstate or foreign commerce any goods, wares, merchandise, securities or money, of the value of $5000 or more, knowing the same to have been stolen, converted or taken by fraud."[16]

17. Burglary (How the Grinch Stole Christmas!)

In 2019, the Grinch caught the attention of the National Judicial College. This esteemed organization is "the only educational institution in the United States that teaches courtroom skills to judges of all types from all over the country, Indian Country and abroad." In its Question of the Month, the NJC challenged its members to figure how the actions in the story violate laws, ordinances, regulations and the like.

In addition to burglary, larceny and trespass, the participants listed a roster of charges for the Grinch including invasion of privacy because he spied on Whoville and destruction of property assuming he damaged gifts when he left Whoville and drove his sled in fast, reckless fashion with the help of his dog Max. Throughout the story, the Grinch mistreats Max until the end when he gives him a healthy slice of the "roast beast" for dinner. So a charge of animal cruelty is another possibility.

One judge chose not to get in the Christmas spirit, refusing to participate in the scenario requiring the application of commonly accepted definitions in criminal law. Rationale: The story depicted no violations. "We are only bound by the law and we have no idea what conduct Whoville statutes, if any, proscribe or require."[17]

However, prosecutors will likely have a tough time making a case against the Grinch. Because of the joyousness expressed by the Whos and their welcoming the thief with his change of heart, it doesn't seem like any of them will want to give testimony.

The Grinch is not alone in his holiday thievery. Journalists have covered several instances of comparably abominable behavior. In 2015, a grand jury in eastern Kentucky indicted two men on charges of second-degree burglary, first-degree burglary and felony theft regarding tools and Christmas gifts. Another man was indicted for receiving the stolen property, according to prosecutors.[18]

Dallas police officers investigated a burglary of a family's Christmas gifts in 2016 and returned the following night with replacements to put under the tree. Their generosity prompted the mother to make a request of the officers: "I asked them for a hug and they said, 'yes,' so I gave them a hug and said, 'thank you.'"[19]

A similar event happened in 2022 when the theft of Christmas gifts from an Indiana home led police in South Bend to replace the stolen items as best they could.[20]

The following year, an Orange County, California, family was robbed of two iPads, a camera and jewelry amounting to "about a few thousand dollars worth of recent purchases." It happened in an empty house during the daytime, when the parents worked and the kids attended school.[21]

Fort Oglethorpe, Georgia, Police Chief Keith Sewell offered a caveat for the holiday season in 2023. In addition to picking up small packages left on the doorstep by UPS, FedEx, Amazon and the U.S. Postal Service as quickly as possible, homeowners ought to pay attention to their post-holiday actions. "Even after the gift-giving season, make sure that you don't put up empty boxes outside and say, 'Hey, I got a new television,'" said Chief Sewell.[22]

In 2022, Porch Research released information that might have holiday gift buyers changing locks and installing alarm systems. Las Vegas suffered the highest cost of stolen property in the country with an estimated $9165 per burglary in December; the national estimate totaled $130.5 million. Rounding out the top ten metropolitan areas were San Diego, Houston, Virginia Beach, Denver, Dallas, Atlanta, Nashville, Indianapolis and Portland. "Almost 5000 homes were burgled either on Christmas Eve or Christmas Day [in 2021], with roughly 2700 break-ins taking place on the 24th and about 2200 on the 25th."

The top five categories were: jewelry (or precious metals), computer technology (hardware-software), clothes and furs, portable electronic communications and money. Atlantic City, New Jersey, residents have a particular reason to be concerned about Grinch-like criminals during December because burglaries double: 120 percent compared to the average for the rest of the year.[23]

But gifts are not the only items vulnerable to thieves. Christmas decorations can be targets and they don't require entry into a dwelling for retrieval. Lights are marketable. Stripping them for the copper wiring may be a lucrative endeavor as well. Some houses have figures of Santa Claus, elves and reindeer, which can be swiped easily in the middle of the night. In 2023, an Antioch, California, family lost its six-foot Santa from the front yard.[24]

Elaborate decorations have pros and cons. Notably, they will likely attract a lot of onlookers, which could dissuade holiday bandits from executing their intentions. On the other hand, they provide tempting targets, especially for a talented thief or team of thieves working quickly. Security cameras and other precautions are warranted for these types of houses. "Criminals aren't stupid, they are smart enough to respond to incentives," said a former police officer in Bowling Green, Kentucky, commenting on holiday thievery in the wake of the Antioch incident. "If they see value in something, they are going to try to take it."[25]

Should the Grinch revert to his old form, he'll have some competition for thefts during the Christmas season.

18

Witness Protection
(*The Sopranos*)

    Salvatore Bonpensiero is many things to Tony Soprano, *caporegime* of the DiMeo mob family in northern New Jersey. Friend. Soldier. Traitor.
    He was nicknamed "Big Pussy" in honor of his Mafia beginnings as a cat burglar; his legitimate business is an automotive body shop. Though never identified as such, the shop is likely part of the Soprano money-laundering machine funneling illegitimate income from bookmaking and other activities through legitimate enterprises to avoid IRS and FBI scrutiny.
    Tony warned Big Pussy not to sell heroin because the risk of getting caught is too high, but the lure of profits proved too large for Big Pussy to ignore because of his kids' college tuition. Facing a prison term of 30 years to life, Big Pussy becomes an FBI informant, targeting the Soprano clan.
    When Tony hears this from his law enforcement contact, a Newark Police Department detective, he initially dismisses the prospect of his longtime friend being a turncoat. Their relationship has historical significance. Soprano soldier Christopher Moltisanti explains to two younger associates that Big Pussy stepped up for "Johnny Boy" Soprano—Tony's father—during a time described as the "Unrest of '83." His action is not clarified. Perhaps he was a fall guy and went to prison instead of Johnny Boy or spoke on his behalf to prevent further chaos either within the DiMeo family or with other mob families.[1]
    During a night of extensive vomiting, sweating and a high fever because of food poisoning, Tony has a dream in which he learns that Big Pussy is working with the FBI to take him down. After he wakes up and the fever breaks, Tony employs measures to confirm his subconscious suspicions; he takes pals Silvio Dante and Paulie Gualtieri to pick up Big Pussy at his home under the pretext of getting their opinions on a boat that he's thinking of buying. Claiming a need to use the bathroom, Tony searches the master bedroom and finds nothing. Then he takes a second look at the

cigar box on the dresser and discovers a false bottom hiding wire equipment. It's apparent to Tony that Big Pussy must be killed to stop the flow of information to the FBI.

On the boat, Big Pussy asserts that he's feeding "misinformation" to take the feds off Tony's scent but admits the veracity of some information including a scam involving calling cards and a pump-and-dump stock scheme. His last gasp for a reprieve fails. The trio shoots Big Pussy several times, wraps him in heavy plastic with weights, and pushes him into the ocean.[2]

In the Christmas episode "…To Save Us All from Satan's Power," Tony recalls the previous year's holiday season when Big Pussy came into Satriale's Pork Store, a Soprano holding and hangout, to carry on the tradition of dressing up as Santa Claus and giving gifts to neighborhood children. This benevolence began with Johnny Boy.

Tony figures that Big Pussy wore a wire because he arrived already garbed in the Santa Claus suit. Plus, he talked fast about an issue Tony had been handling regarding the EPA and Barone Sanitation—another asset in the Soprano portfolio—presumably to record Tony talking about an illegal act. But the discussion never got that far. When Christopher interrupted the conversation, nerves and temper got the better of Big Pussy and he threw an ashtray. "What the fuck is wrong with you?!" exclaimed Tony. "Fuck you!" responded Big Pussy. Provoked by this blatant disrespect, Tony jumped from his chair to punch Big Pussy. Paulie stands between them to prevent the boss' surging anger from escalating to fisticuffs.[3]

During his tenure as an FBI informant, Big Pussy reported to agent Skip Lipari. If he hadn't been killed, Big Pussy would have gotten a new identity courtesy of the federal government in exchange for testifying against Tony. Skip once highlighted the benefits of starting a new life and noted that one informant became recycling and garbage commissioner of a "good-size city in Florida."[4]

Witness Protection began with Public Law 91–452, otherwise known as the Organized Crime Control Act, which President Nixon signed on October 14, 1970. Title V, Section 501, of the statute illustrates broad powers involved in witness protection:

> The Attorney General of the United States is authorized to provide for the security of Government witnesses, potential Government witnesses, and the families of Government witnesses and potential witnesses in legal proceedings against any person alleged to have participated in an organized criminal activity.[5]

Nixon's statement upon signing the bill into law emphasized the 18-month journey that began with "recommendations to the Congress" followed by "a bipartisan effort" resulting in legislation. The president also stressed the impact of organized crime and the new law's expansion of opportunities for civil servants in the government's executive branch to investigate, arrest and prosecute criminals.

> [T]he billions of dollars that organized crime has taken out of American society, what it has done to society in other ways, its, for example, support of the drug traffic in this country, in many of these areas where we have seen organized crime doing so much harm to America, we are going to find now that those who are fighting against crime will have the tools that they need to do the job and they will do the job.[6]

Section 502 provides that witnesses and their families can get access to "protected housing facilities" if the attorney general deems their lives to be in jeopardy. "Any person availing himself of an offer by the attorney general to use such facilities may continue to use such facilities for as long as the attorney general determines the jeopardy to his life or person continues."[7]

Gerald Shur was the primary influence behind the creation of the Witness Protection Program. Like Wernher von Braun with America's rocketry program, Bugsy Siegel with Las Vegas, or Walt Disney with Disneyland, Shur had the appropriate instinct, forethought and perseverance to make his vision a thriving reality. Shur was part of the program, nicknamed WITSEC, for 34 years.

WITSEC proved to be an invaluable tool for FBI agents and federal prosecutors to take on Mafia activities; Shur and his colleagues persuaded Bonpensiero's real-life counterparts to testify against superiors in exchange for minimal or zero time in prison plus relocation to another state under a different identity. Consequently, they greatly weakened the Mafia structure. During Shur's tenure, more than 6400 witnesses went into the program in addition to more than 14,400 dependents. His involvement was critical. "No witnesses got protection in WITSEC without his personal attention," wrote Pete Early in the prologue to *WITSEC: Inside the Federal Witness Protection Program*, a 2002 book that he co-authored with Shur. "[Shur] wrote nearly all of the program's rules, shaped it based on his own personal philosophical views, and guided it with a steady but iron hand."

Further, Shur's oversight created a cocoon of safety for the witnesses and their families. "None of the witnesses who followed his rules was murdered."

What are the duties for an FBI agent involved with WITSEC? Whatever needs to be done. Certainly, there's psychology that needs to be used for persuading a witness that testifying against friends and colleagues is in his or her better interest even if it means uprooting from everything you've ever known and starting a new life with a new identity somewhere else in the country. Early wrote that Shur also got entangled in the personal lives of witnesses:

> At various times, he served as a mob marriage counselor, substitute father, even priest. He helped create false backgrounds for witnesses, arranged secret weddings, oversaw funerals, and personally persuaded corporate executives to hire former mob hit men as delivery route drivers. Once he arranged for the wife of a Los Angeles killer to have breast enlargement surgery to keep her husband happy.[8]

Henry Hill became a household name because of the 1990 film *Goodfellas*, which ends with Hill testifying against Jimmy Conway and Paul Cicero (characters based on mobsters Jimmy Burke and Paul Vario) and then entering the Witness Protection Program. One of their schemes involved paying Boston College basketball players to affect games against Providence, Harvard, UCLA, Fordham, St. John's and Holy Cross during the 1978–79 season.[9]

It was a simple process. Let's say that the Boston College Eagles were favored to win by ten points, then the players would "shave" points to ensure that they won by less than that figure; Hill and his cohorts bet against the spread with a series of bookmakers, giving odds that led to huge payouts.

The Witness Protection Program's deal with Hill required him to testify about the point-shaving scandal, fraud, murder and other crimes. His participation resulted in several convictions with Burke and Vario being the most prominent targets, though the prosecutors never put anyone from Hill's group behind bars for the December 1978 Lufthansa Heist, a major robbery engineered by Burke. More than $5 million in cash and more than $850,000 in jewelry was boosted from the airline's cargo terminal; this was a major storyline in *Goodfellas*.[10]

When Hill got involved with the Witness Protection Program and began delivering robust testimony for federal prosecutors, everyone involved from their end of the robbery had been executed except Burke and himself. The prosecutors were able to convict an airline employee.

Like Bonpensiero in *The Sopranos*, Hill struck a deal with the feds after facing serious charges involving drug trafficking that could have resulted in imprisonment for the rest of his life. He had been on parole after a stint in federal prison; his parole officer recommended cooperating with the federal authorities. After Hill made bail, the feds acted.

Former federal prosecutor Ed McDonald, who plays himself in *Goodfellas*, recalled the events surrounding Hill entering the Witness Protection Program:

We suspected that once he made the street, that he would become a fugitive. What we did was, we quickly put together an application to have him arrested as a material witness and he was arrested because we were afraid that he was going to flee.

Henry was an enormously successful witness. He was enormously helpful in making some major, major prosecutions. And so, the government got its money's worth by putting Henry in the Witness Protection Program despite the fact that he was a headache. I mean, he was a headache in the sense that the first place he went to, he blew his cover. The second place he went to, he blew his cover. Usually, it's two and out. But by that time, probably by '83 or so, Henry was still testifying in significant cases, was still providing significant information helping to make investigations, support wiretap applications, search warrant applications. So, Henry was still a valuable witness.

"So, we went to Washington in conjunction with the FBI and also with the Drug Enforcement Administration and we said, "Look, Henry is still a very valuable witness. Don't kick him out of the program."[11]

In his third city—Seattle—Henry was arrested on drug charges and faced 15 years in prison after a successful prosecution. McDonald sent a letter summarizing the cases in which Hill had provided valuable information and served as a witness; the judge sentenced Hill to probation and drug rehabilitation.[12]

Hill's initial agreement with the Department of Justice Organized Crime Strike Force for the Eastern District of New York excluded federal prosecution regarding crimes for which he offered testimony before and after the agreement was signed. If a city's district attorney office or other law enforcement organization decided to prosecute, then the DOJ would recommend that it cease. If it moved forward, then the DOJ would highlight Hill's cooperation.[13] According to the agreement,

> this office will seek to place you in the Federal Witness Protection Program along with your wife and children and any other associates who become in need of protection as a result of your cooperation with this office. This understanding is predicated upon your complete cooperation with the Government including the immediate, full and truthful disclosure of all information in your possession which is relevant to these matters.[14]

Robert Simels, Hill's court-appointed defense attorney, explained the underlying reason for his client entering WITSEC: "He wants a new life and he can't afford to be involved with crooks."[15]

But Hill couldn't stay on a straight and narrow path. His arrest on drug charges in 1987 and similar arrests in the 1990s precipitated the Witness Protection Program removing him from its roster.[16]

Sammy Gravano also became a household name for his testimony against fellow mobsters and participation in the Witness Protection Program. On December 5, 1990, the *Staten Island Advance* described Gravano, nicknamed "Sammy the Bull," as the consigliere for the Gambino crime family—one of New York's five major Mafia families—and a target for a possible indictment along with Gambino boss John Gotti. A week later, the indictments happened. Gotti was charged with three murders of alleged Mafia figures; Gravano faced charges of two murders and other crimes including loansharking. In total, Gravano had responsibility for 19 murders.[17]

Federal prosecutor John Gleeson plotted to test Gravano's mettle in a courtroom by questioning him in a grand jury scenario when the courthouse would be sparsely populated. "It was a relatively minor case involving the DeCalvacante family in New Jersey and the Genovese family," explains Peter Maas in *Underboss: Sammy the Bull Gravano's Story of Life in the Mafia*. "Gleeson had purposely scheduled it for New Year's Eve. The courthouse was all but vacant. Security would not be much of a factor. The media was not likely to be around." Gleeson clarifies:

> We didn't need Sammy to get an indictment. But I wanted him to testify. I wanted him to be under oath and speak in front of jurors. To be candid about it, I wanted to get a look at him, to see, when it came to crunch time and he had to raise his right hand and testify, how he comported himself. And he comported himself perfectly, of course.[18]

Imprisoned for 11 months waiting for trial and facing the prospect of a prison term likely to be for the rest of his life, Gravano struck a deal to testify against Gotti and others. The *Daily News* quoted an unnamed source in federal law enforcement: "It's true, Sammy's cooperating and John is beside himself—and in deep trouble."[19]

Indeed, he was. Gotti received a guilty verdict on all counts, resulting in life imprisonment, while Gravano got a path to a new life, which erased evidence of his previous life including bank accounts. Gravano would receive the bounty created by selling his assets.[20]

After serving five years in prison, Gravano went into the Witness Protection Program. Destination: Arizona. But he voluntarily abandoned the program in the late 1990s and returned to the criminal life as Hill did, seeking to create a foothold in the Southwest by "setting up a drug operation and collecting protection money from local businesses," according to the Associated Press. Brooklyn assistant U.S. attorney Linda Lacewell declared, "Sammy Gravano got the second chance of a lifetime, and he blew it big time."[21]

Gravano's drug operation focused on an ecstasy ring that he absorbed, expanded and strengthened; revenue reached up to $500,000 a week. It was a family business. In 2001, Gravano and his family faced drug charges, which led to a guilty plea for ten felony counts and a 20-year state prison sentence. His son pleaded guilty to two felony counts; his wife and daughter each entered a guilty plea for one felony count.[22]

Henry Hill, Sammy Gravano and other Mafia figures who went into the Witness Protection Program provided rich fodder for true crime authors, TV news producers and newspaper writers. Big Pussy's partnership with the FBI in *The Sopranos* reflects the reality of a mobster facing a fork in the road—imprisonment for decades or testimony followed by a change in location and identity.

Big Pussy was not the only *Sopranos* character to work with the federal government. Ray Curto, Eugene Pontecorvo and Adrianna La Cerva (Christopher's fiancée) fed information to their FBI handlers, though they never reached the phase of testifying in court. Ray died of a stroke in the passenger seat of a parked car while talking with FBI agent Robyn Sanseverino. Eugene hung himself after getting a $2 million bequest in an aunt's will and learning that Tony would not let him move to Florida. Adrianna confessed her relationship with the FBI to Christopher, who almost choked her to death and then went to Tony's house in North Caldwell barely able to explain the situation. "Feds," he says through tears, knowing that his girlfriend must be killed. Tony assigns the task to Silvio.

19

Prostitution, Narcotics, Organized Crime, Murder (*L.A. Confidential*)

L.A. Confidential is a hotbed of crime.[1]

Based on James Ellroy's novel of the same name, this 1997 film strips away the glamour of early 1950s Los Angeles to reveal its seedy underside. Murder. Prostitution. Police corruption. Political payoffs. Organized crime. They're all in a compelling tale set in 1953, starring Russell Crowe, James Cameron, Danny DeVito, Guy Pearce, Kevin Spacey, David Strathairn and Kim Basinger.

Brian Helgeland and Curtis Hanson—who also directed the film—won the Oscar for Best Writing of a Screenplay Based on Material Previously Produced or Published. Basinger won the Oscar for Best Supporting Actress, a terrific achievement for the former model who began her acting career with TV guest roles on shows before transitioning to a movie career including *Batman*, *9½ Weeks*, *The Natural* and *Never Say Never Again*.

In *L.A. Confidential*, Basinger plays Lynn Bracken, a high-priced call girl working for Pierce Morehouse Patchett. This rich businessman owns Fleur-de-Lis, a prostitution ring that distinguishes its roster of attractive women with plastic surgery to look like movie stars; Basinger's character is a Veronica Lake match complete with peekaboo hairstyle. In one scene with a customer (a city councilman), they engage in a bit of role playing that recreates a moment from one of Lake's movies.

According to California law, a prostitute is an individual

> who solicits, or who agrees to engage in, or who engages in, any act of prostitution with the intent to receive compensation, money, or anything of value from another person. An individual agrees to engage in an act of prostitution when, with specific intent to so engage, he or she manifests an acceptance of an offer or solicitation by another person to so engage, regardless of whether the offer

19. Prostitution, Narcotics, Crime, Murder (L.A. Confidential)

or solicitation was made by a person who also possessed the specific intent to engage in an act of prostitution.[2]

Patchett will also be vulnerable to a pimping charge if Bracken affirms her activities with names, dates and dollar amounts regarding her customers. Section 266(h)(a) of the California Penal Code provides,

> [A]ny person who, knowing another person is a prostitute, lives or derives support or maintenance in whole or in part from the earnings or proceeds of the person's prostitution, or from money loaned or advanced to or charged against that person by any keeper or manager or inmate of a house or other place where prostitution is practiced or allowed, or who solicits or receives compensation for soliciting for the person, is guilty of pimping, a felony, and shall be punishable by imprisonment in the state prison for three, four, or six years.[3]

Notorious mobster Mickey Cohen's early 1950s trip to prison for tax evasion provides a key story point in *L.A. Confidential*: Who will take over his operations, including heroin distribution? In 1978, the Department of Justice's Organized Crime Control Commission summarized Cohen's impact on organized crime in Southern California:

> Well before [Bugsy] Siegel's death [in 1947], Mickey Cohen was sent to the West Coast by Eastern syndicate leaders to keep an eye on Siegel. Cohen was instrumental in setting up narcotic operations through Mexico and California. Joseph and Alfred Sica associated with Cohen in this activity. The Sica brothers were indicted in 1950 for narcotics violations, but the charges were dropped after Abraham Davidian, the key prosecution witness, was assassinated in Fresno.[4]

Cohen and his wife were charged with tax evasion amounting to more than $156,000 across a three-year period, from 1946 to 1948.[5]

On June 13, 1951, the charges against Mrs. Cohen were dropped. Five days later, Mickey Cohen testified on the witness stand and answered questions about bookmaking, gambling, loans and other financial activities. The *Los Angeles Times* reported, "Under questioning by [the U.S. attorney], Cohen spent considerable time disclaiming income testified to by government witnesses."[6]

Cohen's trial lasted 12 days and ended with a guilty verdict thanks to the prosecution's sound and effective legal strategy. "Courtroom observers were amazed at the thoroughness with which the government attorneys had prepared their case," declared the *Citizen-News*, which called itself the "Newspaper of Distinction" and served Southern California. "Nearly 150 government witnesses paraded to the witness stand in rapid-fire order."[7]

Judge Ben Harrison issued a sentence of five years in federal prison and a $10,000 fine. His rationale stemmed partly from the city's lackadaisical approach concerning illegal activities. "He was permitted to operate here as a betting commissioner with what I think was the virtual acquiescence of law enforcement officials," said the judge. "This community has to take its share of responsibility for his predicament."

Cohen's upbringing was another factor.

> Through an investigation by the probation department, I found that the rest of the members of his family turned out pretty well. But Mr. Cohen, brought up in a questionable environment, with little education, went from the sporting field into gambling and he found a fertile field in Los Angeles.[8]

In addition to the void created by Cohen's incarceration, marijuana serves as a story point in *L.A. Confidential*. *Hush Hush* magazine editor Sid Hudgens revels in stories that sensationalize sex, drugs and other topics ripe for consumption by readers looking for truth, innuendo and gossip about Hollywood. With visions of expanding into radio and TV, Hudgens has "a circulation of 36,000 and climbing" thanks to stories like "Movie Premiere Pot Bust" on Christmas Eve.

After getting a tip from a friend who sold marijuana to Matt Reynolds and Tammy Jordan, two young actors under contract at MGM, Hudgens collaborates with LAPD Detective Jack "Big V" Vincennes, an acquaintance and business partner. Hudgens gives Vincennes $100 ($50 for Vincennes, $40 to be split between two patrolmen and $10 for the police station watch commander) to have the opportunity for an exclusive on the Christmas Eve arrest.

Vincennes pulls the couple out of a two-family house; a movie theater down the street is showing *When Worlds Collide*, which gives Hudgens' photographer a terrific opportunity for a photo showing the detective with his latest captures framed by the marquee in the background. It reinforces the celebrity aura for Vincennes, who's also a member of Hollywood's inner circle because of his job as a technical advisor on the TV show *Badge of Honor*, an homage to *Dragnet*.

The Los Angeles District Attorney's office would probably look at the 1953 case of *People vs. Batwin* to determine whether to proceed with a prosecution. The ruling states,

> Possession of a narcotic is established when it is shown that a person has physical control thereof with the intent to exercise such control, or having had such physical control has not abandoned it, and no other person has that possession.[9]

After the arrest, Vincennes goes back into the house where a bag of marijuana is in clear view on a coffee table. The couple's physical control is therefore evident. *People vs. Batwin* further states, "The prosecution must establish that the defendant had knowledge of the presence of the article and that it was

19. Prostitution, Narcotics, Crime, Murder (L.A. Confidential) 119

Jack Webb created the TV series *Dragnet*, which inspired the TV series *Badge of Honor*, depicted in *L.A. Confidential* (courtesy Los Angeles Public Library/*Los Angeles Herald Examiner* Photo Collection).

marijuana." To prove this aspect of the case, the prosecutor could have a forensic scientist testify to the marijuana's authenticity; Hudgens' friend who sold the marijuana could cut a deal for immunity or a lower sentence provided that he confirms the sale and the product.[10]

The scribe who specializes in lewd, lurid and lascivious stories apparently makes peace with Reynolds after the young actor does a stint on the "honor farm." Luring him with $100 and the possibility of a comeback underscored by Vincennes all but guaranteeing a guest role on *Badge of Honor*, Hudgens persuades Reynolds to set up Ellis Loew, the district attorney, in a compromising situation in room 203 at the Hollywood Center Motel. Loew is homosexual; Reynolds is bisexual. Hudgens promises Reynolds that nobody will know, but he plans on making this another explosive *Hush Hush* story. He explains to Vincennes: "Reynolds is acey-deucey, not to mention broke. I'm getting him to fuck the D.A. for a hundred bucks."

Hudgens is susceptible to a pimping charge. It can certainly be argued that he solicits Reynolds with the payment of $100. Plus, he told Vincennes about his scheme. Testimony from the LAPD detective would be substantive corroboration.

Reynolds is killed at the motel. Loew reveals the reason after Detective Wendell "Bud" White assaults him, grabs one of his legs, and dangles him outside the D.A.'s office window to get information about the corruption of Captain Dudley Smith; White worked for the captain. Patchett and

Smith were co-conspirators with Hudgens, who apparently fulfilled his goal to take photos of Reynolds and Loew *in flagrante delicto*. "I wouldn't play ball, so they set me up," cries Loew. "And then I gave in. But the kid heard everything. So they killed him. They're taking over Mickey Cohen's rackets. Because of those pictures, I couldn't prosecute them."

Section 187 of the California Penal Code defines murder as "the unlawful killing of a human being, or a fetus, with malice aforethought." It's obvious from Loew's disclosure that Patchett and Smith satisfy this definition. White and Detective Ed Exley later discover that Patchett has been murdered at his home, but the scene is staged to look like a suicide. They deduce that Smith killed Patchett but probably had somebody help him.[11]

Smith either commits or is responsible for other murders in *L.A. Confidential*. After Vincennes visits the captain's house in the middle of the night to share information about an investigation and get some insight, Smith senses that the detective will soon figure out his endgame. So he shoots and kills Vincennes. In a subsequent scene, it's implied that he also kills Hudgens.

A major storyline connecting the *L.A. Confidential* characters is the slaughter of several people at the Nite Owl Café, including Detective Dick Stensland and his girlfriend Susan, who worked for Patchett. Exley tells his superiors and Loew that an investigation by himself, White, and Vincennes concerning the Nite Owl case led to the conclusion that Stensland had been involved in Smith's illegal activities but "betrayed him over 25 pounds of heroin, the retrieval of which was the ultimate motivation behind the Nite Owl killings."

Exley further explains that two LAPD detectives working for Smith and a third man—possibly Smith himself—committed the murders, not the three young black men arrested (although those suspects are guilty of kidnapping and rape). In a previous scene, Exley interrogated a Nite Owl suspect to determine the location of the young woman they assaulted but does not get substantive information. This failure lights White's fuse. The brawny detective busts into the interrogation room, pushes the suspect against a wall, puts a gun in his mouth and plays Russian Roulette until he gets the answer: The victim is being kept in a house.

White finds the woman tied to bedposts and gagged; she motions toward an adjacent room with her eyes. White sees a man watching TV. He shoots him in the chest; produces a small gun with tape on the handle; shoots at the door frame; and plants the gun in the man's hand. It's a legal violation.

California law states,

A peace officer who knowingly, willfully, intentionally, and wrongfully alters, modifies, plants, places, manufactures, conceals, or moves any physical matter, digital image, or video recording, with specific intent that the action will result in a person being charged with a crime or with the specific intent that the physical matter, digital image, or video recording will be concealed or destroyed, or fraudulently represented as the original evidence upon a trial, proceeding, or inquiry, is guilty of a felony punishable by two, three, or five years in the state prison.[12]

After the arrests of the Nite Owl suspects, they received beatings from the cops. This part of *L.A. Confidential* is based on a real incident nicknamed "Bloody Christmas," which happened soon after the clock struck midnight and turned Christmas Eve technically into Christmas morning. According to a 1997 *Los Angeles Times* article:

> Police Chief William Parker initially denied charges of police brutality and went on television to accuse his department's critics of trying to discredit law enforcement. But he also launched two intensive investigations, which ultimately involved interviews with 405 witnesses and produced a report that ran for 204 single-spaced typewritten pages. After reading it, Parker transferred 54 officers—including two deputy chiefs—and suspended 39 others.[13]

Eight officers were indicted. Separate trials concluded with the clearing of one officer, an acquittal of two others, and five convictions for "assault under the color of authority." At the sentencing of one officer, Judge Thomas Ambrose underlined his disgust at the behavior of those who pledged to serve and protect the public:

> These prisoners were taken into a room, one at a time, like so many small animals in a trap, with no chance to defend themselves, and beaten. I recognize no rights (the policemen) have over anybody else to inflict punishment on these men, who were utterly helpless in their hands.[14]

In the sentencing of another officer, Judge Clement Nye echoed that sentiment: "Surely one thinks this must be some Nazi or Communist dungeon or concentration camp that is being described. The court is appalled at the wild orgy which attended the beatings inflicted in this case."[15]

In addition to using the "Bloody Christmas" incident and portraying real mob figures Mickey Cohen and Johnny Stompanato, filming locations of *L.A. Confidential* contribute to the film's authenticity. White lures a domestic abuser out of his house by yanking on a cord, which brings a display of Santa Claus and reindeer crashing to the ground. After a beating with a warning, White handcuffs him to a post where he'll stay until cops from a local precinct arrive. This scene takes place at a house in Long Beach, not a soundstage.

Sid Hudgens works in the Crossroads of the World, an open-air mall on Sunset Boulevard. Jack Vincennes has a drink at the Frolic Room.

Pierce Patchett lives in the Lovell House, an architectural landmark added to the National Register of Historic Places in 1971. Exley and Vincennes encounter Lana Turner and her boyfriend Stompanato at the Formosa Cafe.

One location needed a transformation. The marquee in the "Movie Premiere Pot Bust" scene did not belong to a movie theater but the California Bank building on Hollywood Boulevard, which had a small tower. The film's production designer, Jeanne Oppewall, navigated around the owner's restriction preventing her team from using nails to secure materials to the façade. Oppewall explained,

> What I ended up doing was designing the movie marquee as a freestanding triangle. We shoved it up against the building, and then we built two pilasters on the back two legs that disappeared directly into the background of the building.... And we had to have a supporting pillar in the front, which we painted black. I specified that we had to always have some extras standing directly in front of it so you wouldn't see that it was actually standing on three legs.[16]

L.A. Confidential captivated audiences. "Ostentatiously cynical, hyper-violent, dripping with attitude, *L.A. Confidential* holds nothing sacred," wrote *Los Angeles Times* film critic Kenneth Turan. "It's intricate plot is so nihilistic and cold around the heart, its nominal heroes so amoral, so willing to sell out anyone and everyone, that the film is as initially unnerving as it is finally irresistible."[17]

20

Community Policing
(*Car 54, Where Are You?*)

The New York Police Department is a staple for storytelling in television.

CBS's *Cagney & Lacey* featured two female detectives, representing the escalation of women in the workforce during the 1980s and spawning four TV movies in the 1990s. ABC's *NYPD Blue* changed the parameters for TV producers with its language and partial nudity; it aired for 12 seasons. Dick Wolf created *Law & Order*, which began its run in 1990; NBC has aired at least one show from the *Law & Order* franchise in prime time ever since. Premiering in 1999, *Law & Order: SVU* is presently the record holder for a prime time drama show and likely will enjoy that achievement in perpetuity. In 2025, the show began its 27th season.

Others had a brief stay on prime time: *Eischeid, Trinity, Brooklyn South, Big Apple, Joe Bash, True Blue, The Job* and *Car 54, Where Are You?* This last entry, a sitcom filmed with a single camera rather than in front of a live audience, aired for two seasons on NBC, from 1960 to 1962. Starring Fred Gwynne as Officer Francis Muldoon and Joe E. Ross as Officer Gunther Toody, *Car 54* revolves around the staff of the fictional 53rd Precinct in the Bronx, their families and the neighborhood residents.

Car 54 benefited from the professional insights of Harold Reidman, a retired NYPD detective who worked on *Car 54* as a technical advisor. In his book about the show, entertainment historian Martin Grams Jr. cites Reidman regarding the image of police work:

> The hardest part of a policeman's job is to overcome the onus of meeting the public only in unpleasant situations, like giving out tickets. As they see it, Toody and Muldoon help to overcome this impression with kindness and understanding, and they feel that, by being depicted on the screen as likable human beings, Toody and Muldoon are putting over the message that other cops are 'nice guys' too."[1]

The link between police and the citizens they protect must be strong for a community to thrive, exemplified in the episode "Christmas at the 53rd" featuring a Christmas Eve revue in the precinct station's lobby marked by songs with lyrics to fit the staff's personalities. Captain Block sings about leadership to the tune of "My gallant crew, good morning.... I am the Captain of the *Pinafore*" from the Gilbert and Sullivan opera *H.M.S. Pinafore*; Toody and Muldoon praise each other in a customized rendition of "Mutual Admiration Society" from the Broadway musical *Happy Hunting*. An officer performs a slapstick routine as he shows the various requirements regarding the NYPD uniform and its accoutrements.[2]

It's unlikely that a holiday performance like this would take place in a real precinct, but Muldoon, Toody *et al.* fostering a bond with residents serves as an inspiration for police officers to do more than know the rules and regulations of their departments plus the laws at the local, state and federal levels. Their actions can be labeled community policing, also known as neighborhood policing. New York City's government website states:

> Neighborhood Policing divides precincts into four or five fully staffed sectors that correspond, as much as possible, to the boundaries of actual established neighborhoods. The same officers work in the same neighborhoods on the same shifts, increasing their familiarity with local residents and local problems. The radio dispatchers, supervisors, and sector officers work together to maintain "sector integrity," meaning that the sector officers and sector cars do not leave the boundaries of their assigned sectors, except in precinct-wide emergencies.[3]

The Department of Justice endorses community policing as a strategy to forge relationships with residents:

> With community policing, there is a shift to the long-term assignment of officers to specific neighborhoods or areas. Geographic deployment plans can help enhance customer service and facilitate more contact between police and citizens, thus establishing a strong relationship and mutual accountability. Beat boundaries should correspond to neighborhood boundaries, and other government services should recognize these boundaries when coordinating government public-service activities.[4]

In the latter half of the 20th century, there was perhaps no greater need for community policing than during a period in the 1990s. The trouble was sparked by four LAPD officers pummeling Rodney King in an apartment complex after a high-speed pursuit; a resident videotaped the 1991 incident. King's beating became a top story on TV news programs. A year later, riots in Los Angeles began when a jury acquitted three officers of excessive force and didn't reach a verdict for the fourth. Strong connections between police departments and their communities escalated to a high priority from Tacoma to Trenton.

In 1991, NYPD Sergeant Andrew McGoey pointed out the obsolescence of driving a police car while waiting for a call on the department radio. "Being a good cop is knowing the community and knowing enough to be able to solve problems rather than just react to them," said McGoey, a Brooklyn-based veteran with more than 20 years of experience. In the same newspaper article that quoted McGoey, the National Center for Community Policing at Michigan State University said that community policing was being used or considered by "nearly two-thirds of the nation's 600 largest police departments."[5]

Austin had been forward-thinking in the community policing arena dating back to the early 1970s even though the idea didn't have a label yet. In the summer of 1992, the *Austin American-Statesman* published a feature on the genesis and growth of the city's program that began in 1972 when Austin opened two storefront police offices.

Although anyone can walk into a precinct house and talk to a police officer, there was an informality creating an inherent value for Austin's police officers by communicating with the public in this environment. "In the '70s, people could come to the storefront offices not just to talk about crime but about any problem, such as a complaint about garbage collection, and work with police to solve the problem," reported the *Statesman*. The link between the police and the public strengthened during the next 20 years as Austin's police department created three similar offices.[6]

But community policing has its critics. In 1994, a comprehensive *Newsday* article quoted New York City Mayor Rudy Giuliani, who said that assigned cops to community policing duties had a counterproductive effect because they perform an overabundance of "social work and don't make enough arrests." Though it might seem soft to some, there's a concrete effect because community policing can impact crime prevention.

A police officer noted that the revival of a Police Athletic League after dormancy for 14 years led to softball games in Brownsville, a neighborhood in Brooklyn: "There was a time when people wouldn't come out to this park. Now, they're in chairs relaxing and watching the games." *Newsday* underscored the positive result of community policing: "The park, which was notorious for blatant daytime drug use, was transformed into a temporary sanctuary. It helped create a renewed respect for the police among community members, who learned that most do care."[7]

While community policing became a common phrase for law enforcement in the 1990s, police departments might suffer the same enemy as corporations regarding effectiveness: bureaucracy. In a *Daily News* (NY) op-ed, criminologist and Northwestern University professor

George L. Kelling stressed that the police officers on a beat in a neighborhood form the first line of crime prevention because they understand its uniqueness. Bureaucracy can have negative—if not disastrous—consequences. For example, a large-scale operation that doesn't convey specifics to beat officers will be unproductive at best. "Patrol officers feel demeaned, frustrated and bitter. The idea of being 'chiefs of their beats' is a joke to most of them."

Kelling also wrote that flexibility at the beat officer level is necessary, rather than "specialized units" that can dominate a precinct's policing. According to Kelling, neighborhood police officers "need the time and resources to discover, understand and deal with local problems. They also need the authority to work with citizens in negotiating priorities and devising solutions."[8]

In South Central Los Angeles, community policing received scrutiny because residents felt that the LAPD did not consider their input. "We don't need no captain, no deputy chief, no mayor to come out here and tell us what we need," said one resident. "What we need is for the police department to listen to us."

At the heart of the matter was the LAPD controlling the selection of members to police advisory boards and the scope of their authority. But the department emphasized that the boards would have little, if any, authority as their mission would be to advise rather than create, implement and execute policy. One community leader asked, "How can the boards represent the community if the LAPD picks the members of the boards? Some of these people are good people, but they don't represent the community, they represent the police department."[9]

Though community policing may be a welcome idea, it takes time and energy for police officers to establish themselves because initially they might be met with distrust, cynicism and skepticism. In the 1980s, Fort Worth's Cavile Place Apartments was plagued by drugs and violence; the police department began a community policing strategy. By the 1990s, it was a safer environment because of increased patrols and a neighborhood watch.

The Fort Worth Police Department used the moniker "neighborhood police officers" to describe this new paradigm of staffing, which fulfilled the mission of building a community where law-abiding citizens who want a life of safety, peace and prosperity can trust their police departments and vice versa. The *Fort Worth Star-Telegram* labeled it "a shining example" of what citizens and police together can do to turn crime around: "When community policing is put into action, crime decreases and quality of life increases. Relationships are established and trust is built."

An additional benefit arises from community policing, noted the

20. Community Policing (Car 54, Where Are You?)

Star-Telegram: "This closeness leads to the officers and residents working on a variety of issues, many of which may not be directly related to crime but may include code violations and quality-of-life issues."[10]

As Internet use became commonplace in the 1990s, it served a valuable function for police departments in gathering, organizing and distributing information. Technology allowed crime statistics to be displayed on a police department's website and questions from residents to be emailed.

But there's also the potential to easily delete information. In 1998, the *Los Angeles Times* reported,

> The LAPD stopped distributing public copies of its crime maps last May after encountering resistance from real estate agents and developers and discovering that the maps were being used as advertising by home security firms. The LAPD does not contain the crime maps that are common features on other police department Internet sites."[11]

Community policing requires funding. At the end of the '90s, a *Chicago Tribune* article noted that that city's police department coffers inflated thanks to an infusion of $73 million piped in from the Community Oriented Policing Services (COPS) program of the U.S. Department of Justice. However, community policing created controversy. The *Tribune* cited research from Northwestern University regarding a downside and negating the positive advances that had been made. The newspaper stated:

> The Northwestern University study found that community policing suffers from lethargic leadership, poor planning and training and a lack of communication between police and residents. The result, researchers said, is that Chicago police in some neighborhoods are failing to carry out a central tenet of community policing: working closely with residents to develop common strategies for attacking local crime problems.[12]

It's difficult to believe that the officers of the 53rd Precinct in the Bronx would ever have been described as such. They were sometimes goofy but always good-hearted.

21

Resisting Arrest, Constitutional Rights (*White Christmas*)

Some men will do just about anything for women in the name of chivalry. To wit, former Army buddies Bob Wallace and Phil Davis break the law as a gesture of kindness for two sisters at the heart of the 1954 film *White Christmas*.[1]

Played by Bing Crosby and Danny Kaye, Bob and Phil become an entertainment sensation after World War II with their Broadway musical smash *Playing Around*. Bob writes the words; Phil writes the music. In Florida to scout the nightclub act of Betty and Judy Haynes (played by Rosemary Clooney and Vera-Ellen), they learn that a sheriff has arrived with an arrest warrant because a landlord claimed the women burned a hole in a rug and caused damages amounting to $200. Bob and Phil had planned a trip to New York City via train. Believing the landlord's complaint is a sham, Phil helps Betty and Judy evade the sheriff by giving them the train tickets.

There are several legal issues stemming from this part of *White Christmas*. Betty and Judy are resisting arrest without violence. Florida law states,

> Whoever shall resist, obstruct, or oppose any officer; member of the Florida Commission on Offender Review or any administrative aide or supervisor employed by the commission; county probation officer; parole and probation supervisor; personnel or representative of the Department of Law Enforcement; or other person legally authorized to execute process in the execution of legal process or in the lawful execution of any legal duty, without offering or doing violence to the person of the officer, shall be guilty of a misdemeanor of the first degree.[2]

The sheriff is clearly within the definition of the clause "personnel or representative of the Department of Law Enforcement; or other person legally

21. Resisting Arrest, Constitutional Rights (White Christmas) 129

authorized to execute process in the execution of legal process or in the lawful execution of any legal duty." There's no physical encounter between the women and the sheriff; subterfuge allows their escape. Likewise, they do not threaten violence. So a charge of resisting arrest without violence is the proper charge.

Phil and Bob could each be in handcuffs as an accessory, which Florida law defines as

> any person not standing in the relation of husband or wife, parent or grandparent, child or grandchild, brother or sister, by consanguinity or affinity to the offender, who maintains or assists the principal or an accessory before the fact, or gives the offender any other aid, knowing that the offender had committed a crime and such crime was a third degree felony, or had been an accessory thereto before the fact, with the intent that the offender avoids or escapes detection, arrest, trial, or punishment, is an accessory after the fact.[3]

Betty and Judy just met the guys, so the phrase "affinity to the offender" likely doesn't apply in a court of law. Phil believes the landlord is making up the story about the rug, sides with the women, and commits an affirmative act: He helps Betty and Judy escape notice of the sheriff and potential arrest, qualifying him to be charged as an accessory before the fact.

Novello, the nightclub owner, will also be complicit as an accessory before the fact because he participates in the smokescreen by stalling the sheriff and preventing him from executing the arrest warrant. Bob later learns about the scheme but does not contact the police, which makes him an accessory after the fact. The women escape; no further mention of the warrant is made in the film.

In Florida, the judicial community must meet a statutory standard for the warrant to be valid:

> A judge, upon examination of the complaint and proofs submitted, if satisfied that probable cause exists for the issuance of an arrest warrant for any crime committed within the judge's jurisdiction, shall thereupon issue an arrest warrant signed by the judge with the judge's name of office.[4]

It's presumed that a judge signed the warrant for the sheriff in *White Christmas*, with proof being either the damaged rug or a photograph of it, but neither is mentioned when the sheriff is in the nightclub manager's office. If the judge goes by the word of the landlord, then the arrest warrant could be invalid. Further, the landlord could be in hot water if he entered the apartment without a good reason, such as imminent danger if he smelled smoke. Betty and Judy could argue that he invaded their privacy and breached the good will of their rental agreement, assuming there's a written contract.

The landlord may enter the apartment under certain circumstances without too much input or resistance from Betty and Judy. Under Florida law,

> [T]he tenant shall not unreasonably withhold consent to the landlord to enter the dwelling unit from time to time in order to inspect the premises; make necessary or agreed repairs, decorations, alterations, or improvements; supply agreed services; or exhibit the dwelling unit to prospective or actual purchasers, mortgagees, tenants, workers, or contractors.[5]

If the landlord went into the apartment, he can argue that he did it for any of these purposes assuming validity is proven. Additionally, access is permissible to guard the property's integrity provided a condition is met:

> The landlord may enter the dwelling unit at any time for the protection or preservation of the premises. The landlord may enter the dwelling unit upon reasonable notice to the tenant and at a reasonable time for the purpose of repair of the premises. "Reasonable notice" for the purpose of repair is notice given at least 24 hours prior to the entry, and reasonable time for the purpose of repair shall be between the hours of 7:30 a.m. and 8:00 p.m.[6]

Even if the sheriff caught and arrested the women, they can exercise their Constitutional rights. The Fourth Amendment states,

> The right of the people to be secure in their persons, houses, papers, and effects, against unreasonable searches and seizures, shall not be violated, and no Warrants shall issue, but upon probable cause, supported by Oath or affirmation, and particularly describing the place to be searched, and the persons or things to be seized.[7]

There's no probable cause if the landlord didn't offer proof. If he had asked the sheriff to examine the alleged damage without consent from Betty and Judy, that could be a violation of the Fourth Amendment.

Let's assume that Betty and Judy never got on the train and the sheriff took them into custody or that he caught up to them later in the story. Betty and Judy would not be required to testify in their own defense at trial. The Fifth Amendment states that no person shall be compelled in any criminal case to be a witness against himself, "nor be deprived of life, liberty, or property, without due process of law; nor shall private property be taken for public use, without just compensation." Moreover, a judge would probably instruct a jury that exercising a Fifth Amendment right should have no bearing on evaluating the facts, arguments and testimony in a trial.[8]

In a scenario where the women are caught and arrested, they have the Constitutional right to legal counsel under the Sixth Amendment:

> In all criminal prosecutions, the accused shall enjoy the right to a speedy and public trial, by an impartial jury of the State and district wherein the crime

21. Resisting Arrest, Constitutional Rights (White Christmas)   131

shall have been committed, which district shall have been previously ascertained by law, and to be informed of the nature and cause of the accusation; to be confronted with the witnesses against him; to have compulsory process for obtaining witnesses in his favor, and to have the Assistance of Counsel for his defence [sic].[9]

If Betty and Judy decide to go to trial, it's likely that the landlord will testify on his own behalf. In turn, the girls' attorney will have the opportunity for cross-examination, including questions about the alleged damage, to reveal weaknesses in the landlord's case.

Of course, the women may have a counterclaim against the landlord for intentional infliction of emotional distress if they can show that the rug is not damaged. They'd have to prove emotional distress mostly through witnesses like Phil and Bob, plus any colleagues with whom they interacted after being notified of the warrant. The *Florida Litigation Guide* outlines the elements for this tort: "(1) defendant's conduct was intentional or reckless; (2) defendant's conduct was outrageous; (3) defendant's conduct caused emotional distress; and (4) plaintiff suffered severe emotional distress."[10]

Also, Betty and Judy could file a complaint for fraud against the landlord if they are innocent; the rug is free of damage; they trust the sheriff; and they can back up their claim with statements and proof including the undamaged rug. The Florida Bar notes that fraud exists in both the criminal and civil arenas:

> Criminal fraud requires criminal intent on the part of the perpetrator, and is punishable by fines or imprisonment. Civil fraud, on the other hand, applies more broadly to circumstances where bad-faith [sic] is usually involved, and where the penalties are meant to punish the perpetrator and put the victim back in the same position before the fraud took place.[11]

Phil and Bob may have some concerns beyond assisting Betty and Judy. When Bob agrees to underwrite the cost of producing a version of *Playing Around* at General Waverly's Columbia Inn in Pine Tree, Vermont, he and Phil take on the responsibility for payroll, insurance, lodging and transportation. Moving elaborate sets to different regions requires expert truck drivers and complex logistics, a paradigm that might not have existed without the Deull family. When theatrical shows traveled in the first half of the 20th century, the crew relied on truckers to bring the show's sets to the nearest train station and transport them via the railroad.

Because the Interstate Commerce Commission regulated trucking, the Deulls inquired about permission to move sets to the next town or city by truck instead. A monopoly emerged after the ICC okayed the venture. "We were the only people who had those rights from '49 to '81, when the trucking industry was deregulated and anybody who wanted to truck goods around could," Norma Deull recalled in 2019, explaining the genesis of her parents creating a new business. "And so that is the way that the business was born and evolved, and it's still going the same way."[12]

White Christmas strikes a sentimental chord. But not all critics fawned over it. Bosley Crowther of the *New York Times* compared the film to *Holiday Inn,* a 1942 offering that also starred Crosby, and blamed the screenwriters. "Everyone works hard at the business of singing, dancing and cracking jokes, but the stuff that they work with is minor," wrote Crowther. "It doesn't have the old inspiration and spark." However, the famed reviewer praised VistaVision: Paramount's technology for showcasing a film on a wide screen inspired him to describe the colors as "rich and luminous" with the images being "clear and sharp."[13]

Philip K. Scheuer, Crowther's counterpart at the *Los Angeles Times*, concurred with the opinion about the story: "[The] inescapable final judgment of the reviewer is that it delivers less than it promises."[14]

Wriston Locklair of the *Charlotte Observer* wrote that *White Christmas* was "not nearly so good" as *Holiday Inn*.[15] In the *Springfield Leader and Press*, Dale Freeman noted that any weakness of the story would be overcome by the cast and the film's visual allure. "*White Christmas* is sort of a stock story, nothing to jump up and click your heels about, but … 'tis almost a certainty it will be a success at the boxoffice."[16]

White Christmas might not have been the favorite of critics across the board when it premiered, but the story punctuated by a rendition of Irving Berlin's title song will bring smiles and maybe some tears for a cathartic, feel-good cry.

22

Self-Defense
(*A Christmas Story*)

All that nine-year-old Ralphie Parker wants for Christmas is a BB gun. More precisely, he wants a Red Ryder Carbine Action 200-shot Range Model air rifle.

Ralphie's desire is at the heart of *A Christmas Story*. This 1983 film showcases a series of tales featuring Ralphie, his family and his circle of friends during the 1940 Christmas season in the town of Hohman, Indiana. Based on Jean Shepherd's 1966 novel *In God We Trust, All Others Pay Cash*, it has a vibe that is both nostalgic and timeless as Ralphie navigates the choppy waters of childhood: dealing with a bully, eccentric family traditions, and disappointment when a secret code from his favorite radio show is deciphered and found to be nothing more than an advertisement for the sponsor.[1]

In one storyline, Ralphie, his friends and his little brother Randy suffer at the hands of Scut Farkus, the school bully, and his sidekick Grover Dill. Ralphie's pent-up frustration explodes on Scut after the constant bullying with the final straw being Scut hitting Ralphie in the face with a snowball followed by taunting him to tears. When Grover tries to intervene, Ralphie knocks him to the ground.

Ralphie's mother happens to walk by and pulls her son from the bloody-faced Scut, who most certainly deserved the assault. Notwithstanding the peculiarities involved in application of the law to juveniles, Ralphie could face a charge of battery, defined as occurring when "a person who knowingly or intentionally touches another person in a rude, insolent, or angry manner."[2]

But Ralphie has a viable claim of self-defense if Scut demands prosecution for the barrage. Indiana case law relies on the statute setting forth conditions for a successful claim. Ralphie appears to be in the clear: "A person is justified in using reasonable force against any other person to protect the person or a third person from what the person reasonably believes to be the imminent use of unlawful force."[3]

Based on Scut's bullying manner seen earlier in the story, it's reasonable for Ralphie to believe that the snowball would have preceded another physical assault. Ralphie's friends Flick and Schwartz could be called as witnesses regarding Scut's previous bullying and their opinions as to a potential outcome if Ralphie hadn't acted.

Ralphie still needs to meet some conditions. In 2024, the Court of Appeals of Indiana stated, "In order to prevail on a claim of self-defense, a defendant must show that he (1) was in a place where he had a right to be; (2) acted without fault; and (3) was in reasonable fear or apprehension of death or great bodily harm."[4]

Interesting. He walked through a residential area of Hohman when the incident happened. He had a right to be there. Scut threw the snowball without any verbal and/or physical provocation from Ralphie, so Ralphie had no fault at the beginning of the clash. It's the third prong that may cause some trouble. Scut would argue that all he did was tease Ralphie, a common occurrence among kids his age. The snowball? A harmless prank.

However, Ralphie has a stronger rebuttal. Not only was Ralphie in reasonable fear of great bodily harm given Scut's previous behavior, he was also clearly vulnerable with tears streaming down his face. Had Ralphie not acted swiftly and preemptively, Scut would most likely have pounded him like he did so many times before.

But there's another potential hurdle. The Court of Appeals in the same case pointed out that a person who claims self-defense might have a weakened argument "if he provokes, instigates, or participates willingly in the violence."[5]

Here, Ralphie would have to argue that his actions in tackling Scut and attacking him did not fall under provocation, instigation or willing participation. In fact, Ralphie is in a severe emotional state that doesn't end until his mom takes him home, gives him a wet washcloth to wipe his face, and implores him to settle down. While Scut could argue that Ralphie's actions reflected willingness, Ralphie again has a stronger argument because he neither sought out the fight nor provoked it. He defended himself in an unwanted situation. Plain and simple.

Additionally, the Indiana statute invalidates a self-defense argument if the person "is the initial aggressor unless the person withdraws from the encounter and communicates to the other person the intent to do so and the other person nevertheless continues or threatens to continue unlawful action."[6]

Scut could again try the argument that teasing classmates and snowball fights are part of children's goofing around with minimal intent to harm in any serious way. But Scut's continued harassment proves that he had an intent to commit emotional and physical injury upon Ralphie.

A prosecutor would likely want a jury to know about Scut's character, supported by testimony of Ralphie and his friends regarding repeated instances of bullying. There's a roadblock here: Indiana's Rules of Evidence. Rule 404(b)(1) states, "Evidence of a crime, wrong, or other act is not admissible to prove a person's character in order to show that on a particular occasion the person acted in accordance with the character."[7]

But the prosecutor has another avenue if there's a different goal for admitting the evidence under Rule 404(b)(2): "motive, opportunity, intent, preparation, plan, knowledge, identity, absence of mistake, or lack of accident." In this scenario, a prosecutor needs to "provide reasonable notice of the general nature of any such evidence." Upon the defense counsel's request, disclosure should take place before the trial begins. It can be disclosed during the trial "if the court, for good cause, excuses lack of pretrial notice."[8] Scut will face a formidable challenge if he wants to keep this evidence from being admitted.

Ralphie's attorney can also point to the 2002 Indiana Court of Appeals case *Adrian Brand vs. State of Indiana*, which noted, "The Indiana Supreme Court has held that evidence of the victim's character may be admitted to show that the victim had a violent character giving the defendant reason to fear him."[9]

A prosecutor would want to know if Scut bullied Ralphie as part of a routine. Rule 406 of Indiana's Rules of Evidence states,

> Evidence of a person's habit or an organization's routine practice may be admitted to prove that on a particular occasion the person or organization acted in accordance with the habit or routine practice. The court may admit this evidence regardless of whether it is corroborated or whether there was an eyewitness.[10]

It can be inferred from the events in *A Christmas Story* that Scut's verbal and physical assaults happened regularly, if not daily. The definition is satisfied. Rule 405 allows two additional avenues to raise the issue of character: (1) reputation or opinion and (2) specific instances of conduct. But the prosecutor will have to abide by a condition. "If, in a criminal case, a defendant provides reasonable pretrial notice that the defendant intends to offer character evidence, the prosecution must provide the defendant with any relevant specific instances of conduct that the prosecution may use on cross-examination."[11]

This will be no problem for the defense counsel. Ralphie, Randy, Flick and Schwartz can list numerous instances of Scut's verbal taunts and physical assaults. There's also another witness who could bolster Ralphie's self-defense argument: Grover Dill. Scut's accomplice has knowledge of what happened before the bullying, specifically, any plans that Scut shared with him.

Scut faces a series of charges that even Clarence Darrow couldn't defend successfully. Battery is at the top of the list. Surely, Scut's previous actions where he attacks Ralphie plus the snowball hitting Ralphie will likely be seen by a court as satisfying the battery requirement of "knowingly or intentionally touches another person in a rude, insolent, or angry manner."[12]

Harassment is another potential charge for Scut, defined by the Indiana Code as conduct directed toward a victim that includes, but is not limited to, "repeated or continuing impermissible contact that would cause a reasonable person to suffer emotional distress and that actually causes the victim to suffer emotional distress."[13]

There's no doubt whatsoever that Scut wanted Ralphie to suffer emotional distress as the result of his repeated bullying. Ralphie cries; Scut laughs. Further, Scut could also face a charge of provocation for his continued bullying. According to the Indiana Code, "A person who recklessly, knowingly, or intentionally engages in conduct that is likely to provoke a reasonable person to commit battery commits provocation."

Grover has a legal snafu as well. Unless a prosecutor offers immunity or a lesser charge in exchange for testifying against Scut, Grover has a substantial chance of being charged with aiding, inducing or causing an offense no matter what happens with his cohort in the legal system. Grover's actions clearly fall within the statutory parameters:

> A person who knowingly or intentionally aids, induces, or causes another person to commit an offense commits that offense, even if the other person has not been prosecuted for the offense; has not been convicted of the offense; or has been acquitted of the offense.[14]

Scut, Ralphie and Grover aren't the only characters whose actions could lead to a courtroom. The man playing Santa Claus at Higbee's—Hohman's main department store—has legal exposure for battery. Ralphie refuses to go down the slide until he tells "Santa" about wanting the BB gun for Christmas; "Santa" nudges Ralphie by pushing a boot on his head after hearing the description of the gun, causing the nine-year-old to traverse the slide into the display full of cotton representing snow. A charge of battery would not be out of the question.

Additionally, if Ralphie sues for intentional infliction of emotional distress, then Higbee's might be drawn into the lawsuit under the legal concept known as *respondeat superior*. Basically, this Latin phrase means that an employer is responsible for employees' actions if they occur within the normal boundaries, obligations and course of employment.

Depending on how long it took Ralphie's attorneys to develop a case, they could ask an Indiana court to adopt a legal trend taking shape in

California a few years after the events depicted in *A Christmas Story*. A 1990 article in the *Santa Clara Law Review* reminds us: "The 1940s brought increased liability for the employer under respondeat superior. The California Supreme Court addressed the issue twice in less than one year." Those cases were decided in July 1946 and March 1947.[15]

The Parkers' neighbors, the Bumpus family, also deserve legal scrutiny. Described as hillbillies by Ralphie's father, they own several large dogs with little or no discipline, as indicated by their constant barking. The rowdy behavior reaches a crescendo on Christmas when they enter the house and devour Mrs. Parker's holiday turkey. Consequently, the Parker clan has Christmas dinner at a Chinese restaurant, apparently the only eating establishment open in Hohman on December 25.

If Hohman has an animal control department, one of the Parkers could call or visit, leading perhaps to a prosecutor's charge of neglect. It would be justified by the dogs' Christmas Day behavior compounded by the barking and the Bumpuses' junk-filled yard. The Indiana Code states, "A person who has a vertebrate animal in the person's custody and recklessly, knowingly, or intentionally abandons or neglects the animal commits cruelty to an animal."[16]

Shepherd co-wrote the *Christmas Story* screenplay with Leigh Brown and Bob Clark, who directed the film. *New York Post* critic Rex Reed called the direction "lame" and the script "corny," as well as lambasted Shepherd's voiceover narration: "[T]he film is seriously marred by the kind of ludicrous, pretentious narration that never allows you the luxury of figuring out what's going on because the narrator is always telling you what the characters are doing and thinking ahead of time."[17]

Reed's counterpart at the *New York Times* had a different take: Vincent Canby wrote,

> Mr. Shepherd is a most engaging raconteur who transforms small stories of everyday life into tall tales of fantastic adventure. In his words, an after-school encounter between Ralphie and a neighborhood bully ... becomes a collision of Olympian deities. Mr. Shepherd himself reads the sometimes very funny voice-over commentaries on the screen action and, you may be sure, is responsible for the bits and pieces of 1940s trivia we see.[18]

Perhaps because of its Midwestern setting, the film struck a chord with critics in the region. "It's chock-full of understated wit but avoids the kind of Disneyesque sentimentality that grown-ups and sophisticated kids gag on," Roxanne T. Mueller wrote in the *Plain Dealer*, Cleveland's leading newspaper.[19]

Gene Siskel told readers of the *Chicago Tribune* that the film "is full of delightful characters and performances." He also emphasized the undercurrent of nostalgia: "It's like looking through a faded family snapshot album, and suddenly your past comes to life."[20]

Shepherd's nostalgia for his childhood with Ralphie as his avatar underscored the appeal of *A Christmas Story*. "What contributes in part to the success of this film is that no one will be able to keep a lid on their own childhood recollections as the film unfolds," wrote John A. Douglas in the *Grand Rapids Press*. "It gently pries open your memory bank to fill in some of the holes in the film."[21]

23

Music Publishing Rights—Recorded Songs (*Love Actually*)

Remakes abound across the entertainment spectrum.

Filmmakers have offered fresh interpretations of *The In-Laws, 3:10 to Yuma, Cape Fear, The Parent Trap, Ocean's Eleven, The Longest Yard, Invasion of the Body Snatchers, The Bad News Bears, Death Wish, Point Break, Footloose, The Thomas Crown Affair, Sabrina* and *The Taking of Pelham One Two Three*. *The Shop Around the Corner* has been remade twice: *In the Good Old Summertime* and *You've Got Mail*. There have been four versions of *A Star Is Born*.

Broadway revivals have included *Guys and Dolls, West Side Story, The Odd Couple, Carousel, Cabaret, Gypsy, Fiddler on the Roof, The Sunshine Boys, All My Sons, Death of a Salesman, Annie, The Man of La Mancha, South Pacific, Glengarry Glen Ross, Inherit the Wind, Once Upon a Mattress* and *The Front Page*.

Television producers have remade *One Day at a Time; Battlestar Galactica, The Bionic Woman, The Fresh Prince of Bel Air, Hawaii Five-O, MacGyver, Lost in Space, Dark Shadows, The Fugitive, Dynasty, Ironside, Kojak, Adam-12, Dragnet, Knight Rider, Perry Mason, Route 66, Fantasy Island, Family Affair, Charmed, The Odd Couple, Magnum, P.I.,* and *Charlie's Angels*.

In music, a remake is called a "cover." Big Mama Thornton recorded "Hound Dog" before Elvis Presley made it a top seller. Dolly Parton wrote and recorded "I Will Always Love You" in 1973 though Whitney Houston's version on the soundtrack of the 1992 film *The Bodyguard* is better known. At the height of his fame thanks to a starring role in ABC-TV's *The Partridge Family* (1970-74), David Cassidy covered "Cherish," a number-one song for the Association in 1966.

Creedence Clearwater Revival recorded "Proud Mary" before Ike and

Tina Turner converted the song to their energetic performance. Sammy Kaye preceded Fats Domino for "Blueberry Hill," however, the latter's version became a signature song of the 1950s. Music buffs may know that the Regents recorded "Barbara Ann" earlier than it became synonymous with the Beach Boys.

At weddings, high school reunions and other gatherings with a dance floor and DJ, it's probable that you'll hear the Beatles sing "Twist and Shout" rather than the Top Notes. George Benson's "On Broadway" outweighs the version by the Drifters for popularity; a similar calculus exists for Rod Stewart vs. the Persuaders regarding "Some Guys Have All the Luck" and Frank Sinatra vs. Liza Minnelli for "New York, New York."

Aging rock'n'roll singer Billy Mack covers "Love Is All Around" at the beginning of the 2003 film *Love Actually*.[1] His offering of the song composed by Reg Presley and first released by the Troggs in 1967 is retitled "Christmas Is All Around." Aiming for distribution during the holiday season, Mack—played by Bill Nighy—or his producer would need to obtain a mechanical license, which ensures that songwriters and copyright owners are compensated for their creative work. In this arena, "Love Is All Around" falls under the authority of the Harry Fox Agency, a Goliath that "represents nearly 50,000 affiliated publishers and licenses more than 2500 record labels."[2]

HFA uses a food analogy on its website to explain the basis for mechanical licenses if you are recording someone else's song:

> Imagine if every time you ate a piece of pizza, you had to give money to the person who made it. Oh wait … that's actually how it works! Mechanical licenses are, at their core, quite the same. Except you can't eat music. Of course it's more interesting than that. Originally conceived for the rolls inside of player pianos, mechanical licenses now cover a variety of different uses, from CDs to streaming. It's simple: if you're recording and distributing music in any format you'll need to purchase a mechanical license.[3]

Information regarding the song will be in this license to protect both parties, including the licensor warranting that it has the right to grant the license; the song having a valid U.S. copyright; and either party being able to assign its rights, benefits and obligations.

Digital technology—streaming services, YouTube, iTunes and musicians' websites—has increased the availability of music for consumers and, in turn, the complexities of rights management for musicians. It's part of a paradigm shift that also affects other areas of entertainment. According to Michael Simon, president and CEO of the Harry Fox Agency,

> Many technologies originally thought to be destructive have had major long-term positive impacts on the music industry, and we've been there for all

of them. Advances that were previously viewed with skepticism are now the backbone of an entirely new way of doing business. We've been on the ground floor the entire time, building a streamlined, global network for music licensing and royalty distribution, and we will continue to be here during this exciting transition.[4]

Rights administrators are adamant about protecting their clients. A good example is the lawsuit between Delta Entertainment Corporation and HFA, beginning in 1996 and ending with an undisclosed settlement in 2003. HFA had given notice that it would audit Delta's account from July 1, 1991, to June 30, 1997; there was an extension of the audit period to December 31, 1997. After a four-year audit, a discrepancy emerged: HFA concluded that Delta owed more than $15 million in unpaid royalties and accumulated interest whereas Delta said it actually overpaid by $1.182 million.

A lawsuit began; judicial power led the parties to a settlement in 2003. A. Barry Cappello, a partner in Cappello & Noël (Delta's law firm), said that when the case was first filed,

> it had the appearances of a long, drawn-out legal battle. The magistrate who presided over the case forced the principals of Delta and HFA to meet until an agreement was reached. They met three times–in Los Angeles, New York and London—and hammered out a solution. This is a great example of how mediation, when in the right hands, can work wonderfully. Delta is delighted with the settlement and continues to do business with the Harry Fox Agency.[5]

Copyright infringement is an evergreen concern for the music industry. In 2003, the Harry Fox Agency received a grant of its motion to dismiss a case involving this issue in the District Court of New Jersey. The case revolved around two songs written by Richard "Dickie" Goodman in the 1950s, "The Flying Saucer Part I" and "The Flying Saucer Part II." Goodman died in 1998; his son Jon claimed to be "the lawful representative of my father's sound recordings ... acknowledged by both a court of law as well as various major music business organizations."[6]

Jon was indeed the administrator of his father's estate, but he did not assert a copyright registration for the sound recordings in his lawsuit. Even if he did, its validity would be questionable. The Sound Recording Act of 1971 amended the 1909 Copyright Act: "[N]o sound recording fixed before February 15, 1972, shall be subject to copyright under this title." Copyright principles in state law and common law governed those offerings.

The court cited the U.S. Supreme Court case of *Dowling vs. United States* in its decision granting the motions to dismiss the case filed by the Harry Fox Agency—and other defendants—but it also noted that Jon Goodman could amend his complaint and mount future litigation based on common law copyright precedents regarding applicable state laws.[7]

However, Goodman would need to qualify. The court states that any such claim could only be maintained "if the requirements of diversity jurisdiction are met, namely, that no defendant is a citizen of the same state as plaintiff, and that the claim against each defendant is for an amount exceeding $75,000 pursuant to [federal law]."[8]

In *Harry Fox Agency vs. Mills Music*, a 1982 case, the District Court for the Southern District of New York observed that the process of a negotiated license often overlooks the compulsory license provision outlined in Section 115 of the 1976 Copyright Act in addition to Sections 1(e) and 101(e) of its predecessor—the 1909 Copyright Act. There's a policy reason behind it:

> Usually, record producers apply to and obtain the right to use copyrighted material from music publishers (the copyright proprietors) under licenses which contain modifications of the statutory terms. These modifications are designed to encourage exploitation of musical compositions by, among other matters, lowering the statutory royalty rate, dispensing with statutory notice requirements, or reducing the frequency with which accountings and payments are made.[9]

A new asset in rights management happened with the Music Modernization Act of 2018 and the subsequent creation of the Mechanical Licensing Collective, a nonprofit organization that began functioning on January 1, 2021, with a blanket license regarding digital audio services in the U.S. The Harry Fox Agency website explains that the MLC is responsible for collecting the mechanical royalties due under the blanket license from those digital services "and then distributing [them] to music publishers, administrators, self-administered songwriters and others who are entitle to receive them."[10]

So, what does "digital services" mean? Essentially, services that allow streaming and downloading. The MLC's board of directors gets input from three advisory committees thanks to the Music Modernization Act. Their makeup is described on the MLC website[11]:

- Unclaimed Royalties Oversight Committee: five songwriters, five representatives of music publishers
- Dispute Resolution Committee: five songwriters, five representatives of music publishers
- Operations Advisory Committee: six representatives of music publishers, six representatives of digital music providers

In February 2023, the MLC exceeded $1 billion in total royalties distributed. It went over the $2 billion mark in March 2024.[12] MLC board of directors chair Alisa Coleman said in a joint interview with CEO Kris Ahrend for the MLC's 2023 Annual Report:

23. Music Publishing Rights—Recorded Songs (Love Actually) 143

In addition to our royalty distributions, another achievement this past year has been the impressive growth in The MLC's membership. In 2023 alone, we welcomed more than 10,000 new Members, bringing our total to more than 34,000 Members. I suspect many of these new Members were previously not receiving their mechanical royalties from streaming platforms. This influx underscores the dedicated efforts of The MLC team, who diligently identified and assisted these missing rightsholders in becoming active Members. This outreach not only strengthens our collective voice but also reinforces The MLC's pivotal role in ensuring fair compensation for all music creators.[13]

New members strengthen the MLC's impact, said Kris Ahrend:

An important focus of our outreach and education efforts is reaching these rightsholders, helping them understand what we do, and then enrolling them as Members so we can pay them the mechanical royalties they have earned. Each new Member helps us increase the number of registered songs in our database, which enables us to achieve higher match rates and distribute even more royalties to our Members.[14]

Further to the mechanical license, Billy Mack and his producer would also need to procure a synchronization ("sync") license from the publisher, composer or representatives of "Love Is All Around" to use the new, Christmas-themed version in the music video that we see in *Love Actually*.

"Christmas Is All Around" reaches the #1 slot in England on Christmas Eve, igniting a comeback for Billy Mack underscored by an invitation from Elton John to attend a holiday party at his home. Did Nighy base his portrayal on anyone in particular? "No inspiration I'm afraid," said the actor, whose subsequent credits include *Notes on a Scandal* and two films in the *Pirates of the Caribbean* franchise. Nighy continued:

He was just an amalgamation of people I've observed over the years. I do a shocked stance which is a bit like Gary Glitter, as if someone had just come up behind him. Then there's some Elvis Costello. He was a fantastic rock dancer of mine—post ironic, putting [the] knees together and sticking his bum out. It was strangely, deeply satisfying.[15]

In 2022, Nighy expressed his deep affection for the movie, revealing that he will "never be sick of people talking about" *Love Actually*: "It was a big and important thing for me and changed the way I went to work. ... People have used it for all sorts of purposes to get through dark times ... there's nowhere in the world where people don't watch it on a regular basis, every Christmas."[16]

Mack realizes that his love connection revolves around a platonic friendship with his manager, Joe. After briefly going to the Christmas party, Mack arrives unannounced at Joe's house to reveal his affection, closeness and appreciation for the man who not only stood by him when his fame faded but also engineered the comeback with the brainstorm of "Christmas Is All Around."

Chicago Tribune film critic Mark Caro isolated it among the many tales of interconnected characters throughout the film: "The most satisfying relationship turns out to be a non-romantic one, between Nighy's rock star and his manager." Jocelyn Noveck of Associated Press wrote that Mack has "the best story" in the film and praised Nighy for "a deliciously funny and dirty portrayal." In the *Oregonian*, Kim Morgan paralleled Caro and Noveck, labeling Billy and Joe as "what is oddly the film's most touching pair."[17]

Love Actually has become a holiday staple for laughs, hopes and a good cry. Its characters are connected either directly or indirectly. One example is Karen, who's married to Harry. While they're Christmas shopping at Selfridges, Karen leaves him alone and buys gifts for their mothers. An overwhelmingly polite and committed salesman helps Harry, who wants to buy a necklace and agrees to have it gift-wrapped for his secretary Mia, but backs out when Karen reemerges. Harry and Mia are either having an affair or about to have one.[18]

Karen is also the sister of Britain's newly installed prime minister and the friend of a widower whose ten-year-old stepson wants to say goodbye before "the love of his life"—a female classmate—leaves on a family vacation. He is prevented by an airline worker because he doesn't have a boarding pass, but a gentleman distracts the worker so that the boy can fulfill his mission and see her. It's the salesman who served Harry.

Love Actually also stars Colin Firth, Hugh Grant, Keira Knightley, Laura Linney, Liam Neeson, Alan Rickman, Emma Thompson and Rowan Atkinson.

24

Music Publishing Rights—Public Performance (*Jack Frost*)

Concerts are a lucrative pillar of the music industry.
At the beginning of the 1998 film *Jack Frost*, a rhythm-and-blues version of "Frosty the Snowman" performed by the Jack Frost Band overwhelms a Denver audience seemingly comprised of a few hundred people. Michael Keaton portrays Jack, who energizes the crowd with his vocal interpretation of Frosty's tale, complemented by outstanding musicians playing the keyboard, violin, guitars and drums; Jack plays the harmonica when he's not singing. A record executive in the audience wants to sign the band to a contract.[1]

Sacrificing a Christmas trip with his wife Gabby and son Charlie for another gig, Jack has second thoughts and starts for home. He dies in a car accident, only to be reincarnated as a snowman thanks to the film's special effects team from Industrial Light & Magic and Jim Henson's Creature Shop. In his new form, Jack tries to make up for lost time by guiding Charlie, a sixth-grader, through some growing pains. On the following Christmas Eve, his snowman façade disappears; Gabby and Charlie see an ethereal version of Jack, who says that he'll never be gone from their lives because he'll be in their hearts. He then disappears in a flurry of snow.

Whether a public performance takes place at a state fair, bowling alley, nightclub, sports arena, stadium or other venue, a license is usually needed.

Regarding public performances, the U.S. Copyright Act is clear:

> To perform or display a work "publicly" means—(1) to perform or display it at a place open to the public or at any place where a substantial number of persons outside of a normal circle of a family and its social acquaintances is gathered; or (2) to transmit or otherwise communicate a performance or display of the work to a place specified by clause (1) or to the public, by means of any

device or process, whether the members of the public capable of receiving the performance or display receive it in the same place or in separate places and at the same time or at different times.[2]

It's evident that the Jack Frost Band's appearance satisfies the requirements to be considered a public performance under the Copyright Act. In turn, the venue would have sought permission from the American Society of Composers, Authors and Publishers (ASCAP), the music rights organization governing the licensing for "Frosty the Snowman," written by Steve Nelson and Walter E. Rollins. (Gene Autry first recorded the song in 1950.) ASCAP's General License Agreement for Restaurants, Bars, Nightclubs and Similar Establishments protects the ASCAP members if their music is used, but there are limitations, conditions and caveats for the venue to consider. Examples are Limitations on License, License Fees and Payments, and Interference in ASCAP's Operations.

One curb under this General License Agreement is the lack of authority to distribute the performance of ASCAP–represented music on television. If a Denver TV station wanted to host a special featuring the Jack Frost Band and performers in the venue, then a separate license would be negotiated for permission. The relevant clause of the agreement reads:

> This license does not authorize the broadcasting, telecasting or transmission by wire or otherwise, of renditions of musical compositions in the ASCAP Repertory to persons outside of the Premises, other than by means of a music-on-hold telephone system operated by LICENSEE at the Premises.[3]

Also, the venue's representative will need to be aware of a restriction regarding the mode of ticket sales for nightclubs, etc.: "This license does not authorize live concert performances at the Premises when tickets for such live concert performances can be purchased from or through Outside Ticket Services." The agreement's Definitions section states, "'Outside Ticket Services' shall mean third-party services distributing tickets to the public for events at the Premises, such as, but not limited to, Ticketmaster, Ticketweb and Ticketron."[4]

The license will be for one year. ASCAP's license fee can be paid outright or in installment payments of 25 percent on a quarterly basis. If it is paid in full, then ASCAP will allow a discount according to its internal Rate Schedule, "provided that no license fees remain due and owing under this or any other prior ASCAP license." An installment plan or a venue's license for "seasonal or occasional performances" blocks the opportunity for the discount.[5]

In the license agreement, ASCAP reserves the right to end the license if government actions deem it burdensome. The specific language dictates,

24. Music Publishing Rights—Public Performance (Jack Frost) 147

Governmental Entities from time to time may enact laws that create obstacles to ASCAP's licensing of public performances. Accordingly, in the event of either (a) any major interference with the operations of ASCAP in the Governmental Entity in which LICENSEE is located, by reason of any law of such Governmental Entity; or (b) any substantial increase in the cost to ASCAP of operating in such Governmental Entity, which is applicable to the licensing of performing rights, ASCAP shall have the right to terminate this Agreement immediately and shall refund to LICENSEE any unearned license fees paid in advance.[6]

ASCAP plays a vital role in protecting the rights of its membership exceeding one million songwriters, composers and music publishers who deserve to be compensated for their artistic contributions, especially if other people and entities are benefiting from them. The Jack Frost Band presumably had a manager negotiate an appearance fee; the venue sold tickets and perhaps beverages including soda and beer. ASCAP has more than 100 licenses with a fee schedule for each one, but similar venues in different locations will pay the same fee. ASCAP explains, "[R]ates for restaurants of the same size, with the same use of music are the same regardless of whether the restaurant is in Oshkosh or New York City."

However, there's an exemption for worship services if the music is not broadcast on TV, radio or the Internet. Also, teachers may use music in the classroom for a non-profit educational institution.[7]

Performers have an opportunity to participate in the licensing process. Their song information is crucial for ASCAP in determining payments for its members. ASCAP's website explains:

ASCAP collects set lists from both headliners and opening acts of the top tours and concerts each year, and pays the ASCAP writers of every song that was performed—even if it's a cover song. In addition to that, ASCAP members at any stage of their career can submit set lists from live performances through our ASCAP OnStage program. No matter how big or small the venue or where in the country it's located, if we license it, then our members can get paid by ASCAP when they perform there.[8]

Using the Jack Frost Band as an example, let's say that the Denver appearance kicks off a Colorado tour with future stops in Boulder, Lakewood, Westminster, Aurora, Fort Collins and Colorado Springs. It's logical to believe that the band plays the same list of songs at each performance. Although this scenario may not be considered a "top tour," it's probable that the band will be on ASCAP's radar, especially after a radio station plays a bootleg copy of the song in a subsequent scene.

So all parties benefit financially from this structure. Revenue is generated from ticket fees for the venue; the ASCAP license fee for EMI; and a performance fee for the Jack Frost Band. Even though EMI owns the song

"Frosty the Snowman," copyright law creates an opportunity that allows another potential revenue stream for the creative community.

In *Jack Frost*, the band's R&B version of "Frosty the Snowman" required an in-depth transformation of the song for a six-piece band, which triggers protection under the U.S. Copyright Act's Section 103, titled "Subject matter of copyright: Compilations and derivative works." It encompasses new versions, including musical arrangements, while protecting the copyright owner of the original work, in this case, Gene Autry's 1950 version. The section reads in part:

> The copyright in a compilation or derivative work extends only to the material contributed by the author of such work, as distinguished from the pre-existing material employed in the work, and does not imply any exclusive right in the preexisting material. The copyright in such work is independent of, and does not affect or enlarge the scope, duration, ownership, or subsistence of, any copyright protection in the preexisting material.[9]

Whomever composed the new arrangement for the Jack Frost Band would be wise to register it for copyright protection, assuming it is original and does not substantially overlap another version. If the band records the song (even though it would be without Jack), then the contract with the record company will determine who registers the performance for copyright protection. It would not be surprising to learn that the Jack Frost Band records "Frosty the Snowman" for a record company. In 2023, it was the 14th most popular ASCAP holiday song ahead of "White Christmas," "Here Comes Santa Claus (Down Santa Claus Lane)" and "Silver Bells."[10]

The Jack Frost Band would be in good company as "Frosty the Snowman" has been an extraordinarily popular song since its debut, inspiring versions sung by the Beach Boys, the Ronettes, the Jackson 5, Nat King Cole, Billy Idol, Bing Crosby, Fiona Apple and Ray Conniff, to name but a few. In the 1990 film *Goodfellas*, the Ronettes' version plays in the background as mobsters congregate at the Suite Lounge after the Lufthansa heist.

Section 115 of the Copyright Act codifies compulsory licenses with language that would give the Jack Frost Band an opportunity to protect a new arrangement without permission from EMI:

> A compulsory license includes the privilege of making a musical arrangement of the work to the extent necessary to conform it to the style or manner of interpretation of the performance involved, but the arrangement shall not change the basic melody or fundamental character of the work, and shall not be subject to protection as a derivative work under this title, except with the express consent of the copyright owner.[11]

The musical arrangement for the Jack Frost Band can have decent legal protection provided the owner consents and it's substantially original from other versions, which are also allowed from a policy standpoint. Restricting interpretations is antithetical to a vibrant, lucrative and inspiring creative community, explained in the 1950 U.S. District Court for the Southern District of California decision *Supreme Records vs. Decca Records*, which paralleled music to acting:

> If recognition were given to the right of ownership in a musical arrangement, we would have to disregard all these cases. We would have to hold that Mr. Charles Laughton, for instance, could claim the right to forbid anyone else from imitating his creative mannerisms in his famous characterization of Henry VIII, or Sir Laurence Olivier could prohibit anyone else from adopting some of the innovations which he brought to the performance of Hamlet.[12]

The Jack Frost Band's R&B version of "Frosty the Snowman" represents the beauty of differing tastes across the musical spectrum. Joan Jett's 1990s interpretation of "Love Is All Around" (the theme song to the 1970s sitcom *The Mary Tyler Moore Show*, not the 1967 song popularized by the Troggs) offers a hard rock sound contrasting the gentle version offered by Sonny Curtis, who also wrote the song. Bobby Freeman's fast-moving anthem "Do You Want to Dance?," also popularized by the Beach Boys, was transformed into a romantic ballad by Bette Midler on *The Divine Miss M*, her 1972 debut album. The same paradigm happened in the 2007 film *Across the Universe*; T.V. (Teresa Victoria) Carpio presented a tender, mournful version of "I Wanna Hold Your Hand," better known for the version with an upbeat style by the Beatles.

"Frosty the Snowman" is appreciated as a cornerstone of America's Christmas songbook even though the lyrics don't reference Christmas. Its holiday status changed in 1969, when CBS premiered the animated special *Frosty the Snowman*. It was produced by Arthur Rankin Jr. and Jules Bass, who had also produced the iconic 1964 stop-motion animation special *Rudolph the Red-Nosed Reindeer*. Jimmy Durante narrated the Rankin-Bass story about the famous snowman, taking place during Christmas Eve and Christmas Day; his rendition of "Frosty the Snowman" uses the word "Christmas."

25

Unpublished Works (*The Bishop's Wife*)

When parishioners and congregants need guidance, they go to their clergy—rabbi, pastor, reverend, minister, etc. Clergy call on a higher authority.

It is this situation that begins the 1947 film *The Bishop's Wife*, set in an unnamed metropolis. Bishop Henry Brougham of St. Timothy's Church faces a massive challenge of raising money to build a new cathedral and asks the Lord for guidance; it comes from an angel named Dudley whose presence, actions, and words make everyone who meets him feel lighter. Everyone except the bishop.

David Niven plays Henry. Cary Grant—whose previous films included *Bringing Up Baby, His Girl Friday, The Philadelphia Story, Arsenic and Old Lace* and *Notorious*—plays Dudley, who charms without being saccharine, persuades without being overbearing, and reveals his heavenly identity to nobody except the bishop.[1]

Dudley tells a story about an ancient coin to Professor Wutheridge (Monty Woolley) and Julia (Loretta Young), the bishop's wife; it inspires the former and charms the latter. After years of procrastination, the scholar resumes writing a history book. Henry remains suspicious and skeptical as he disapproves of Dudley, particularly a blooming though platonic relationship with Julia, who appears to be on the brink of falling for the dashing aide. And vice versa. The angel begins his journey back to heavenly headquarters upon realizing that he envies a mortal—specifically, Henry's marriage to Julia—and explains to Henry that all memories of his visit will be erased from those with whom he interacted.

Niven's frustration as the bishop is palpable, particularly when he seeks to mine the extraordinary wealth of Agnes Hamilton, a widow who wants a cathedral built not as a symbol of devotion, kindness or charity but as a testament to her deceased husband. Played with aplomb by Gladys Cooper, the affluent matron is dour, condescending and selfish, striking

25. Unpublished Works (The Bishop's Wife)   151

down suggestions that do not place her deceased husband's name in a prominent place. When the building committee meets about the project and discusses the site, one member suggests an alternative location for the George B. Hamilton Memorial Chapel within the boundaries of the blueprints. "It will be completely out of sight there," argues the donor. "I won't stand for it."

Henry responds, "Mrs. Hamilton, surely you understand that this cathedral cannot be designed for the glory of an individual. It has to be created for all the people." She reminds him that he was a parson in the slums before she used her influence to elevate him to the position of bishop. Henry later accedes to her requests, apologizing and emphasizing that the building of the cathedral supersedes his objections.

Dudley visits the moneyed woman and discovers sheet music for a song called "Lost April," authored by Allan Cartwright; going by a message on the first page, the angel deduces that Allan was her first and only love. Dudley plays the song on the harp, shocking Mrs. Hamilton, because Cartwright died before he could become known and appreciated. She confesses her personal story to Dudley and sheds tears from trying to cover her feelings by building things to honor her husband, a man she never truly loved.

There was an engagement decades ago, but the talented musician had no money and seemed to have few prospects. Poverty frightened her. So she traded emotional attachment for financial security and married a wealthy man. Apparently Dudley and Mrs. Hamilton have an off-screen conversation, because instead of building a cathedral honoring George B. Hamilton, she wants her donations to be used for altruistic projects with Henry supervising the distribution of the money.

It is not stated whether "Lost April" was ever registered for copyright or published, which makes the song's legal protection an interesting topic for exploration. Presuming that Mrs. Hamilton is in her late 50s like the actress playing her (Cooper was born in 1888), let's also suppose that she dated Cartwright in her early 20s or late teens, which would place the relationship sometime in the late 1910s or the beginning of the 1920s.

In this scenario, the 1909 Copyright Act governs the song's copyright status. There are two requirements: publication and affixation. The relevant language is in Section 9 of the statute:

> That any person entitled thereto by this Act may secure copyright for his work by publication thereof with the notice of copyright required by this Act; and such notice shall be affixed to each copy thereof published or offered for sale in the United States by authority of the copyright proprietor, except in the case of books seeking ad interim protection under section twenty-one of this Act.[2]

It does not appear that "Lost April" satisfied this requirement. Taking an expansive view of the word "publication" as meaning available to the public, the dialogue suggests that only Cartwright and his paramour knew about the song. The title on the sheet music is handwritten by Cartwright along with a personal inscription of affection. This theory is reinforced when Mrs. Hamilton hears Dudley playing the composition and says that nobody else alive knows the song, causing him to commiserate with her that only the two of them know "the lost genius of Allan Cartwright." It's safe to conclude that there are no recordings and no copies of the sheet music other than the one in Mrs. Hamilton's house.

Assuming Cartwright had no viable heirs who would be the song's rightful owners to publish the song and gain federal copyright protection, then Mrs. Hamilton had a viable avenue to see that the composer's work be available to the public. She could have used her wealth to get it recorded, distributed and registered for copyright with proceeds going to Cartwright's estate. Surely a woman of her means would have attorneys, accountants, and investment advisers to establish an estate account in Cartwright's name, register "Lost April" for copyright in the estate's name, and monitor royalties.

Further, there would have been a compulsory mechanical license under the 1909 statute; musicians could play "Lost April" without getting permission of the Cartwright estate. Section 1(e) states that whenever the owner of a musical copyright

> has used or permitted or knowingly acquiesced in the use of the copyrighted work upon the parts of instruments serving to reproduce mechanically the musical work, any other person may make similar use of the copyrighted work upon the payment to the copyright proprietor of a royalty of two cents on each such part manufactured, to be paid by the manufacturer thereof.[3]

But nothing could happen legally until the copyright owner green-lit the initial mechanical reproduction. In 2005, Marybeth Peters, the Register of Copyrights at the U.S. Copyright Office, testified before the Senate about music licensing reform and explained the background of mechanical licensing in the 1909 Copyright Act:

> Starting in 1905, copyright owners began seeking legislative changes which would grant them the exclusive right to authorize the mechanical reproduction of their works. The impetus for this movement was the emergence of the player piano and the ambiguity surrounding the extent of copyright owners' right to control the making of copies of their works on piano rolls.[4]

In 1908, the Supreme Court struck a blow against copyright owners by ruling that perforated piano rolls were not considered "copies" under the 1831 Copyright Act, then the governing statute. Instead, the majority

25. Unpublished Works (The Bishop's Wife)

opinion written by Justice William Day, formerly Secretary of State in President William McKinley's cabinet, classified the rolls as different from copies of sheet music:

> It is true that there is some testimony to the effect that great skill and patience might enable the operator to read this record as he could a piece of music written in staff notation. But the weight of the testimony is emphatically the other way, and they are not intended to be read as an ordinary piece of sheet music, which, to those skilled in the art, conveys, by reading, in playing or singing, definite impressions of the melody. These perforated rolls are parts of a machine which, when duly applied and properly operated in connection with the mechanism to which they are adapted, produce musical tones in harmonious combination. But we cannot think that they are copies within the meaning of the Copyright Act.[5]

In his concurrence, Justice Oliver Wendell Holmes, Jr., noted the restrictive impact of his fellow justice's decision. "On principle, anything that mechanically reproduces that collocation of sounds ought to be held a copy, or, if the statute is too narrow, ought to be made so by a further act, except so far as some extraneous consideration of policy may oppose.[6]

There's an alternative argument for Mrs. Hamilton to see that "Lost April" gets copyright status under the 1909 Copyright Act. She can claim ownership. Presuming no viable heirs exist, Mrs. Hamilton can argue that Cartwright gave her the sheet music as a gift and bolster her contention with the inscription on the sheet music: "This was composed for you, my darling—and you only."

Even if a long-lost Cartwright relative emerges with a claim on the copyright and argues that there's no written instrument establishing the conveyance of rights to "Lost April," her possession of the sheet music plus the personal message will likely be enough to overcome any claim. But Mrs. Hamilton would do herself a favor by finding people she knew in her youth to make statements that she and Cartwright were involved in a romance. It would be helpful, though likely not vital.

By asserting ownership of the sheet music via gift, Mrs. Hamilton could register it for copyright, then invest in having the song recorded for public distribution and register those recordings as well. Since Dudley has stirred her feelings of altruism, she could then use the profits to establish scholarships for music students at a local university or donate the copyrights to a local university's music department. Mrs. Hamilton's lawyers and their counterparts will want to make sure that a gift is airtight through conversations that will clarify the university's mechanisms, paperwork and intricacies for such a donation.

The 1909 Copyright Act also has a deposit requirement. Section 10 states in part:

That such person may obtain registration of his claim to copyright by complying with the provisions of this Act, including the deposit of copies, and upon such compliance the register of copyrights shall issue to him the certificate provided for in section fifty-five of this Act.[7]

Depositing a copy of the sheet music would be a step toward copyright protection for the composition. Whether Mrs. Hamilton would receive a copyright registration for a recording would depend upon an agreement with the musicians performing "Lost April." Section 55 of the 1909 Copyright Act states in part that a printed certificate, sealed with the seal of the copyright office, shall, upon payment of a fee, "be given to any person making application for the same, and the said certificate shall be admitted in any court as prima facie evidence of the facts stated therein." Additionally, the copyright office would provide receipts to the claimant depositing the work; the registration fee would have been one dollar.[8]

The Bishop's Wife premiered in New York City in December 1947; it went into nationwide release two months later. Given the timing, Mrs. Hamilton would have a potential blue-chip opportunity to leverage a valid copyright for "Lost April" because NBC launched *Texaco Star Theater* in the following June; Milton Berle hosted and became television's first star after finding success in vaudeville, movies, nightclubs and radio.

NBC paved a path for comedy-variety shows featuring guest entertainers, so it's reasonable to presume that Mrs. Hamilton or the recipient of her donated copyright would try to get the leading pianists of the day to play "Lost April" on a nationally broadcast TV show. This exposure would lead to Cartwright posthumously getting his rightful recognition.

Section 1(e) of the 1909 Copyright Act grants the right of public performance: "[t]o perform the copyrighted work publicly for profit if it be a musical composition." Consequently, the copyright owner would have the right to license a performance. As the copyright owner under the gift theory, Mrs. Hamilton could receive the license fees and distribute the money as she sees fit or add it to the bounty for the bishop's oversight.[9]

Of course, there's a potential downside to Mrs. Hamilton's reputation should she wish to navigate the challenges of copyright law and give the world an opportunity to enjoy the "lost genius" of a great composer. Even though her motives for publishing the work of her lost love will be charitable, questions will arise regarding her relationship with Cartwright and the reason for ending it. That's not really a matter of expertise for lawyers, but any counseling on legal matters would have to at least highlight the issue and refer her to a public relations expert on how best to manage the information.

Praise showered on *The Bishop's Wife* like a 12-inch snowfall in Central Park. The *Daily News* (New York) highlighted the film's producer Sam

25. Unpublished Works (The Bishop's Wife)   155

Goldwyn, who had tremendous commercial and critical success with *The Best Years of Our Lives*, a 1946 film chronicling the lives of three soldiers returning home to the Midwest after World War II. It won seven Academy Awards. *The Bishop's Wife* continued that quality: "Bearing the Goldwyn hallmark, which has become a symbol of good film craftsmanship, you may be sure that care has been lavished on the comedy's production details," wrote Kate Cameron. "It has been well made, down to its simplest background item."[10]

The Associated Press declared, "The general effect of the movie, however, is so heart-warming that any possible objections are likely to be overlooked." *Los Angeles Times* film critic Philip K. Scheuer lauded the director: "[Henry Koster directs] with an impeccable, sly humor.... An inflection of voice, a pause, a movement of the eyes—they are all there, and beautifully timed. Even the opening or closing of a door is significant in the building of a laugh."[11]

The *Pasadena Star-News* described David Niven as "convincingly harassed by his dream of building a cathedral and by the pettiness of a rich parishioner." The *Pittsburgh Post-Gazette* opined, "Mr. Niven is a droll figure of quizzical exasperation. If this is anybody's picture, it's certainly his."[12]

26

Public Domain (*Scrooged*)

Scrooged is a 1988 film starring Bill Murray in the paradigm of network television.[1]

Murray plays Frank Cross, the IBC TV network president overseeing a live Christmas Eve production of *A Christmas Carol*, retitled *Scrooge*. This $40 million broadcast will star Buddy Hackett in the title role, Jamie Farr as Cratchit, Mary Lou Retton as Tiny Tim, dancers from the 1980s TV show *Solid Gold*, and Sir John Houseman as narrator. Frank has risen to the top of the media ladder to become the youngest TV network president in broadcast history while dismissing the intangibles that could have filled his life with joy instead of high Nielsen ratings.

Like Scrooge, Frank takes a journey through time helmed by four ghosts. It begins with his mentor, followed by apparitions showing Christmases of the past, present and future. These wraiths reveal the emotional debris that Frank created, including a failed relationship with a girlfriend, Claire. Frank interrupts the *Scrooge* broadcast, praises the spirit of Christmas, and urges the viewers to be kinder to each other.

The *Hollywood Reporter* lauded *Scrooged*:

> With his deadpan, cut-through-it style, Murray is hilarious as the network czar. His deadpan putdowns—his voice pulsating with flat disdain and his open glare shooting darts—are scrumptiously condescending. Despite the juicy, on-the-edge craziness, Murray is able to layer his outrageous histrionics with an inner sensibility, making his ultimate transformation not only believable but Christmas-cheer uplifting.[2]

Producing a live broadcast inspired by *A Christmas Carol* does not subject IBC to a license fee; Dickens' story is in the public domain. The U.S. Copyright Office explains,

> The public domain is not a place. A work of authorship is in the "public domain" if it is no longer under copyright protection or if it failed to meet the requirements for copyright protection. Works in the public domain may be used freely without the permission of the former copyright owner.[3]

26. Public Domain (Scrooged)

Frank's real-life counterparts in the entertainment industry—executives, writers and producers of *Scrooged* and other variations of *A Christmas Carol*—factor this financial freedom into their decisions about adding another interpretation of Dickens' iconic tale instead of producing a TV, film or stage version of an original work under copyright protection, such as a recent novel with new characters.

The concept of public domain is rooted in what's nicknamed the "copyright clause" in Article 1, Section 8 of the Constitution, which reads in part: "The Congress shall have Power.... To promote the Progress of Science and useful Arts, by securing for limited Times to Authors and Inventors the exclusive Right to their respective Writings and Discoveries."[4] Using the phrase "limited Times" indicates that authors would not have rights to exploit their work in perpetuity. Congress first codified this philosophy with the Copyright Act of 1790, setting the boundary for a copyright at 14 years with the option to renew the copyright for another 14 years.

However, a new work of authorship that is based on a work in the public domain can enjoy copyright protection to the extent of original elements in the new work. As IBC's president, Frank would certainly be conscious of the copyright implications involved in protecting and exploiting a version of *A Christmas Carol*; IBC's copyright lawyers would seek protection under the Copyright Act of 1976. Section 106 gives exclusive rights to the copyright owner of the new work to make and distribute copies or make derivative works such as a sequel or prequel. In addition, IBC has the right "to perform the copyrighted work publicly" and "display the copyrighted work publicly."[5]

Assuming the routines from the *Solid Gold* dancers are owned by IBC, either through a work-for-hire arrangement or an in-house choreographer, then Section 102(a) will give the network an added asset because choreography falls under the umbrella of protection offered to numerous expressions:

> Copyright protection subsists, in accordance with this title, in original works of authorship fixed in any tangible medium of expression, now known or later developed, from which they can be perceived, reproduced, or otherwise communicated, either directly or with the aid of a machine or device. Works of authorship include the following categories: literary works; musical works, including any accompanying words; dramatic works, including any accompanying music; pantomimes and choreographic works; pictorial, graphic, and sculptural works; motion pictures and other audiovisual works; sound recordings; and architectural works.[6]

CHRISTMAS AND GOVERNMENT

27

Gifts to State Government Employees (*Parks and Recreation*)

America has had a great many optimists in its history. Among them are Franklin Delano Roosevelt proclaiming that we have nothing to fear but fear itself; John F. Kennedy declaring that the torch of liberty has been passed to a new generation; and Ronald Reagan describing Washington as a shining city upon a hill.[1]

Leslie Knope mirrors them in the NBC sitcom *Parks and Recreation*, which aired from 2009 to 2015.

As Pawnee, Indiana's Deputy Director of Parks and Recreation, Leslie shows an unyielding positivity regarding civil service. Her sunny outlook on Pawnee and her department's importance cannot be swayed by red tape, legitimate objections and a boss indifferent to government action. In the 2011 episode "Citizen Knope," Leslie has been suspended for two weeks for an ethical violation: She did not disclose her relationship with co-worker Ben Wyatt to her superiors.[2]

When she comes to the office in the early morning trying to get work done before anyone arrives, she's surprised to find Chris Traeger, a state employee a few rungs above her on the civil service ladder. Chris says, "You are specifically prohibited from doing your job." Pawnee's resident optimist counters with a flimsy excuse that probably makes sense to her because she doesn't plan to give her usual 100 percent. "Oh, I'm not gonna do my job. I'm just gonna oversee the department and check in on the parks and attend any meetings that require the deputy director."

Despite the mandate, Leslie cannot stay away from working for the public good; she creates a citizens group called Parks Committee of Pawnee. It backfires because the members become nuisances. Leslie's energetic spirit—which she basically has all year round—also inspires her to buy Christmas gifts for her co-workers. This series of events happens in the middle of her campaign for a spot on Pawnee's city council. Though Leslie has a tremendous drive to serve Pawnee, her actions are questionable under Indiana law and may place her in legal jeopardy.

Presuming that Leslie and her co-workers are employees and appointees of the state rather than Pawnee for the purposes of a legal discussion regarding her gifts, it's important to note the state's legal restrictions:

> A state employee or special state appointee, or the spouse or unemancipated child of a state employee or special state appointee, shall not knowingly solicit, accept or receive any gift; favor; service; entertainment; food; drink; travel expenses; or registration fees; from a person who has a business relationship with the employee's or special state appointee's agency or is seeking to influence an action by the employee or special state appointee in his or her official capacity."[3]

Leslie often uses her powers of persuasion to bring people to her side of an issue, even if they do so with reluctance or appeasement. But a hard-nosed, cynically minded government investigator could hypothesize that her position in the Pawnee government creates an inherent business relationship with her staff, especially with her seeking higher office. Further, any gifts could be seen as Leslie trying to "influence an action," thereby making her culpable under the statute.

Andy Dwyer monitors City Hall's shoe polishing stand and heads up a local rock group called Mouse Rat. In honor of his latter vocation, Leslie gives him a gold album commemorating 100 copies sold. Leslie notes the fashion sense of Parks and Recreation department manager Donna Meagle by giving her a robe with a leopard print and pink feather cuffs. "You Can Get It" in rhinestones adorns the back of the robe. Tom Haverford, who reports to Leslie, couldn't get tickets to the Watch the Throne Tour starring Kanye West and Jay-Z, so Leslie bestows a pocket watch with the words Baller Time replacing the clock face and a throne that seems to be from a jewelry store. April Ludgate is the apathetic, sarcastic, but basically good-hearted assistant to department director Ron Swanson, a libertarian. She receives a commissioned painting featuring her killing the Black Eyed Peas rock group. "It's a Christmas miracle," says April.

Ron admits that Leslie gets him "something thoughtful and personal" during the holiday season. "This year, she outdid herself," Ron says before he chokes up. "It's so beautiful." The gift: Both of Ron's doors on opposite sides of his office will close when an electronic fob is pushed. Ron's aversion to meetings and personal interactions makes the gift a bullseye.

The co-workers would need to understand that receiving the gifts will not violate the statute as long as two conditions are met. The relevant part reads:

27. Gifts to State Government Employees (Parks and Recreation) 161

Gifts, favors, services, entertainment, food, or drinks from relatives, or a person with whom the employee or special state appointee has an ongoing social relationship, so long as: the gifts or other items of value are not deducted as a business expense; and the gift giver is not seeking to influence an action by an employee or special state appointee in that person's official capacity.[4]

It's reasonable to presume that Leslie would not deduct the gifts, but the second requirement would again prompt a skeptical investigator to seek proof that she did not mean to influence the co-workers in an official capacity. Leslie could offer an affidavit listing her gifts during previous years plus receipts or personal credit card statements indicating the amount spent as evidence for an argument that she gave the gifts as part of her annual Christmas tradition, paid a reasonable amount, and did not use government funds.

However, these gifts are not nominal. You wouldn't expect to find them in a "Secret Santa" gift exchange like a $25 gift certificate to a local restaurant or a baseball cap representing the recipient's favorite sports team. Leslie's gifts probably cost more than $100 each, perhaps a few hundred dollars in some cases.

There's no question that Leslie is an outstanding civil servant whose passion for serving the public is a paragon for anyone wanting to work inside the government at the local, state or federal level. Although her sense of friendship informs her generosity, it violates an unspoken norm about the boundaries of cost while spending money on holiday gifts. In turn, one can make a solid argument that she's violating both the letter and spirit of the law that's supposed to protect government employees from undue influence.

But her gifts are not always extravagant. For example, six months before "Citizen Knope" aired, the episode "Eagleton" showed her tricking Ron Swanson, her celebration-averse boss, by making him think that she planned an extravagant birthday party for him. Instead, she arranged a night of uninterrupted solitude in the office consisting of a steak dinner with sides—including bacon, his favorite food—and whisky in addition to DVDs of *The Bridge on the River Kwai* and *The Dirty Dozen*.[5]

However, an investigator's interrogation of Ron would reveal that Leslie's generosity is generally above and beyond the norm. He tells the members of the department, "We need to get Leslie something that erases the enormous emotional debt that has built up over years of this gift-giving imbalance." Therefore, an investigator could argue that Leslie's superiority of thoughtfulness is really a ploy to put others in a situation where they will owe her favors.

Starting a citizen action committee doesn't help. While it's a noble effort to keep involved in city government during her hiatus, she's lobbying the department that she will work for again. It's a clear conflict of interest. Leslie corrals a group of volunteers and attends a public forum arranged by the Parks and Recreation Department concerning potential improvements. She later tells the group about tactics: a volunteer to call Chris every 15 minutes and protesters along the route that he jogs plus volunteers in every GNC outlet within a five-mile radius of Pawnee.

Chris is a dedicated fitness enthusiast, so Leslie figures that these will be the best options for getting their voices heard. But to show there are no hard feelings (and perhaps to strengthen her position on future issues where she will need Chris' approval), her Christmas gift is a stopwatch that monitors his jogging times and uploads the information to his computer.

A probe into Leslie's past dealings is reasonable considering her misjudgment in not disclosing the relationship with Ben and her excessiveness in gift-giving. Her ethical reputation would be at stake as well as culpability. So, another line of defense for Leslie would be her list of achievements while in office to prove that her conduct has been above board and unaffected by her gifts.

Leslie would benefit by thinking strategically, putting herself in the shoes of an investigator, and anticipating questions that might be asked concerning her work in Pawnee's Parks and Recreation Department. Has she helped conceive, maintain and complete projects within the proposed constraints of budget, time and resources? How have those projects added to the quality of life in Pawnee? How has she helped manage the overall budget of the department, including fundraisers? How does Pawnee's budget compare to other Indiana cities of the same size? What has been her greatest achievement as a Pawnee civil servant? Is her job vital or can the duties be administered by other people in the department? What are her annual reviews from Ron? Has she given gifts to civil servants in other departments of Pawnee's city government?

Leslie's actions amount to a cautionary tale for the members of the Parks and Recreation Department. Let's take Ron as an example. He's an expert craftsman with a fondness for woodworking. If he made jewelry boxes for everyone in the office and distributed them as Christmas gifts, it might seem to him like nominal labor. But an investigator would have to inquire about the specifics. What kind of wood did he use? What kind of varnish or shellac? How much time did it take him? Does he sell these or other similar items for profit and if so, what is the price?

Men can use the jewelry boxes for cuff links and watches while women can use them for rings, necklaces and bracelets. What might seem like a gift representing kindness and practicality can actually be a breach of the code, but Ron's aversion to relationships with co-workers beyond the bare minimum lends credence to an argument that the gift is reasonable.

27. Gifts to State Government Employees (Parks and Recreation) 163

The episode "Flu Season" exemplifies this attitude. "The less I know about other people's affairs, the happier I am," said Ron. "I'm not interested in caring about people. I once worked with a guy for three years and never learned his name. Best friend I ever had. We still never talk sometimes."[6]

Depending on the level of extravagance that Ron used in crafting the jewelry boxes, it could be posited that he's using them to bank favors in the future, perhaps to get a project disapproved or to perform tasks that fall under his areas of responsibility. But that argument is flimsy, given Ron's distrust of government.

Tom presents another interesting topic. In the episode "Beauty Pageant," he discloses that he sometimes has meetings at Talent and Poise, a strip club near the local Veterans Administration hospital. Besides the obvious public disgust that will emerge from a government official conducting business and using government funds at a strip club, Tom will be in hot water depending on how much he spends for the goods and services plus the specifics regarding them. Beer or champagne? A booth on the main floor or a private room for a government contractor and a dancer in the back of the club? If the meetings take place during the holiday season, then an investigation into Leslie may prompt similar inquiries into Tom's actions.[7]

Played by Amy Poehler, who became a TV star with a stellar tenure on *Saturday Night Live* from 2001 to 2008, Leslie Knope had enthusiasm that alternated between inspiring and annoying. TV critic Verne Gay aptly called the character "a clueless dork with a big heart." But it's the combination of those qualities that fuel her generosity, which may consequently lead to a violation of the statute if a prosecutor believes her motives to be impure.[8]

Say nope to Knope? Hardly. Her character witnesses will consist of the people in the Parks and Recreation Department, a likely fountain of positivity even though they may be bothered by her unbridled energy whether she's promoting a small horse named Li'l Sebastian as Pawnee's mascot or adding to her stream of compliments about her best friend Ann Perkins. They will go along with her even if they don't share her vision without regard to her gifts. TV critic Tom Shales wrote that Knope "is gung-ho all the way and able to summon false enthusiasm even after, say, tumbling into a giant ditch that's supposedly going to become a new recreation center."[9]

In the show's early days, Poehler addressed her character's political ambition: "She's got a 40-year plan." It seems that this plan extended her career even further than she might have imagined. In the two-episode series finale, Leslie's upward trajectory includes two terms as Indiana governor; an honorary doctorate from the Indiana University School of Public

Policy; and an IU library renamed in her honor. When Leslie and Ben visit Pawnee in 2048 for the burial of their former co-worker Garry Gergich, who died on his 100th birthday, the presence of Secret Service agents may indicate that either Leslie or Ben occupies the office of president of the United States.[10]

28

Gifts to the President of the United States (*Family Ties*)

In NBC's sitcom *Family Ties* (1982-89), Steven and Elyse Keaton have kept their values of peace, love and togetherness ever since they were hippies in the late 1960s. He's an executive at the public television station in Columbus, Ohio; she's an architect. They live in a nice house with their children Jennifer, Mallory and Alex, who is 17 years old when the series begins and 180 degrees from his parents on political issues. The Keatons have a baby boy, Andy, in the show's third season.

Fond of lower taxes and a rising Dow Jones Industrial Average, Alex P. Keaton could have been a caricature with another actor's portrayal but Michael J. Fox injected warmth, depth and dimension into his performance, resulting in three Emmy Awards. Writers tailored stories and scenes to leverage Fox's talent and complement the character's intellectual arrogance with emotional vulnerability, humor and likability.

When Alex visits Andy's preschool, he entertains the kids with his trademark sarcasm as he teaches a lesson in building a business, including the importance of tax avoidance. "A tax is a terrible, hairy, liberal monster with big teeth," says Alex, who makes the kids laugh when he imitates a monster's growl. "And the only thing—the only thing that can stop the terrible tax monster is a Republican. Who wants to be a Republican?" The kids laugh again with delight and jump on Alex to show their affection.[1]

Alex's passion for finance manifests in the Christmas episode "Miracle in Columbus" when he works as a shopping mall's Santa Claus and tells a kid, "Santa is gonna bring you shares of Aramco Petroleum. Now Santa invests heavily in this, and ho, ho, ho! Santa has done very well." Another kid receives a salutation fitting Alex's persona: "Okay, Merry Christmas and good luck in the fiscal new year."[2]

His interest in financial health reflects a conservative political philosophy, both serving as hallmarks of the character exemplified by idolatry of Ronald Reagan, whose presidency (1981–89) coincided with the show's lifespan. In another "Miracle in Columbus" scene, Alex laments that the Reagans only sent him a Christmas card after he sent them gifts—jams and jellies.[3]

The White House protocol might have surprised Alex and disappointed him further. According to the Ronald Reagan Presidential Library & Museum website, safety concerns prevented consumption by the First Family. "To protect the President and his family, the Secret Service requires destruction of food and drink gifts, combustible items which may release fumes, and colognes and other substances that are applied to the skin."[4]

Alex's generosity would also be subject to the restrictions of federal law. Under the Code of Federal Regulations, the Office of Government Ethics ensures that government workers are not in danger of being bribed through gifts of money or objects. The parameters for Gifts from Outside Sources are clearly defined in Subpart B of Title 5, Chapter 16, Section 2635, which prohibits employees from soliciting or accepting gifts donated by a "prohibited source" or gifts donated because of the employees' official position. Section 2635.203(d) specifies that the term "prohibited source" is defined as someone engaging in the following activities:

- Is seeking official action by the employees agency.[5]
- Does business or seeks to do business with the employee's agency.[6]
- Conducts activities regulated by the employee's agency.[7]
- Has interests that may be substantially affected by the performance or nonperformance of the employee's official duties.[8]

Additionally, an entity will be subject to this definition if it is "an organization a majority of whose members are described" in the abovementioned classifications.[9]

Alex must be careful with his gift-giving. Although his love of money is a character trait launching him towards an undoubtedly prosperous career in finance (which is solidified in the 1989 series finale when he leaves the Keatons' Columbus home for a job on Wall Street), it's not out of the realm of possibility that he would have sought a position with Reagan's successor George H.W. Bush, making him a subject of scrutiny as a person seeking to do business.

However, Alex may be able to use an exception to the prohibition depending on the value of the jams and jellies that he sent to the Reagans. Section 2635.204(a) allows that a gift with a value of $20 or less will not be subject to the rule. There's no mention of the cost that Alex incurred in buying the jams and jellies, but we can presume from his persona that

28. *Gifts to the President of the United States* (Family Ties) 167

he leaned toward an expensive brand and exceeded the $20 barrier, perhaps buying them from a boutique store. Had he known about the rule, it's likely that he would have purchased a less expensive gift so he could use the exception.[10]

Providing some guidance on the issue, the introductory paragraph urges a recipient to exercise caution:

> Even though acceptance of a gift may be permitted by one of the exceptions contained in this section, it is never inappropriate and frequently prudent for an employee to decline a gift if acceptance would cause a reasonable person to question the employees integrity or impartiality.[11]

The term "gift" is defined to include nearly anything of market value. However, it does not include items that clearly are not gifts, such as publicly available discounts and commercial loans. Certain inconsequential items also warrant exclusion such as coffee, donuts, greeting cards and contest prizes.[12]

It's reasonable to presume that Alex also sent gifts to Republican lawmakers espousing his conservative financial philosophy. If Alex's holiday magnanimity extended to members of the Senate, he would have benefited by studying the rules of the Senate's Select Committee on Ethics. His gift of jams and jellies may fall under an exception if it costs less than the $20 in the CFR. The committee's exception for Items of Little Intrinsic Value states a Member, officer or employee "may accept an item of little intrinsic value, such as a greeting card, baseball cap, or T-shirt. This exception also includes food and non-food items valued at $10 or less, including flowers and perishables provided to a Senate office."[13]

Additionally, Alex could have shown initiative by ordering a gift from a Senator's state because it will be allowable under the Senate's rules. But the purpose must be clear. Alex needs to expect no remuneration either in kind or deed:

> A Member may accept donations of products (e.g., apples, peanuts, popcorn, coffee, candy, orange juice) from the state that the Member represents that are intended primarily for promotional purposes, such as display or free distribution, and are of minimal value to any individual recipient. These products must be from the Senator's home state, must be from home state producers or distributors, and must be available to office visitors.[14]

There's no doubt that Alex's love of conservative politics would have inspired him to think about potential gifts if he wanted to expand his holiday generosity beyond 1600 Pennsylvania Avenue. Kansas wheat bread for Bob Dole; Wyoming bison burgers for Alan Simpson; Pennsylvania Shoo-fly pie for John Heinz; Idaho potatoes for James McClure; Mississippi mud pie for Thad Cochran ... all viable possibilities to enjoy the exception.

Since Alex is destined for a successful Wall Street career, his gifts will likely increase in value over time. Therefore, prudence dictates considering whether the gifts will amount to bribery by looking at Title 18, Section 666(a)(1)(B) of the U.S. Code between his readings of *The Wall Street Journal* and *Fortune*. If Alex targets somebody employed by a state, local or Indian tribal government for a holiday gift, he'd be in violation of the statute if he

> corruptly gives, offers, or agrees to give anything of value to any person, with intent to influence or reward an agent of an organization or of a State, local or Indian tribal government, or any agency thereof, in connection with any business, transaction, or series of transactions of such organization, government, or agency involving anything of value of $5,000 or more.[15]

While Alex may want to show his affection, idolatry or kinship concerning a Republican politician, it's doubtful that he would jeopardize their good will with an ostentatious gift either financial or in kind. He may be sly, but he's not slick. The gift of jams and jellies is not only reasonable but also reflective of the gifts received by America's fortieth president.

During Reagan's two terms as president, donors ranging from Americans that he never met to close friends to heads of state offered more than 75,000 gifts. In 1998, the Ronald Reagan Presidential Library & Museum put a roster of items on display in an exhibit titled "Within the Vault": a gold clock from British Prime Minister Margaret Thatcher; 15 pairs of cowboy boots; a painting of Mount Rushmore with Reagan's face added to it; and white satin jackets for the president and First Lady Nancy Reagan, donated by Frank Sinatra in honor of Reagan's second inaugural gala.[16]

The connection between Michael J. Fox and Ronald Reagan went beyond the political references on *Family Ties*. In the 1985 film *Back to the Future*, Fox's character travels from 1985 to 1955 and tells Doc Brown that Ronald Reagan is the president of the United States—a laughable proposition in the 1950s as Reagan was then a film and TV actor. He served two terms as the governor of California (1967-75) before pursuing the presidency. Also, President Reagan referenced *Back to the Future*'s closing line in his 1986 State of the Union Address: "Where we're going, we don't need roads."[17]

Fox's portrayal of Alex became the launching pad for a movie career in the 1980s and '90s, bolstered by vehicles where he played different versions of a guy with good-heartedness, integrity and warmth underneath a layer of smarminess, ambition and condescension. *Doc Hollywood*, *The Secret of My Success*, *For Love or Money* and the *Back to the Future* trilogy showcase the appeal of the actor, who showed loyalty to *Family Ties* by staying with the show for its entire seven-year run rather than abandon it for a movie career.

But fans of Alex P. Keaton might have been dismayed when Fox appeared

28. Gifts to the President of the United States (Family Ties)

Michael J. Fox won three Emmys for his portrayal of politically conservative Alex P. Keaton on *Family Ties*. Fox and actress Nancy McKeon met President Ronald Reagan and First Lady Nancy Reagan at a state dinner in 1985 (Ronald Reagan Presidential Library & Museum).

as a Democratic political operative in the 1995 movie *The American President* and the ABC sitcom *Spin City* (1996-2002). Written by Aaron Sorkin and directed by Rob Reiner, *The American President* stars Michael Douglas as President Andrew Shepherd, an idealistic, Democratic chief executive who has grand visions of legislation involving gun control and limiting the use of fossil fuels. Fox has a supporting role as presidential aide Lewis Rothschild.

In *Spin City*, Fox plays New York City Deputy Mayor Mike Flaherty, a key factor in the Democratic administration of Mayor Randall Winston. Because of the worsening effects of Parkinson's Disease, Fox left the show in 2000 with a two-episode story concluding the fourth season and offering a storyline for his character's exit. When it's alleged with substantiation that the Winston administration has ties to the mob, Mike resigns to provide political cover for the mayor.

At the end of the story, his fate is revealed. Six weeks after leaving City Hall, Mike sends an email to his girlfriend—Caitlin Moore (Heather Locklear), a Winston administration colleague—explaining that he loves being an environmental lobbyist but endures friction with some conservative lawmakers. "I just met this junior senator from Ohio. What a stiff. Alex P. Keaton."[18]

29

United States Postal Service (*Miracle on 34th Street*)

There is a Santa Claus. Well, there is one officially recognized by a Manhattan judge in the 1947 film *Miracle on 34th Street*. He calls himself Kris Kringle.[1]

In Manhattan, the man hired to portray Santa Claus in Macy's Thanksgiving Day Parade shows up drunk. Kris happens to walk by and gets hired on the spot as a replacement by Doris Walker, the Macy's executive in charge of the parade; she later gives him a job as the store's Santa Claus for the holiday season. But Macy's psychiatrist Dr. Sawyer raises questions regarding Kris' mental fitness and thinks Kris should be committed.

Doris calls Kris' residence in Great Neck (Brookfield Memorial Home for the Aged) to get some answers from Dr. Pierce, a geriatrician treating Kris. In a meeting at the Macy's headquarters (34th Street and Seventh Avenue), Pierce tells Doris, her colleague Julian Shellhammer and Dr. Sawyer that Kris is harmless. "People are institutionalized to prevent them from harming themselves or others," explains Pierce. "Mr. Kringle is incapable of either. His is a delusion for good. He only wants to be friendly and helpful."

At a hearing, young, idealistic attorney Fred Gailey defends Kris from a charge of mental incompetence. If the judge rules against him, Kris could be committed to Bellevue Hospital on a long-term basis. Fred begins by calling department store magnate and Kris' employer R.H. Macy to the stand; Macy has visions of negative headlines and plummeting sales if he opposes Kris, so he testifies that he believes him to be Santa Claus.

Also on Fred's roster of witnesses is Tommy Mara, the young son of District Attorney Thomas Mara. Tommy's testimony reveals that the elder Mara credited Santa Claus with bringing his Christmas gift last year and promises he will do so again this year. Realizing that continuing his legal arguments against Kris will shatter his son's trust, the District Attorney relents but with a condition:

29. United States Postal Service (Miracle on 34th Street) 171

Your honor, the state of New York concedes the existence of Santa Claus. But in so conceding, we ask that Mr. Gailey cease presenting personal opinion as evidence. The state could bring in hundreds of witnesses with opposite opinions. But it's our desire to shorten this hearing rather than prolong it. I therefore request that Mr. Gailey now submit authoritative proof that Mr. Kringle is the one and only Santa Claus.

Judge Henry X. Harper concurs, forcing Fred to abandon emotion and sentiment in his legal strategy. On December 24, Fred is due to present his case; his outlook is as dreary as the sky when Santa asks Rudolph to light the way. Before the judge enters the courtroom, a court officer approaches Fred about another matter: Bags with thousands of letters have been delivered to Santa Claus at the courthouse.

Earlier that morning, a post office clerk sorting mail (presumably at the branch on 34th Street and Eighth Avenue, just a block from Macy's) selected a letter addressed to Santa Claus at the New York County Courthouse and showed his boss, who presents a newspaper article about the legal proceeding. It gives the postal worker an idea which thrills the supervisor: gather the letters addressed to Santa Claus now taking up space in the dead letter office and send them to the courthouse for the guy claiming to be the genuine article.

This inspires Fred to present facts about the genesis, authority and commerce regarding the post office in addition to three letters addressed to Santa Claus as tangible evidence. "Your honor, the figures I have just quoted indicate an efficiently run organization," declares Fred. "United States postal laws and regulations make it a criminal offense to willfully misdirect mail or intentionally deliver it to the wrong party. Consequently, the department uses every possible precaution."

When the district attorney scoffs at this trio of missives as substantive evidence, Fred says, "I have further exhibits but I hesitate to produce them." Mara responds, "We'll be very happy to see them." Judge Harper agrees and directs Fred to bring them to his desk at the front of the courtroom. The attorney motions for the court officers to bring in the bags. Piles of envelopes obscure the judge from the camera's view as Fred continues his argument: "Your honor, every one of these letters is addressed to Santa Claus. The post office has delivered them. Therefore, the Post Office Department, a branch of the federal government, recognizes this man, Kris Kringle, to be the one and only Santa Claus!"

Judge Harper pushes the mounds of evidence aside to make his ruling: "Since the United States government declares this man to be Santa Claus, this court will not dispute it. Case dismissed."

Fred's argument about misdirecting mail reflects in the U.S. Code: "Whoever knowingly and willfully obstructs or retards the passage of the mail, or any carrier or conveyance carrying the mail, shall be fined under this title or imprisoned not more than six months, or both."[2]

So, where does the post office get its authority to deliver mail? It's a fascinating trek through political and legal history. Fred accurately describes the beginning of its operations authorized by the Second Continental Congress, which convened in Philadelphia's Independence Hall on May 10, 1775, a few weeks after the Battles of Lexington and Concord ignited the Revolutionary War. Among the achievements at this gathering of delegates from the 13 colonies were the creation of a Continental army and election of George Washington as its commander.

On July 26, the Congress created the post office. Benjamin Franklin received the job of postmaster general; his familiarity with the postal paradigm dated back four decades. In 1737, when the American colonies were under British rule, America's deputy postmaster general, Alexander Spotswood, selected Franklin to be Philadelphia's postmaster. This job had perquisites for Franklin, a newspaper publisher banned from distributing his publication in the mail. Because of the nexus to his business, the 31-year-old future statesman took the job,

> and found it of great advantage; for, tho' the salary was small, it facilitated the correspondence that improv'd my newspaper, increas'd the number demanded, as well as the advertisements to be inserted, so that it came to afford me a considerable income.[3]

Under Postmaster General Elliott Benger, Franklin worked as comptroller, then ascended after Benger took ill and died in 1753. Franklin worked jointly with Virginia's William Hunter in the top position. By no means did Franklin treat his job as mere patronage or a platform for distribution of his newspaper; his contributions included surveying post offices and the distance between them as well as adding night rides for mail carriers. Franklin's biographer Walter Isaacson emphasizes:

> Franklin drew up typically detailed procedures for running the service more efficiently, established the first home-delivery system and dead letter office, and took frequent inspection tours. Within a year, he had cut to one day the delivery time of a letter from New York to Philadelphia. The reforms were costly, and he and Hunter incurred £900 in debt over their first four years. But then they started turning a profit, earning at least £300 a year apiece.[4]

Hunter died in 1761. Despite Franklin's credentials, impact and longevity (nearly a quarter century in the postal arena), he did not get to run the postal operation by himself. Instead, the mandate from the office of the governor paired his secretary, John Foxcroft, with Franklin. According to Isaacson, "There was much work to be done. With Canada now part of the British Empire, they set up a system for extending mail delivery to Montreal."[5]

Franklin's political stances favoring independence caused him to lose his job as postmaster general for the Crown in 1774, a year before getting the job for the colonies. The Second Continental Congress developed the Articles of Confederation, which formed the legal structure for the colonies in 1777 and included a provision for a post office:

> The united states [sic] in congress assembled shall also have the sole and exclusive right and power ... of establishing and regulating post-offices from one state to another, throughout all the united states, and exacting such postage on the papers passing thro' [sic] the same as may be requisite to defray the expences [sic] of the said office.[6]

In 1787, representatives from 12 of the original 13 states signed the Constitution. (Rhode Island did not have representatives at the Constitutional Convention in Philadelphia.) Ratification took place in 1788. Article I, Section 8 follows its predecessor in giving the federal government power concerning postal activities: "The Congress shall have Power to establish Post Offices and post roads."[7]

George Washington became the country's first president in 1789 with 75 post offices and approximately 2400 miles of post roads populating the land. Highlighting the post office in his third annual address to Congress in 1791, Washington emphasized,

> The importance of the post office and post roads on a plan sufficiently liberal and comprehensive, as they respect the expedition, safety, and facility of communication, is increased by their instrumentality in diffusing a knowledge of the laws and proceedings of the Government, which, while it contributes to the security of the people, serves also to guard them against the effects of misrepresentation and misconception. The establishment of additional cross posts, especially to some of the important points in the Western and Northern parts of the Union, cannot fail to be of material utility.[8]

By signing the Post Office Act of 1792, Washington cemented the role of the Congress in overseeing the nation's postal activities, which incorporated newspapers for the public benefit. The Smithsonian Institution's National Postal Museum states that the new law admitted newspapers into the mail at extremely low rates, "facilitating the spread of information essential to the creation of an informed citizenry. The Act also forbade the opening of letters as a tool of surveillance."[9]

According to Devin Leonard's wonderful book *Neither Snow Nor Rain: A History of the United States Postal Service,*

> Within a few years, the General Post Office was delivering mail in new states like Vermont, Kentucky, and Tennessee. Settlers on the western frontier

inundated Congress with petitions pleading for post offices so they, too, could receive mail. By the turn of the century, there were 903 post offices and 20,817 miles of post roads in the United States, a phenomenal increase in less than a decade.[10]

In *Miracle on 34th Street,* Fred's invocation of the post office's early history creates a terrific opportunity to dive into a compelling part of America's development. It also recognizes recent statistics and a key figure during the 1940s: Robert Hannegan, the postmaster general at the time.

A political icon in Democratic circles, the St. Louis native was a well-connected operative. He began his professional career as a lawyer who got involved in the city's Democratic political machine—including membership on the party's city committee—and later helped fellow Missourian Harry Truman get the vice-presidential nomination in 1944. "He swung support to the Missouri senator through adroit work with key delegates and with President Roosevelt," stated the Associated Press in its obituary for Hannegan.

Roosevelt died in 1945. Truman succeeded him in the presidency and won the 1948 election against New York Governor Thomas E. Dewey, whom Roosevelt had defeated in 1944. In 1949, a week before Hannegan died of heart failure at age 46, he and Truman attended a testimonial dinner honoring incoming Democratic Party chairman William Boyle; Truman credited Hannegan by saying that the veteran advisor "had something to do" with him being the nation's 33rd president.[11]

Hannegan resigned from the postmaster general job in 1947; Truman responded with a letter showing terrific respect for his political ally. "Now for more than two years you have justified my own faith through your admirable administration of the office of Postmaster General, whose duties are onerous as well as complex."[12]

In 1970, the country's postal operations got an overhaul when President Richard Nixon signed the Postal Reorganization Act, which ended the Post Office Department and created the U.S. Postal Service. Previously, the nation's postal operations had been run by an agency equal to a Cabinet department backed with federal tax revenue. The USPS had a different makeup: "part independent federal agency, part self-supporting business: a government-owned corporation." Further, the law addressed the underlying aim to unite Americans: "The Postal Service shall have as its basic function the obligation to provide postal services to bind the Nation together through the personal, educational, literary and business correspondence of the people."[13]

One USPS outlet has a name that stands out for fans of *Miracle on 34th Street* and other Christmas offerings: Santa Claus, Indiana. The post office for this small town in the Hoosier State has become a destination

29. United States Postal Service (Miracle on 34th Street) 175

because of its artistic Christmas-theme postmarks on envelopes, a tradition complementing an operation dating back to the early 20th century. Although the Santa Claus Post Office began operating in 1856, it took almost 60 years for it to achieve fame. The Santa Claus website explains,

> The town's name did not peak interest ... until 1914 when Santa Claus' 14th postmaster, James Martin, took it upon himself to answer the children's letters. Soon after, people flocked to the Santa Claus Post Office to get the special postmark; so much that in the early 1930s the US Postal Department suggested changing the name of the town to avoid the Christmas season frenzy. Fortunately, for everyone, that did not happen![14]

This venture continues because of volunteers with Santa's Elves Inc., a nonprofit organization, and the Santa Claus Museum. Operation Santa also embodies the Christmas spirit; postmaster general Frank Hitchcock began this project in 1912 when he gave the green light for post offices in communities to respond to children who write to Santa Claus. Since 2019, Operation Santa has been accessible online.

In 2024, Toys "R" Us partnered with the U.S. Postal Service. Volunteers could go on a website designed for the operation, buy gifts for the children, and send them through the USPS for Operation Santa. The future is bright. According to Sheila Holman, USPS marketing vice president, in a September 2024 press release,

> This year, we're excited to offer a curated selection of toys and playthings, and next year, we'll be expanding to include clothing, shoes, books and more. Our goal is to make it even easier for people to personalize their gift giving and help more families experience the magic of the holidays through USPS Operation Santa.[15]

In *Miracle on 34th Street,* Fred's climactic speech about the post office caps a tale reflecting a post–World War II sentiment of optimism after the horrors that killed thousands of Allied soldiers battling the Axis powers in Europe and the South Pacific. "What this country, and the rest of the world, needs right now is a few more stories like this one of [*Miracle on 34th Street* writer] Valentine Davies," wrote Ann Helming in the *Citizen-News,* a popular Los Angeles area newspaper. Edwin Schallert told *Los Angeles Times* readers, "If you don't believe in Santa Claus before you see it at Loew's State, Chinese, Uptown or Loyola, you certainly will credit his existence while you are watching the film unfold."[16]

There were similar reviews across the country. The *Memphis Press-Scimitar*'s Edwin Howard noted the movie's underlying message of hope: "[It] captures a considerable amount of the cynical commercialism that has come to surround Christmas in this country, backs it into a corner and kills it with warm faith and human kindness."[17] Fellow Memphis film critic

Harry Martin wrote, "I haven't the heart to reveal the outcome, but I feel fairly certain it will make you agree, too, there must be a Santa Claus."[18]

Miracle on 34th Street won three Oscars: Edmund Gwenn for Best Supporting Actor, George Seaton for Best Writing (Screenplay), and Valentine Davies for Best Writing (Original Story). Gwenn and Seaton also won Golden Globes.

There's a romantic storyline involving Fred and Doris. While Doris embodies cynicism because of divorce or abandonment (the source is never clarified), she comes to believe in the hope that Kris represents and Fred prizes. Doris' eight-year-old daughter Susan is wise beyond her years but lacking imagination, a result of Doris' parenting paradigm to avoid fantasies so she won't be heartbroken by reality. As Susan softens throughout the movie, so does Doris.

On Christmas morning, a party is held at Brookfield Memorial Home. Doris, Fred and Susan attend. Earlier in the film, Susan had asked Kris for a house like the one in a magazine drawing because she doesn't want to live in an apartment any longer, but there's no indication that he came through on his promise. Kris gives Fred directions for a more efficient route back to Manhattan, soon bringing them to a street with a house just like the one in the picture. Susan demands that they stop and then runs inside. There's a FOR SALE sign in front. Fred tells Doris that they shouldn't disappoint Susan, followed by a passionate embrace implying an imminent marriage and move from Manhattan into Susan's dream house.

"I must be a pretty good lawyer," says Fred. "I take a little old man and legally prove that he's Santa Claus. Now, you know that…" He interrupts his monologue when he sees a cane in the corner, just like the one that Kris brandished throughout the film. Coincidence? Maybe Kris really *was* Santa Claus!

Because the U.S. Post Office is "an efficiently run organization" as Fred stated, there won't be any reason for concern about directing the post office to change their addresses and forward their mail to the new home.

30

Blacklisting (*Seinfeld*)

Elaine Benes had quite the roster of gentlemen suitors on *Seinfeld*.

The Policemen's Benevolent Association Orchestra conductor who demanded to be called "Maestro," a fellow gym member who talked about himself in the third person, a furniture mover who contravened her political beliefs by being pro-life, a former baseball star who offended her by smoking cigarettes, a 66-year-old writer who suffered a stroke while they were walking on Manhattan's Upper West Side, and a blind date who took out his penis in the car at the end of the evening are among the men who tried to romance the charming brunette.[1]

In the episode "The Race," Elaine dates a Communist named Ned Isakoff. When her friend Kramer becomes a department store Santa Claus during the holiday season, Ned tells him about the horrible working conditions at the store and influences his outlook. A child says that he wants a racing car set; Kramer responds that that the toys are built by child labor in Taiwan and sold at a magnificent profit. It prompts the child to shout, "Commie! Commie! Traitor to our country!"[2]

Ned's Communism becomes the focus for another story point when Elaine's complaint about the wrong food delivery from Hop Sing's Chinese restaurant leads to her getting blacklisted. "Elaine, when my father was blacklisted, he couldn't work for years," says Ned. "He and his friends used to sit in Hop Sing's every day figuring out how to survive."

"Your father was blacklisted?"

"Yes, he was. And you know why? He was betrayed by people he trusted. They named names."

Elaine tries to place another order for her Upper West Side address: 16 West 75th Street, Apartment 2G. When the delivery guy answers the phone and recognizes the address but not her voice, she says that Elaine Benes doesn't live there anymore and places an order under her new boyfriend's name. Believing her ruse, he delivers the food. Ned opens the door but the delivery guy notices Elaine in the apartment. Enraged, he snatches the bag from Ned and blacklists him. "You tried to trick Hop

Sing! You're on our list—Elaine Benes! And now you're on our list—Ned Isakoff."

"You got me blacklisted at Hop Sing's?" Ned asks, shocked.

"She named name!" declares the delivery guy.

The phrase "naming names" and its derivations result from the Red Scare, a panic that gripped the nation during the 1940s and 1950s as post–World War II America confronted a perceived threat of Communism during the early years of the Cold War. Blacklisting resulted.

Republican Senator Joe McCarthy of Wisconsin spearheaded a mission to uncover Communists in the government and other influential arenas. The House Un-American Activities Committee looked for Communist influences in Hollywood. Formed in the late 1930s as a select committee, HUAC became a permanent standing committee on January 3, 1945. McCarthy was a Senator, so he did not sit on the House committee. Their missions were similar but separate.[3]

Hollywood writers and producers suspected of being Communists (or who refused to name names of suspected Communists) often got blacklisted. They included a group dubbed the Hollywood Ten: Dalton Trumbo, Adrian Scott, Samuel Ornitz, Albert Maltz, Alvah Bessie, Herbert Biberman, Lester Cole, Edward Dmytryk, John Howard Lawson and Ring Lardner Jr.

Attorney Joseph Welch (left) and Senator Joe McCarthy (right) during the Army-McCarthy Hearings in 1954 (U.S. Senate Historical Office).

30. Blacklisting (Seinfeld) 179

Millions of TV viewers watched the developing political drama underscored by McCarthy's constant bellowing about Communists. It began in Wheeling, West Virginia, on February 9, 1950, when McCarthy gave a speech to the Women's Republican Club for a Lincoln's Birthday event in which he declared that 205 members of the Communist Party worked in the State Department. He warned, "Today we are engaged in a final, all-out battle between Communistic atheism and Christianity. The modern champions of Communism have selected this as the time. And, ladies and gentlemen, the chips are down—they are truly down."[4]

But McCarthy's figures often fluctuated. Wisconsin newspaper editor and radio executive William Evjue explained McCarthy's changes in a radio editorial that Madison's *Capital Times* reprinted on February 20:

> Later, he sent a letter to Pres. Truman which said that 57 employees in the State Department are card-carrying members of the Communist Party. Later, in a speech at Reno, Nev., McCarthy repeated that there are 57 card-carrying Communists on the State Department payroll and he mentioned four persons in the department. Three of the four named are not even employed in the department and the fourth person named has been cleared by [an] FBI investigation.[5]

Edward R. Murrow, longtime CBS radio and TV journalist, hosted *See It Now*, a news program tackling the complex issues of the day. On March 9, 1954, Murrow focused his show on McCarthy, who appeared on the April 6 broadcast but didn't offer substantive information regarding his accusations of Communism. Moreover, his verbal attacks on Murrow were full of misstatements of facts. Murrow offered a lengthy response in his April 13 broadcast, highlighting his familiarity with the impact of Communism after nearly 20 years working for CBS:

> Having watched the aggressive forces at work in Western Europe, having had friends in Eastern Europe butchered and driven into exile, having broadcast from London in 1943 that the Russians were responsible for the Katyn massacre, having told the story of the Russian refusal to allow allied aircraft to land on Russian fields after dropping supplies to those who rose in Warsaw—and then were betrayed by the Russians—and having been denounced by the Russian radio for these reports, I cannot feel that I require instruction from the Senator on the evils of Communism.[6]

McCarthy had maneuvered himself to be the chair of the Committee on Government Operations' Permanent Subcommittee on Investigations and used broad powers to direct his investigation of Communism in the U.S. government and the media. The Army-McCarthy Hearings resulted from McCarthy's diatribes and factored in his downfall. Looking for anti–American influences within the Army created an atmosphere of tension and dread culminating on June 9, 1954; Joseph Welch, the Army's attorney and a partner at the prominent Boston law firm Hale and Dorr, confronted the pugnacious Senator, who had mentioned a young Hale and Dorr lawyer's past membership in a left-leaning lawyers organization.

Welch provided the verbal equivalent of a boxer's jabs, uppercuts and a right cross that put McCarthy on the political canvas for a knockout:

> Little did I dream you could be so reckless and so cruel as to do an injury to that lad. It is true he is still with Hale and Dorr. It is true that he will continue to be with Hale and Dorr. It is, I regret to say, equally true that I fear he shall always bear a scar needlessly inflicted by you. If it were in my *power* to forgive you for your reckless cruelty, I would do so. I like to think I'm a gentle man, but your forgiveness will have to come from someone other than me.

The knockout punch came after McCarthy persisted and Welch declared, "You've done enough. Have you no sense of decency, sir, at long last? Have you left no sense of decency?"[7]

WCBS-TV news anchor Don Hollenbeck is an indirect example of fallout from McCarthy's diatribes. Subsequent to the March 9 broadcast, CBS viewers who stayed tuned for the local news saw Hollenbeck begin his broadcast with an emphatic endorsement of Murrow's work. Readers of the *New York Journal-American* found resolute opposition in the words of entertainment columnist Jack O'Brian, after turning the pages of the March 10 edition populated by stories about the daughter of legendary comedian Jack Benny getting married; a potential hydrogen bomb test in the Marshall Islands; a revival of the opera *Norma*; Yankees shortstop Phil Rizzuto hoping to play in all 154 games of the upcoming baseball season; and the Harlem Globetrotters biographical film *Go, Man, Go!*[8]

O'Brian targeted Hollenbeck and accused him of being soft on Communism; his newspaper had potency given its status as a cornerstone of the Hearst organization. Calling attention to Hollenbeck's tenure with "the demised pinko publication *P.M.*" and Murrow's leadership of CBS news "filled for years with pink and liberal editorializing," O'Brian further opined about the network broadcast and the local news anchor's reaction:

> When his explosively one-sided propaganda, edited with deviously clever selectivity from McCarthy's march against Communism, was finished last evening, by equally Machiavellian coincidence the following telecast featured Murrow's *P.M.* protege Hollenbeck. In an obviously gloating mood, Hollenbeck hoped viewers had witnessed his patron's triumph from and for the left.
>
> He then proceeded through an equally tilted review of the day's events with McCarthy dominating his words, actions, attitude and camera.[9]

On June 22, Hollenbeck committed suicide by turning on the gas oven in his efficiency apartment on East 48th Street. O'Brian was a factor,

30. Blacklisting (Seinfeld)

but probably not the only one. In his 1986 biography *Murrow: His Life and Times*, A.M. Sperber wrote,

> In the background were a failed marriage, a recent hospital stay for bleeding ulcers, bouts of heavy drinking, and severe depression—all aggravated by attacks in Jack O'Brian's column in the Hearst *Journal-American*, starting in the morning after Hollenbeck's on-the-air salute to the McCarthy show and keeping up all through the weeks that followed.[10]

A resolution to censure McCarthy was introduced on July 30, 1954. A committee formed to study the charges and issued a 68-page report, which led to a vote of censure on December 2 by a 67–22 vote.[11]

The 2005 film *Good Night and Good Luck*—which takes its title from Murrow's signature goodbye line for his broadcasts—stars David Strathairn as Murrow and George Clooney as Murrow's producer, Fred Friendly. Clooney's production company brought the story to the silver screen, but they interspersed footage of McCarthy rather than cast an actor. Clooney explained,

> [T]he hard part is—and the reason we didn't have an actor playing McCarthy is because if you had an actor actually do an exact impersonation of Joe McCarthy, every critic in the country would say that we're making him too much of a buffoon and too arch. You wouldn't really believe that someone could reach that kind of power acting the way he did.[12]

HUAC's headlines had a bit of glamour because of the Hollywood targets. On October 23, 1947, HUAC members learned that Communism had, to a minor degree, infiltrated the filmmaking community. George Murphy, Robert Montgomery and Ronald Reagan each provided a similar analysis. "We have had in the Screen Actors Guild a very militant, a very small minority, well organized, well disciplined," said Reagan.[13]

Robert Taylor also testified on that date. The star of the World War II drama *Bataan* (1943) named names: Howard da Silva and Karen Morley. Taylor's testimony described da Silva as one who "seems to have something to say at the wrong times" and Morley's behavior at Screen Actors Guild meetings to be a "disrupting influence." Morley's career effectively ended but da Silva continued to work in film with roles including Benjamin Franklin in *1776*, Meyer Wolfsheim in *The Great Gatsby* and Louis B. Mayer in *Mommie Dearest*. He also had a robust list of TV guest-starring roles, among them *The Defenders*, *The Outer Limits*, *Ben Casey*, *The Man from U.N.C.L.E.*, *The Fugitive*, *Mannix* and *Archie Bunker's Place*.[14]

With the authority to subpoena witnesses, HUAC had more than 40 members of the Hollywood community testify in Washington; if they didn't show, a contempt of Congress order might be the next step. In 1947, Hollywood's elite formalized their barrier with the Waldorf Declaration, which essentially became the foundation for blacklisting. It said, in part: "We will not knowingly employ a Communist or member of any party or group which advocates the overthrow of the government of the United States by force or by any illegal or unconstitutional methods."[15]

Though not part of the Hollywood Ten, Zero Mostel emblemized the impact of the Red Scare penetrating the creative community. He invoked the Fifth Amendment before HUAC in 1955 when questioned about his knowledge of, endorsement of, or participation in groups associated, informally or otherwise, with the Communist Party. A suggestion from a committee member to split from organizations with Communist foundations prompted Mostel to reply, "My dear friend, I believe in the antiquated idea that a man is in his profession because of his ability and not because of his political beliefs."[16]

In 1958, Mostel rebounded from being blacklisted with an Obie Award for an off–Broadway performance in *Ulysses in Nighttown*. He won three Tony Awards in the 1960s.

Larry Parks also suffered from being blacklisted. During his testimony before the committee in 1951, Parks—who had starred as legendary entertainer Al Jolson in *The Jolson Story* (1946) and *Jolson Sings Again* (1949)—attempted to distinguish his past involvement with Communism from the present-day atmosphere amplifying concern regarding the brutal wielding of power underlying the ideology. Parks explained,

> As I say, I am not a Communist. I was a member of the Communist Party when I was a much younger man, ten years ago. …Being a member of the Communist Party fulfilled certain needs of a young man that was liberal in thought, idealistic, who was for the underprivileged, the underdog. I felt that it fulfilled these particular needs. I think that being a Communist in 1951 in this particular situation is an entirely different kettle of fish when this is a great power that is trying to take over the world. This is the difference.

Parks added that he wasn't particularly interested in it after he became a member. "I attended very few meetings, and I drifted away from it the same way that … I drifted into it…. To the best of my recollection, I petered out about the latter part of 1944 or 1945."[17]

Arguably, Parks testified under duress. In addition to talking about his own history, he named names. According to a wire service report, "Mr. Parks, who at first pleaded with the investigators not to force him to 'crawl through the mud to be an informer' on other entertainment figures, later went behind closed doors to give them the names of 'four or five' Hollywood Communists he had known."[18]

Under contract to Columbia Pictures, Parks saw his acting career evaporate. He had a pay-or-play deal—one film a year or get paid for not working. Columbia chose the latter. Parks made one film for MGM and two more in the United Kingdom before ending his film career. His obituary noted that he continued performing in nightclubs, television and summer stock.[19]

Despite his talent, integrity and good character, Parks suffered ignominy for a much longer period than others directly targeted or indirectly impacted by HUAC. After he died in 1975, Hollywood legend Lloyd Bridges—who guest starred on two episodes of *Seinfeld* later in his career—and his wife Dorothy lauded their friend in a letter to the editor of the *Los Angeles Times*: "[F]or 24 years Larry wasn't allowed to forget 'The Investigation.' For 24 years he was made to pay—not for any wrong that he had committed, but for the ugly notoriety that was thrust upon him. He was strong. He was a proud man, uncomplaining and tight-lipped."[20]

In 1969, HUAC underwent a rebranding. Its new moniker: Committee on Internal Security. Operations ceased in 1975.

Victor Navasky's 1980 book *Naming Names*, a comprehensive study on this piece of American history, noted the impact of the committee and criticized its tactics. "These were not information-gathering investigations so much as they were degradation ceremonies," wrote Navasky. "Ironically it was the informer who was degraded, because the informer represented a threat not merely to the person he named but to the community. He was regarded as a polluter—and became a perpetual outsider."[21]

Ned doesn't mention his father's vocation in "The Race" but it's easy to imagine being outed and blacklisted if he worked in the media and entertainment industry, which undoubtedly would lead to the name of the elder Isakoff appearing in *Red Channels: The Report of Communist Influence in Radio and Television*. This 1950 publication made the rounds in Hollywood and New York, spotlighting people considered to be dangerous in the media and entertainment industries:

> [T]he Communist party has made intensive efforts to infiltrate every phase of our life, and because of its great propaganda value has concentrated on radio and television. Networks, individual stations, advertising agencies, "package producers," radio-TV unions and even the trade press have been more and more "colonized" by the Party. The "colonists" need not be party members or even deliberate cooperators. It is sufficient if they advance Communist objectives with complete unconsciousness.[22]

Chapter Notes

Chapter 1

1. *Scrooge*, Paramount Pictures, 1935; *A Christmas Carol*, MGM, 1938; *Scrooge*, Renown Pictures (United Kingdom), known as *A Christmas Carol* in the U.S., 1951; *Scrooge*, Cinema Center Films, 1970.
2. Charles Dickens, *A Christmas Carol* (London: Chapman & Hall, 1843; New York: Garden City Publishing Company, 1938), 4. Citations refer to the Garden City Publishing Company edition.
3. Dickens, 27.
4. Dickens, 110.
5. Dickens, 111.
6. "Usury," Legal Information Institute, Cornell Law School, https://www.law.cornell.edu/wex/usury (last accessed December 4, 2024).
7. Lionel Barrymore, introduction to *A Christmas Carol*, by Charles Dickens, xiii–xiv.
8. Barrymore, xix.
9. Exodus 22:25.
10. *Marquette National Bank vs. First of Omaha Service Corporation*, 439 U.S. 299 (1978).
11. *Marquette National Bank vs. First of Omaha Service Corporation*.
12. *Marquette National Bank vs. First of Omaha Service Corporation*.
13. *Marquette National Bank vs. First of Omaha Service Corporation*.
14. Dickens, 28.
15. Dickens, 28.
16. Dickens, 3.
17. Dickens, 13.
18. Dickens, 6.
19. Dickens, 7.
20. Dickens, 101.

Chapter 2

1. *Die Hard*, Twentieth Century Fox, 1988, based on the novel *Nothing Lasts Forever* by Roderick Thorp (New York: W.W. Norton & Company, 1979).
2. *Marques vs. Federal Reserve Bank of Chicago*, United States Court of Appeals for the Seventh Circuit, 286 F.3d 1014 (2002).
3. *Marques vs. Federal Reserve Bank of Chicago*.
4. *Marques vs. Federal Reserve Bank of Chicago*.
5. Harry F. Themal, "Willis moonlights his way to stardom," *Evening Journal* (Wilmington, DE), July 14, 1988: D1.
6. Ronald Reagan, "Remarks at the Ford's Theatre Gala," June 24, 1988, Ronald Reagan Presidential Library & Museum, https://www.reaganlibrary.gov/archives/speech/remarks-fords-theatre-gala (last accessed December 4, 2024).

Chapter 3

1. *Emmet Otter's Jug-Band Christmas*, CBC, 1977; HBO, 1978; Russell Hoban and Lillian Hoban, *Emmet Otter's Jug Band Christmas* (New York: Parents' Magazine Press, 1971); O. Henry, *The Gift of the Magi*, originally published as "Gifts of the Magi," *The New York Sunday World*, December 10, 1904.
2. 2024 Minnesota State Fair, Amateur Talent Contest Entry Rules, https://talent.mnstatefair.org/rules (last accessed September 5, 2024).
3. Dyer County Fair (Tennessee) 2024 Contest Rules, https://www.dyercofair.com/wp-content/uploads/2024/

06/2024-CONTEST-RULES-1.pdf (last accessed September 5, 2024).
  4. 2024 Rice County Fair, Rice County Fair Talent Show, https://ricecountyfair.net/talent-show (last accessed September 6, 2024).
  5. Arkansas State Fair (2021), Youth Talent Contest, Qualifications and Rules, https://www.arkansasstatefair.com/youth-talent-contest/ (last accessed September 6, 2024).
  6. Northeast Arkansas District Fair, Youth Talent Contest, https://neadistrictfair.com/youth-talent-contest-2/ (last accessed September 6, 2024).
  7. Southeast Alaska State Fair, Southeast's Got Talent Contest!, https://seakfair.org/talentshow/ (last accessed September 6, 2024).
  8. 2024 Iroquois County Agricultural and 4-H Club Fair, Iroquois County Fair Talent Contest Rules, https://www.iroquoiscofair.com/talent-contest-rules (last accessed September 6, 2024).
  9. North Texas Performing Arts, North Texas' Got Talent, Contest Rules, https://ntpa.org/got-talent/ (last accessed September 6, 2024).
  10. Patrick Sauer, "This Cult Classic Christmas Special Is Quintessential Jim Henson," *Smithsonian*, December 20, 2017, https://www.smithsonianmag.com/arts-culture/cult-classic-christmas-special-quintessential-jim-henson-180967602/ (last accessed December 4, 2024).
  11. Noel Murray, "Emmet Otter's Jug-Band Christmas," AV Club, December 22, 2011, https://www.avclub.com/emmet-otter-s-jug-band-christmas-1798229042 (last accessed December 4, 2024).
  12. Tara Bennett, "Emmet Otter's Jug-Band Christmas Oral History: Behind the Scenes of Jim Henson's Holiday Classic," Syfy, December 13, 2023 (updated), https://www.syfy.com/syfy-wire/jim-hensons-emmet-otter-jug-band-christmas-oral-history (last accessed December 4, 2024).

Chapter 4

  1. *The Beverly Hillbillies*, "The Clampetts Strike Oil," CBS, September 26, 1962; Vernon Scott, "Ebsen Says Hillbillies O.K. Show," United Press International, *Chicago Tribune*, December 8, 1963: N15.
  2. *The Beverly Hillbillies*, "The Clampetts Are Overdrawn," CBS, November 13, 1963; *The Beverly Hillbillies*, "The Clampett Curse," CBS, January 18, 1967.
  3. "'The Beverly Hillbillies': Do You Know Just How Rich the Clampetts Were Supposed to Be?," Internet Movie Database, https://www.imdb.com/news/ni64162826/# (last accessed September 6, 2024).
  4. *The Beverly Hillbillies*, "Home for Christmas," CBS, December 19, 1962.
  5. Jenn Underwood, "What Is Private Banking and How Does It Work?," *Forbes*, July 11, 2024, https://www.forbes.com/advisor/banking/private-banking/ (last accessed September 6, 2024).
  6. Underwood, "What Is Private Banking and How Does It Work?"
  7. Federal Deposit Insurance Corporation, "Due Diligence Programs for Private Banking Accounts," https://www.fdic.gov/sites/default/files/2024-03/fil23040a.pdf (last accessed September 6, 2024).
  8. Code of Federal Regulations, Title 31, Money and Finance: Treasury, Section 1010.620, Due diligence programs for private banking accounts, Legal Information Institute, Cornell Law School, https://www.law.cornell.edu/cfr/text/31/1010.620 (last accessed September 6, 2024).
  9. U.S. Code, Title 12, Banks and Banking, Section 1829b(d)(1) and (2), Retention of records by insured depository institutions; Reproduction of checks, drafts, and other instruments; record of transactions; identity of party, https://www.govinfo.gov/content/pkg/USCODE-2020-title12/pdf/USCODE-2020-title12-chap16-sec1829b.pdf (last accessed September 6, 2024).
  10. Wells Fargo, The Private Bank, https://www.wellsfargo.com/the-private-bank/solutions/private-banking/ (last accessed September 7, 2024).
  11. Karmen Alexander, "Merrill Signs JPMorgan Private Banker Managing Nearly $9 Billion in Los Angeles," AdvisorHub, https://www.advisorhub.com/merrill-signs-jpmorgan-private-banker-managing-over-4-billion-in-los-angeles/ (last accessed September 7, 2024).
  12. Alexander.
  13. *Return of the Beverly Hillbillies*, CBS, October 6, 1981.

14. *The Legend of the Beverly Hillbillies*, CBS, May 24, 1993.
15. Susan King, "Legendary 'Hillbillies,'" *Los Angeles Times*, May 23, 1993: J15.
16. *The Beverly Hillbillies*, Twentieth Century Fox, 1993.

Chapter 5

1. *Cheers*, "The Spy Who Came In for a Cold One," NBC, December 16, 1982.
2. Legal Information Institute, Cornell Law School, "Offer," https://www.law.cornell.edu/wex/offer#:~:text=Offer%20is%20part%20of%20contract,something%20in%20exchange%20for%20consideration (last accessed September 8, 2024).
3. The 193rd General Court of the Commonwealth of Massachusetts, "Offer and Acceptance in Formation of Contract," Section 2–206(1)(a) https://malegislature.gov/Laws/GeneralLaws/PartI/TitleXV/Chapter106/Article2/Section2-206 (last accessed September 8, 2024).
4. *Cheers*, "Bad Neighbor Sam," NBC, November 15, 1990.
5. Massachusetts Association of Realtors, "Contract to Purchase Real Estate #501," Section 7(b), Inspections, https://www.marealtor.com/wp-content/uploads/2024/07/501-Contract-to-Purchase-RO.pdf (last accessed September 8, 2024).
6. The 193rd General Court of the Commonwealth of Massachusetts, "Agreement for purchase and sale of real estate; acknowledgment; recordation," Section 17A, https://malegislature.gov/Laws/GeneralLaws/PartII/TitleI/Chapter184/Section17A (last accessed September 8, 2024).
7. *Minnesota Linseed Oil Co. vs. Collier White Lead Co.*, Circuit Court, District of Minnesota (1876).
8. Gina M. Grother, "Interference with Contract in the Competitive Marketplace," *William Mitchell Law Review*, Mitchell Hamline School of Law, Volume 15, Issue 2 (1989).
9. Shawn J. Bayern, "Offer and Acceptance in Modern Contract Law: A Needless Concept," *California Law Review*, 2015, https://ir.law.fsu.edu/cgi/viewcontent.cgi?article=1039&context=articles (last accessed September 8, 2024).
10. *Cheers*, "Cry Harder," NBC, May 3, 1990.
11. Martin F. Nolan, "A Fitting City for 'Cheers,'" *Boston Globe*, May 19, 1993: 1.
12. *Cheers*, "No Contest," NBC, February 17, 1983; *Cheers*, "Bar Wars VI: This Time It's for Real," NBC, April 30, 1992; *Cheers*, "Sam Time Next Year," NBC, February 14, 1991; *Cheers*, "Daddy's Little Middle-Aged Girl," NBC, December 10, 1992; *Cheers*, "Bar Wars," NBC, March 31, 1988; *Cheers*, "Now Pitching, Sam Malone," NBC, January 6, 1983; *Cheers*, "Cheers Fouls Out," NBC, September 27, 1990; *Cheers*, "Where Have All the Floorboards Gone?," NBC, November 7, 1991; *Cheers*, "Woody for Hire, Meets Norman of the Apes," NBC, January 7, 1988.
13. *Cheers*, "Any Friend of Diane's," NBC, November 4, 1982; *Cheers*, "Bar Bet," NBC, February 14, 1985; *Cheers*, "Two Girls for Every Boyd," NBC, November 23, 1989; *Cheers*, "Sam at Eleven," NBC, October 21, 1982; *Cheers*, "Old Flames," NBC, November 17, 1983; *Cheers*, "'I' on Sports," NBC, October 1, 1987; *Cheers*, "Unplanned Parenthood," NBC, October 24, 1991; *Cheers*, "Loathe and Marriage," NBC, February 4, 1993; *Cheers*, "Sam at Eleven," NBC, October 21, 1982; *Cheers*, "The Boys in the Bar," NBC, January 27, 1983; *Cheers*, "Pick a Con…Any Con," NBC, February 24, 1983; *Cheers*, "How Do I Love Thee?...Let Me Call You Back," NBC, December 8, 1983. Harry Anderson also appeared during and after the run of *Night Court* (1984–1992): *Cheers*, "A Kiss Is Still a Kiss," NBC, December 3, 1987; *Cheers*, "Bar Wars VII: The Naked Prey," NBC, March 18, 1993.

Fred Dryer had a voiceover as a caller on a radio show: *Cheers*, "Love Thy Neighbor," NBC, November 21, 1985.

Chapter 6

1. *It's a Wonderful Life*, Liberty Films, 1946.
2. "Social Security History: The Depression," Social Security Administration, https://www.ssa.gov/history/bank.html (last accessed October 28, 2024).
3. "False Rumor Leads to Trouble at Bank," *New York Times*, December 11, 1930: 5.

4. "Bank of U.S. Closes Doors; State Takes Over Affairs; Aid Offered to Depositors," *New York Times*, December 12, 1930: 1.

5. "Bank Opened in 1913 Grew By Mergers," *New York Times*, December 12, 1930: 2.

6. Gary Richardson, "Banking Panics of 1930–31: November 1930-August 1931," Federal Reserve History, https://www.federalreservehistory.org/essays/banking-panics-1930-31 (last accessed October 29, 2024).

7. R. Daniel Wadhwani, "Soothing the People's Panic: The Banking Crisis of the 1930s in Philadelphia," *Closed for Business: The Story of Bankers Trust Company During the Great Depression*, Historical Society of Pennsylvania, http://digitalhistory.hsp.org/bnktr/essay/soothing-peoples-panic-banking-crisis-1930s-philadelphia (last accessed October 30, 2024).

8. William L. Silber, "Why Did FDR's Bank Holiday Succeed?," Federal Reserve Bank of New York, https://www.newyorkfed.org/medialibrary/media/research/epr/09v15n1/0907silb.pdf (last accessed December 4, 2024).

9. President Franklin D. Roosevelt, Radio Address, "Fireside Chat on Banking," March 12, 1933, The American Presidency Project, University of California, Santa Barbara, https://www.presidency.ucsb.edu/documents/fireside-chat-banking (last accessed October 30, 2024).

10. *A Brief History of Deposit Insurance in the United States*, Chapter 3, "Establishment of the FDIC: Deposit Insurance Provisions of the Banking Act of 1933," https://www.fdic.gov/resources/publications/brief-history-of-deposit-insurance/book/brief-history-deposit-insurance-3.pdf (last accessed December 4, 2024).

11. Banking Act of 1933; History, 1930–1939, August 23, 1935, FDIC, https://www.fdic.gov/history/1930-1939 (last accessed October 29, 2024); Unite States Code Code, Title 12, Chapter 16, Section 1813(b)(3)(A), Definitions of Bank and Related Terms, Definition of Savings Associations and Related Terms, State Savings Association, Legal Information Institute, Cornell Law School, https://www.law.cornell.edu/uscode/text/12/1813 (last accessed October 29, 2024).

12. Larceny; defined, New York Penal Law § 155.05(2)(b), https://www.nysenate.gov/legislation/laws/PEN/155.05#:~:text=1.,from%20an%20owner%20thereof (last accessed October 30, 2024).

13. Matthew Goldberg, "The History of FDIC Insurance Limits," Bankrate, March 24, 2023, https://www.bankrate.com/banking/fdic-limits-history/ (last accessed October 29, 2024).

Chapter 7

1. David Bianculli, "White House Like It Oughtta Be," *Daily News* (New York), September 22, 1999: 76.

2. Rob Owen, 'The West Wing' Holds Promise as TV Drama," *Pittsburgh Post-Gazette*, September 22, 1999: E3; Richard Reeves, "TV show 'West Wing' a Case of Art Imitating Life," *Asheville* [NC] *Citizen-Times*, September 28, 1999: 7.

3. David Hinckley, "A Veterans Day Salute to Classic 'West Wing,'" *Daily News* (New York), November 10, 2011: 84.

4. *The Diane Rehm Show*, "Former West Wing Actor Richard Schiff," February 4, 2013, https://dianerehm.org/shows/2013-02-04/former-west-wing-actor-richard-schiff (last accessed September 10, 2024).

5. *The West Wing Weekly*, a podcast hosted by Joshua Malina and Hrishkesh Hirway, episode 1:10, "In Excelsis Deo" (with Richard Schiff), May 25, 2016, transcript, https://static1.squarespace.com/static/56e27eb82fe131d8eec3a4e3/t/59f0c64ff9a61eaaa713fd8a/1508951632588/1.10+-+In+Excelsis+Deo.pdf (accessed February 4, 2020).

6. United States Code, Title 10, Section 1491: Funeral honors functions at funerals for veterans; Public Law 106–65, Section 578, October 5, 1999, https://uscode.house.gov/view.xhtml?req=granuleid:USC-prelim-title10-section1491&num=0&edition=prelim; https://www.congress.gov/106/plaws/publ65/PLAW-106publ65.pdf (last accessed December 4, 2024).

7. 1st Marine Division, 2nd Battalion, 7th Marines, "Overview—Infantry: 1st, 5th and 7th Marine Regiments," https://www.1stmardiv.marines.mil/About/Overview/ (last accessed September 10, 2024).

Chapter Notes 189

8. James S. Santelli, *A Brief History of the 7th Marines* (Washington, D.C.: History and Museums Division Headquarters, United States Marine Corps, 1980), 36, https://www.usmcu.edu/Portals/218/A%20 Brief%20History%20of%20the%207th%20 Marines%20%20PCN%2019000308200.pdf (last accessed December 5, 2024).

9. "2nd Platoon—Firing Party," United States Navy, https://ndw.cnic.navy.mil/ About/Tenant-Commands/United-States-Navy-Ceremonial-Guard/Bravo-Company/2nd-Platoon-Firing-Party/ (last accessed September 10, 2024).

10. "What to Expect During Military Funeral Honors," Military One Source, January 5, 2023, https://www.military onesource.mil/transition-retirement/ veterans/what-to-expect-during-military-funeral-honors/ (last accessed September 10, 2024).

11. "What to Expect During Military Funeral Honors."

12. "What to Expect During Military Funeral Honors."

13. Sgt. Clevon Wright, 367th Mobile Public Affairs Detachment, "Significance of the Military Funeral Honors Team," September 21, 2022, U.S. Army Reserve, https://www.usar.army.mil/News/News-Display/Article/3166790/significance-of-the-military-funeral-honors-team/ (last accessed September 10, 2024).

14. *The West Wing*, "Somebody's Going to Emergency, Somebody's Going to Jail," NBC, February 28, 2001.

Chapter 8

1. *Stalag 17*, Paramount Pictures, 1953.

2. Eric Ethier, "Stalag 17-B," *America in WWII*, February 2006, http://www. americainwwii.com/articles/stalag-17-b/ (last accessed October 25, 2024).

3. Cameron Crowe, "Conversations with Billy," *Vanity Fair*, October 1999, https://www.vanityfair.com/news/1999/10/ billy-wilder-199910?srsltid=Afm BOooPs1EOKXzsybN7ucY_G-__ BQR8M8xljqDOYImfVmLP7Hh2bpdW (last accessed December 5, 2024).

4. Bosley Crowther, "'Stalag 17' Emerges as Taut Film with William Holden—Has Bow at Astor," *New York Times*, July 2, 1953: 19.

5. "History of the ICRC, The Founding," International Committee of the Red Cross, October 29, 2016, https://www. icrc.org/en/document/history-icrc (last accessed October 26, 2024); International Committee for the Red Cross, "Convention for the Amelioration of the Condition of the Wounded and Sick in Armies in the Field, Geneva, 6 July 1906," https:// ihl-databases.icrc.org/pt/ihl-treaties/gc-1906?activeTab=historical (last accessed December 5, 2024).

6. 1929 Geneva Convention Relative to the Treatment of Prisoners of War, Title III, Captivity, Section II, Prisoners of War Camps, Chapter 2, Food and Clothing of Prisoners of War, Article 11, July 27, 1929, https://ihl-databases.icrc.org/assets/ treaties/305-IHL-GC-1929-2-EN.pdf (last accessed December 5, 2024).

7. 1929 Geneva Convention Relative to the Treatment of Prisoners of War, Title III, Captivity, Section II, Prisoners of War Camps, Chapter 2, Food and Clothing of Prisoners of War, Article 12, July 27, 1929, https://ihl-databases.icrc.org/assets/ treaties/305-IHL-GC-1929-2-EN.pdf (last accessed December 5, 2024).

8. Capture, Title II, Article 5, 1929 Geneva Convention Relative to the Treatment of Prisoners of War, July 27, 1929, page 179, United States Naval War College, https://digital-commons.usnwc.edu/cgi/ viewcontent.cgi?article=1923&context=ils (last accessed October 25, 2024).

9. Executive Order 9547, Harry S. Truman Presidential Library and Museum, National Archives, https://www.truman library.gov/library/executive-orders/ 9547/executive-order-9547 (last accessed December 15, 2024); The National World War II Museum, The Nuremberg Trials, https://www.nationalww2museum. org/war/topics/nuremberg-trials#:~: text=Subsequent%20Nuremberg%20 Trials&text=The%20trials%20uncovered %20the%20German,and%2098%20 other%20prison%20sentences (last accessed December 15, 2024).

10. 1929 Geneva Convention Relative to the Treatment of Prisoners of War, Section IV, External Relations of Prisoners of War, Article 38.

11. 1929 Geneva Convention Relative to the Treatment of Prisoners of War, Title VI, Bureaus of Relief and

Information Concerning Prisoners of War, Article 77.

12. 1929 Geneva Convention Relative to the Treatment of Prisoners of War, Title I, General Provisions, Article 2, July 27, 1929.

13. Fred L. Borch III, "The 'Malmedy Massacre' Trial: The Military Government Court Proceedings and the Controversial Legal Aftermath," *The Army Lawyer*, March 2012, 22–23; https://maint.loc.gov/law/mlr/pdf/03-2012.pdf (last accessed December 5, 2024); "Justice After the 1944 Malmedy Massacre," The National World War II Museum, https://www.nationalww2museum.org/war/articles/justice-after-1944-malmedy-massacre (last accessed October 26, 2024).

14. "The Perils of Liberation: In the Crossfire Outside Stalag III-C," The National World War II Museum, August 23, 2023, https://www.nationalww2museum.org/war/articles/perils-liberation-crossfire-outside-stalag-iii-c (last accessed October 26, 2024).

15. *Rules of Land Warfare*, Chapter 1, Basic Rules and Principles, Clause 1, General, War Department Field Manual, FM27–10, War Department, October 1, 1940, 1, https://www.ibiblio.org/hyperwar/USA/ref/FM/PDFs/FM27-10.pdf (last accessed December 5, 2024).

16. "Marching to Victory: WWII At 75, Prisoners of War, September 4, 1945," Truman Library Institute, September 4, 2020, https://www.trumanlibraryinstitute.org/wwii-75-marching-victory-23/ (last accessed October 26, 2024).

17. United States Constitution, Article 1, Section 8.

18. President Franklin D. Roosevelt, Message to U.S. Congress, December 11, 1941; "Text of War Message," *Los Angeles Times*, December 12, 1941: 4.

19. "Pre-U.S. Entry Into WWII," Naval History and Heritage Command, National Museum of the U.S. Navy, https://www.history.navy.mil/content/history/museums/nmusn/explore/photography/wwii/wwii-atlantic/battle-of-the-atlantic/pre-us-entry-into-wwii.html (last accessed October 26, 2024).

20. *Bevan vs. Columbia Broadcasting System*, U.S. District Court, Southern District of New York, July 30, 1971.

21. "Survivor recalls WWII Stalag 17," United Press International, February 6, 1989, https://www.upi.com/Archives/1989/02/06/Survivor-recalls-WWII-Stalag-17/3375602744400/ (last accessed October 25, 2024).

Chapter 9

1. *M*A*S*H*, "Quo Vadis, Captain Chandler," CBS, November 7, 1975; *M*A*S*H*, "That's Show Biz," CBS, October 26, 1981; *M*A*S*H*, "Heroes," CBS, March 15, 1982; *M*A*S*H*, "Morale Victory," CBS, January 28, 1980.

2. *M*A*S*H*, "Fallen Idol," CBS, September 27, 1977.

3. *M*A*S*H*, "Sometimes You Hear the Bullet," CBS, January 28, 1973.

4. *M*A*S*H*, "Death Takes a Holiday," CBS, December 15, 1980.

5. "The Unit Chaplain: Roles and Responsibilities," Military One Source, November 9, 2023, https://www.militaryonesource.mil/relationships/married-domestic-partner/the-unit-chaplain-roles-and-responsibilities/ (last accessed October 27, 2024).

6. Uniform Code of Military Justice, Article 107, False Statements, https://ucmj.us/907-article-107-false-statements/ (last accessed October 27, 2024).

7. *United States vs. Spicer*, United States Court of Appeals for the Armed Forces (February 6, 2013), https://law.justia.com/cases/federal/appellate-courts/caaf/12-0414-AR/12-0414-AR-2013-02-06.html (last accessed December 5, 2024).

8. *M*A*S*H*, "Mr. and Mrs. Who?," CBS, November 12, 1979.

9. "Life Insurance—Additional VA Life Insurance: Veterans' Special Life Insurance (Korean War Program)," U.S. Department of Veterans Affairs, https://www.benefits.va.gov/INSURANCE/vsli.asp (last accessed October 27, 2024).

10. D. Rose, "Aid and Attendance Benefits for Widows of Korean Conflict Vets," American Veterans Aid, January 3, 2019, https://americanveteransaid.com/newblog/aid-and-attendance-benefits-for-widows-of-korean-conflict-vets/ (last accessed October 27, 2024).

11. "VA Employee Charged with Falsifying Medical Records of Numerous Veterans," Press Release, United States Attorney's Office, Southern District of

Georgia, July 17, 2015, https://www.justice.gov/usao-sdga/pr/va-employee-charged-falsifying-medical-records-numerous-veterans (last accessed October 27, 2024).

12. United States Code, Title 18, Section 1035(a)(1) and (2), False statements relating to health care matters, Legal Information Institute, Cornell Law School, https://www.law.cornell.edu/uscode/text/18/1035 (last accessed December 5, 2024).

13. *United States vs. Henderson*, United States Court of Appeals, 11th Circuit (February 21, 2018), quoting *United States vs. Moran*, United States Court of Appeals, 11th Circuit (February 17, 2015).

14. "Rhode Island Woman Sentenced to Federal Prison for Falsifying Military Service; False Use of Military Medals; Identity Theft; and Fraudulently Collecting More Than $250,000 in Veteran Benefits and Charitable Contributions," Press Release, United States Attorney's Office, District of Rhode Island, March 14, 2023, https://www.justice.gov/usao-ri/pr/rhode-island-woman-sentenced-federal-prison-falsifying-military-service-false-use (last accessed October 27, 2024).

15. President Harry S. Truman, Statement by the President on the Situation in Korea, June 27, 1950, The American Presidency Project, University of California, Santa Barbara, https://www.presidency.ucsb.edu/documents/statement-the-president-the-situation-korea (last accessed October 27, 2024).

16. United States Constitution, Article II, Section 2.

17. Senator Karl Mundt, Speech, May 9, 1951, Congressional Record, Volume 97, pp. 5078–5088, reprinted by Teaching American History, https://teachingamericanhistory.org/document/speech-on-the-constitutionality-of-korean-war/ (last accessed October 27, 2024).

18. Armistice Agreement for the Restoration of the South Korean State (1953), National Archives, https://www.archives.gov/milestone-documents/armistice-agreement-restoration-south-korean-state (last accessed October 27, 2024).

19. President Dwight D. Eisenhower, Radio and Television Address to the American People Announcing the Signing of the Korean Armistice, July 26, 1953, The American Presidency Project, University of California, Santa Barbara, https://www.presidency.ucsb.edu/documents/radio-and-television-address-the-american-people-announcing-the-signing-the-korean (last accessed October 27, 2024).

20. Harold B. Hinton, "Doctor Draft Bill Goes to President," *New York Times*, September 2, 1950: 6.

21. Walter H. Waggoner, "President Orders Draft Registering of Doctors Oct. 16," *New York Times*, October 7, 1950: 1; "2,348 Medical Men Register in Draft," *New York Times*, October 17, 1950: 14.

22. Richard Hooker, *MASH* (New York: William Morrow and Company, 1968; New York: William Morrow and Company, 1996), 103. Citation refers to the 1996 edition.

23. *M*A*S*H*, "Death Takes a Holiday"; *M*A*S*H*, "Sometimes You Hear the Bullet."

Chapter 10

1. *All in the Family*, "The Draft Dodger," CBS, December 25, 1976.

2. United States Code, Sections 302–315 (1940), Selective Training and Service Act of 1940; "Resistance and Revolution: The Anti-Vietnam War Movement at the University of Michigan, 1965–1972—The Military Draft During the Vietnam War," University of Michigan, https://michiganintheworld.history.lsa.umich.edu/antivietnamwar/exhibits/show/exhibit/draft_protests/the-military-draft-during-the- (last accessed September 10, 2024).

3. Andrew Glass, "President Carter Pardons Draft Dodgers, Jan. 21 1977," Politico, https://www.politico.com/story/2018/01/21/president-carter-pardons-draft-dodgers-jan-21-1977-346493 (last accessed September 10, 2024).

4. President Richard Nixon, "Special Message to the Congress on Draft Reform," April 23, 1970, The American Presidency Project, University of California, Santa Barbara, https://www.presidency.ucsb.edu/documents/special-message-the-congress-draft-reform (last accessed September 10, 2024).

5. Robert B. Semple, Jr., "Draft Act Signed, Pay Rise Frozen," *New York Times*, September 29, 1971: 15.

6. "U.S. Cuts Shipment of Men to Vietnam," Associated Press, *New York Times*, January 25, 1973: 23; David E. Rosenbaum, "Nation Ends Draft, Turns to Volunteers," *New York Times*, January 28, 1973: 1.

7. Rosenbaum.

8. "Proclamation 4313—Announcing a Program for the Return of Vietnam Era Draft Evaders and Military Deserters," September 16, 1974, President Gerald R. Ford, The American Presidency Project, University of California, Santa Barbara, https://www.presidency.ucsb.edu/documents/proclamation-4313-announcing-program-for-the-return-vietnam-era-draft-evaders-and-military (last accessed November 28, 2024).

9. "The Fall of Saigon (1975): The Bravery of American Diplomats and Refugees," National Museum of American Diplomacy, April 29, 2021, https://diplomacy.state.gov/stories/fall-of-saigon-1975-american-diplomats-refugees/ (last accessed September 11, 2024).

10. "Tonkin Gulf Resolution (1964)," National Archives, Milestone Documents, https://www.archives.gov/milestone-documents/tonkin-gulf-resolution (last accessed September 11, 2024); Joint Resolution of Congress, H.J. RES 1145, August 7, 1964.

11. "Proclamation 4483: Granting Pardon for Violations of the Selective Service Act," Office of the Pardon Attorney, U.S. Department of Justice, January 21, 1977, https://www.justice.gov/pardon/proclamation-4483-granting-pardon-violations-selective-service-act (last accessed September 11, 2024).

12. Lee Lescaze, "President Pardons Viet Draft Evaders," *Washington Post*, January 22, 1977: A1.

13. Austin Scott, "Reaction to the Pardon Runs Gamut From Joy to Outrage," *Washington Post*, January 22, 1977: A5.

14. *Route 66*, "Fifty Miles from Home," CBS, March 22, 1963; *Route 66*, "What a Shining Young Man Was Our Gallant Lieutenant," CBS, April 26, 1963.

15. *The Munsters*, "Herman the Rookie," CBS, April 8, 1965.

16. Renny Temple, Telephone interview with author, October 19, 2018.

Chapter 11

1. The National D-Day Memorial Necrology Project, The National D-Day Memorial, https://www.dday.org/learn/necrology-project/ (last accessed December 6, 2024).

2. Air Force Historical Support Division, 1965—Operation Rolling Thunder, https://www.afhistory.af.mil/FAQs/Fact-Sheets/Article/458992/1965-operation-rolling-thunder/ (last accessed September 17, 2024).

3. "Resolution 1441," Reuters, *Washington Post*, November 9, 2002: A1; U.S. Military Casualties—Operation Iraqi Freedom (OIF) Casualty, As of December 3, 2024, Defense Casualty Analysis System, Defense Manpower Data System, Department of Defense, https://dcas.dmdc.osd.mil/dcas/app/conflictCasualties/oif/byCategory (last accessed December 6, 2024).

4. *Operation Christmas Drop*, Netflix, 2020.

5. Andersen Air Force Base, About Operation Christmas Drop, https://www.andersen.af.mil/ocd/ (last accessed September 17, 2024).

6. Andersen Air Force Base, About Operation Christmas Drop.

7. Richard Roeper, "Sugar Rush," Universal Press Syndicate, *Albuquerque Journal*, December 25, 1978: 28.

8. United States Code, Title 10, Section 402(a) and (b)(1)(A-E inclusive), Transportation of humanitarian relief supplies to foreign countries, https://www.govinfo.gov/content/pkg/USCODE-2023-title10/pdf/USCODE-2023-title10-subtitleA-partI-chap20-sec402.pdf (last accessed September 17, 2024).

9. United States Transportation Command, Denton Humanitarian Assistance Program, United https://www.ustranscom.mil/mov/denton.cfm (last accessed September 17, 2024).

10. Department of Defense, Defense Security Cooperation Agency, Humanitarian Mine Program, https://www.dsca.mil/humanitarian-mine-action-hma-program (last accessed September 17, 2024).

11. Department of Defense, Defense Security Cooperation Agency, Excess Property (EP) Program, https://www.dsca.

mil/excess-property-ep-program (last accessed September 17, 2024).

12. Department of Defense, Defense Security Cooperation Agency, Humanitarian Assistance Transportation Programs, https://www.dsca.mil/humanitarian-assistance-transportation-programs-hatp (last accessed September 17, 2024).

13. Department of Defense, Defense Security Cooperation Agency, Foreign Disaster Relief (FDR), https://www.dsca.mil/foreign-disaster-relief-fdr (last accessed September 17, 2024).

14. United States Code Title 10, Section 12304, Selected Reserve and certain Individual Ready Reserve members; order to active duty other than during war or national emergency, https://uscode.house.gov/view.xhtml?req=(title:10%20section:12304%20edition:prelim)#:~:text=§12304.,during%20war%20or%20national%20emergency (last accessed December 15, 2024).

15. Army Reserve, Defense Support of Civil Authorities, https://www.usar.army.mil/DSCA/ (last accessed September 17, 2024).

16. Jelena Pejic, "Humanitarian Assistance: Between the Law and Reality," Lieber Institute for Land & Law Warfare, West Point, Articles of War, https://lieber.westpoint.edu/humanitarian-assistance-between-law-reality/ (last accessed September 17, 2024).

17. Pacific Air Forces, Public Affairs, Press Release, "Operation Christmas Drop 2023: Pacific Air Forces preparing to deliver humanitarian assistance," November 14, 2023, https://www.pacaf.af.mil/News/Article-Display/Article/3588829/operation-christmas-drop-2023-pacific-air-forces-preparing-to-deliver-humanitar/ (last accessed September 17, 2024).

18. Tech Sgt. Taylor Altier, 374th Airlift Wing Public Affairs, U.S. Indo-Pacific Command, "Operation Christmas Drop 2023 ends with Allied elephant walk, formation flight over the Pacific," December 11, 2023, https://www.pacom.mil/Media/News/News-Article-View/Article/3614218/operation-christmas-drop-2023-ends-with-allied-elephant-walk-formation-flight-o/#:~:text=Zach%20"Badger"%20Overbey%2C%20U.S.,difference%20they're%20making" (last accessed September 17, 2023).

Chapter 12

1. *The Man Who Came to Dinner*, Warner Brothers, 1942.

2. *Scheibel vs. Lipton*, 156 Ohio St. 308, 102 N.E.2d 453 (Ohio 1951), https://casetext.com/case/scheibel-v-lipton (last accessed December 6, 2024).

3. Ohio Laws & Administrative Rules, Ohio Revised Code, Section 2307.011(C)(1), Civil action definitions, Economic loss, https://codes.ohio.gov/ohio-revised-code/section-2307.011 (last accessed September 25, 2024).

4. Ohio Laws & Administrative Rules, Ohio Revised Code, Section 2307.011(C)(2), Civil action definitions, Economic loss, https://codes.ohio.gov/ohio-revised-code/section-2307.011 (last accessed September 25, 2024).

5. Ohio Laws & Administrative Rules, Ohio Revised Code, Section 2315.33, Contributory fault effect on right to recover, https://codes.ohio.gov/ohio-revised-code/section-2315.33#:~:text=The%20contributory%20fault%20of%20a,all%20other%20persons%20from%20whom (last accessed September 25, 2024).

6. *Scheibel vs. Lipton*.

7. Brooks Atkinson, "Moss Hart and George S. Kaufman Discuss 'The Man Who Came to Dinner,'" *New York Times*, October 17, 1939: 31.

8. Herbert L. Monk, "'Who Came to Dinner' Film Tops Stage Play," *St. Louis Globe-Democrat*, January 30, 1941: 6C.

9. Kaspar Monahan, "That Man Whiteside Is Here for Dinner!," *Pittsburgh Press*, January 31, 1942: 10.

10. Ardis Smith, "The Man Who Came to Dinner Is Funnier Movie Than Play," *Buffalo Evening News*, February 3, 1942: 19.

Chapter 13

1. *The Apartment*, United Artists, 1960.

2. "The Apartment," *Variety*, May 18, 1960, https://variety.com/1960/film/reviews/the-apartment-1200419766/# (last accessed September 24, 2024).

3. Thomson Reuters, Glossary of legal terms, Sublease, https://legal.thomsonreuters.com/blog/legal-glossary/#S-terms (last accessed September 24, 2024). The glossary is described as "over 900 of the

most common legal terms and definitions derived from *A Dictionary of Basic Law Terms*, sources from *Practical Law*, and *Black's Law Dictionary*."

4. Subleases & Roommates, Legal Referral Service, New York City Bar Association, https://www.nycbar.org/get-legal-help/article/landlord-tenant/subleases-and-roommates/ (last accessed September 23, 2024).

5. Subletting FAQ, NYC Rent Guidelines Board, https://rentguidelinesboard.cityofnewyork.us/resources/faqs/subletting/ (last accessed September 23, 2024).

6. Landlord and Tenant, Right to Sublease or Assign, NY Real Property Law, § 226-B(2)(a) and (2)(c) (2023), https://law.justia.com/codes/new-york/rpp/article-7/226-b/ (last accessed September 24, 2024).

7. Carolyn Debra Karp, "NYRPL § 226-b: No Right to Sublease Without Consent," 9 Fordham Urb. L.J. 753 (1981).

Chapter 14

1. *Home Alone*, Twentieth Century Fox, 1990.

2. Illinois Compiled Statutes, Use of force in defense of dwelling, Section 7–2(a), https://www.ilga.gov/legislation/ilcs/fulltext.asp?DocName=072000050K7-2 (last accessed December 6, 2024).

3. Illinois Compiled Statutes, Use of force in defense of other property, Section 7–2(b), https://www.ilga.gov/legislation/ilcs/fulltext.asp?DocName=072000050K7-2 (last accessed December 6, 2024).

4. Illinois Compiled Statutes, Use of force by aggressor, Section 7–4, https://www.ilga.gov/legislation/ilcs/documents/072000050K7-4.htm (last accessed December 6, 2024).

5. Semayne's Case, reprinted in part, Online Library of Liberty, https://oll.libertyfund.org/quotes/sir-edward-coke-declares-that-your-house-is-your-castle-and-fortress-1604 (last accessed September 22, 2024). The ruling uses spelling that may be unfamiliar to modern American readers.

6. National Conference of State Legislatures, "Self-Defense and 'Stand Your Ground," https://www.ncsl.org/civil-and-criminal-justice/self-defense-and-stand-your-ground, updated March 1, 2023 (last accessed September 22, 2024).

7. Robert J. Spitzer, "Stand-Your-Ground, the Castle Doctrine, and Public Safety," Rockefeller Institute of Government, May 3, 2023, https://rockinst.org/blog/stand-your-ground-the-castle-doctrine-and-public-safety/ (last accessed September 22, 2024).

8. Self-Defense, Association of Prosecuting Attorneys, https://www.apainc.org/programs-2/gun-violence/837-2/ (last accessed September 22, 2024).

9. Self-Defense, Association of Prosecuting Attorneys.

10. Franchise: Home Alone, Box Office Mojo, https://www.boxofficemojo.com/franchise/fr2588380933/ (last accessed September 22, 2024).

11. Joe DeChick, "'Home Alone' Lacks Discipline, in Need of Baby Sitter," *Cincinnati Enquirer*, November 16, 1990: 27; Doug Brode, "'Home Alone' Falls Apart in the Middle," *Post-Standard* (Syracuse), November 16, 1990: D4.

12. Roger Ebert, "Child Star Only Redeeming Feature of 'Home Alone,'" *Rock Island* [Illinois] *Argus*, November 18, 1990: G6

13. Jeffrey Westhoff, "'Home Alone' tries too hard to do it all," *Northwest Herald* (McHenry and Northern Kane Counties, Illinois), November 23, 1990: 21.

14. Larry Rohter "Young Muscle: 'Home' Success Surprises All But Producer Hughes," *Florida Today*, December 17, 1990: 33.

Chapter 15

1. *The Andy Griffith Show*, "Man in a Hurry," CBS, January 14, 1963.

2. *The Andy Griffith Show*, "Christmas Story," CBS, December 19, 1960.

3. Alcohol and Tobacco Tax and Trade Bureau, United States Department of the Treasury, "Home Distilling," https://www.ttb.gov/distilled-spirits/penalties-for-illegal-distilling (last accessed September 11, 2024); United States Code, Title 26, Section 5601, Criminal Penalties, Legal Information Institute, Cornell Law School, https://www.law.cornell.edu/uscode/text/26/5601 (last accessed December 6, 2024).

4. United States Code, Title 26, Section 5602, Penalty for tax fraud by distiller, https://www.law.cornell.edu/uscode/text/26/5602#:~:text=Whenever%20any%20person%20engaged%20in,not%20more%20than%205%20years%2C (last accessed December 6, 2024).
5. Bureau of Alcohol, Tobacco, Firearms and Explosives, Mission Areas, Alcohol & Tobacco, https://www.atf.gov/alcohol-tobacco (last accessed September 11, 2024).
6. North Carolina General Assembly, Chapter 18B, Regulation of Alcoholic Beverages, 18B-306, Making wines and malt beverages for private use, https://www.ncleg.gov/EnactedLegislation/Statutes/PDF/BySection/Chapter_18B/GS_18B-306.pdf (last accessed December 6, 2024).
7. "Moonshine in North Carolina: The Illegal Whiskey That Shaped a State," North Carolina Department of Natural and Cultural Resources, https://www.dncr.nc.gov/explore/trip-ideas/moonshine-and-motorsports-trail/moonshine-north-carolina-illegal-whiskey-shaped-state (last accessed September 11, 2024).
8. Hayley Fowler, "Master Distiller Churned Out 9,000 Gallons of Illegal Moonshine on NC Farm, Feds Say," *Charlotte Observer*, September 15, 2021, https://www.charlotteobserver.com/news/state/north-carolina/article254212698.html (last accessed September 11, 2024).
9. Jule Hubbard, "5 Sentenced in Wilkes Moonshine Case," *Wilkes Journal-Patriot* (North Wilkesboro, NC), June 18, 2022, https://www.journalpatriot.com/news/5-sentenced-in-wilkes-moonshine-case/article_d5c9a8b1-9372-518d-b555-16e771d90397.html (last accessed September 11, 2024).
10. Hubbard, "5 Sentenced in Wilkes Moonshine Case."
11. "20 Found Guilty of Conspiracy," *Roanoke Times*, July 2, 1935: 1.
12. "Lee Expresses Gratification at Verdict of Jury," *Roanoke Times*, July 2, 1935: 1.
13. *Hobby Distillers Association vs. Alcohol and Tobacco Tax and Trade Bureau*, No. 4:2023cv01221-Document 49 (N.D. Tex. 024), https://law.justia.com/cases/federal/district-courts/texas/txndce/4:2023cv01221/384014/49/ (last accessed September 12, 2024).
14. *Hobby Distillers Association vs. Alcohol and Tobacco Tax and Trade Bureau*, Footnote 1.
15. *Hobby Distillers Association vs. Alcohol and Tobacco Tax and Trade Bureau*, quoting *Trop vs. Dulles* 356 U.S. 86 (1958).
16. *Hobby Distillers Association vs. Alcohol and Tobacco Tax and Trade Bureau*.
17. *Hobby Distillers Association vs. Alcohol and Tobacco Tax and Trade Bureau*.
18. Ed Grabianowski, "How Moonshine Works," Walton's Distillery, https://www.waltonsdistillery.com/how-moonshine-works/ (last accessed September 12, 2024).

Chapter 16

1. *Deck the Halls*, Twentieth Century Fox, 2006.
2. Rick Bentley, "'Deck the Halls' Stars Aren't Obsessed in Real Life," *Fresno Bee*, November 24, 2006: D3.
3. The 193rd General Court of the Commonwealth of Massachusetts, General Laws, Section 127A, Destruction of or tampering with, electric or gas lines, meters, etc.; theft of electricity or gas, https://malegislature.gov/Laws/GeneralLaws/PartI/TitleXXII/Chapter164/Section127A (last accessed October 9, 2024).
4. Camille Furst, "An $1,800 Electric Bill? Here's How Much Those Crazy Holiday Light Displays Really Cost N.J. Families," December 22, 2022, https://www.nj.com/news/2022/12/an-1800-electric-bill-heres-how-much-those-crazy-holiday-light-displays-really-cost-nj-families.html (last accessed October 9, 2024); *The Great Christmas Light Fight*, ABC, December 16, 2020.
5. Andy Morgan, "'Electric Detectives' Track Down Power Thieves," Oncor, March 6, 2020, https://www.oncor.com/content/oncorwww/wire/en/home/safety/electric-detectives-track-down-power-thieves.html (last accessed October 9, 2024).
6. Abby Frye, "Police Say Man Siphoned Electricity from Neighbor's Home," *Elizabethton Star*, February 1, 2018, https://www.elizabethton.com/2018/02/01/police-say-man-siphoned-electricity-from-neighbors-home/ (last accessed October 10, 2018).
7. Matt McCabe, "Man Arrested, Accused of Stealing Electricity from

Neighbors," News9 (Oklahoma City), August 11, 2023, https://www.news9.com/story/64d6dc1922e25175ba9bc3b2/man-arrested-accused-of-stealing-electricity-from-neighbors (last accessed October 10, 2024).

8. Elizabeth Pace, "Thieves Use New Tactics to Steal Electricity from Neighbors," Everything Lubbock, January 10, 2018, updated January 15, 2018, https://www.everythinglubbock.com/news/klbk-news/thieves-use-new-tactics-to-steal-electricity-from-neighbors/ (last accessed October 10, 2024).

9. "Pirating Electricity Is a Crime," LCEC, April 28, 2022, https://www.lcec.net/blog/pirating-electricity-is-a-crime/ (last accessed October 10, 2024).

10. Luke Jones, "3 Accused of Stealing Nearly $3K Worth of Power by Wiring Line from Pole to Home, Records Allege," ABC13 (Houston), June 19, 2024, https://abc13.com/post/harris-county-trio-accused-wiring-line-pole-home/14976679/ (last accessed October 10, 2024).

11. California Penal Code, Section 1202.4(f), https://casetext.com/statute/california-codes/california-penal-code/part-2-of-criminal-procedure/title-8-of-judgment-and-execution/chapter-1-the-judgment/section-12024-restitution (last accessed October 10, 2024); *People vs. Cam*, California Court of Appeal, Third District (2021), https://casetext.com/case/people-v-cam-2182#:~:text=Defendant%20Luc%20Cam%20pleaded%20no,the%20amount%20of%20%24219%2C%20035.32 (last accessed December 6, 2024).

12. *People vs. Cam*.

13. "Electricity Theft," CenterPoint Energy, https://www.centerpointenergy.com/en-us/business/safety/electric-safety/electricity-theft?sa=HO (last accessed October 11, 2024).

14. Jennifer Rothacker, "Duke Energy Team Hunts for Electric Thieves," Duke Energy, February 6, 2019, https://illumination.duke-energy.com/articles/duke-energy-team-hunts-for-electric-thieves (last accessed October 11, 2024).

15. Emily (no last name given in the byline), "Illinois Man Caught Stealing This from His Next Door Neighbors," 97 ZOK, March 23, 2023, https://97zokonline.com/illinois-man-steals-from-neighbors/ (last accessed October 10, 2024).

16. "Paying the Price of Power Theft," Safe Electricity, https://safeelectricity.org/public-education/tips/paying-the-price-of-power-theft/ (last accessed October 10, 2024).

Chapter 17

1. *How the Grinch Stole Christmas!* CBS, December 18, 1966.
2. Hal Humphrey, "Seuss Menagerie to Star on Sunday," *Los Angeles Times*, December 12, 1966: D26.
3. Isobel Ashe, "Dr. Seuss' Grinch in Video 'First,'" *Kenosha News* (TV Telescope Section), December 17, 1966: 14.
4. Ruth Thompson, "TV Version of Dr. Seuss' Story: A Pre-Christmas Treat," *Evening Sentinel*, "TV Magazine," (Carlisle, PA), December 17, 1966: 2.
5. "Children's Show Stars Voice of Boris Karloff," *Columbus* [Georgia] *Enquirer*, December 17, 1966: 19.
6. Donald Freeman, "Seuss' 'Grinch' A TV Triumph," *Daily Breeze* (South Bay—Los Angeles), December 22, 1966: 14.
7. Bill Greeley, "Television Reviews—Dr. Seuss' How the Grinch Stole Christmas," *Variety*, December 21, 1966: 36.
8. Burglary in the Third Degree, New York Penal Law, Section 140.20, https://www.nysenate.gov/legislation/laws/PEN/140.20 (last accessed October 2, 2024).
9. Larceny; defined, New York Penal Law, Section 155.05, https://www.nysenate.gov/legislation/laws/PEN/155.05#:~:text=1.,from%20an%20owner%20thereof. (last accessed October 2, 2024).
10. Grand larceny in the fourth degree, New York Penal Law, Section155.30, https://www.nysenate.gov/legislation/laws/PEN/155.30 (last accessed October 5, 2024).
11. Grand larceny in the third degree, New York Penal Law, Section155.35, https://www.nysenate.gov/legislation/laws/PEN/155.35 (last accessed October 5, 2024).
12. Grand larceny in the second degree, New York Penal Law, Section155.40, https://www.nysenate.gov/legislation/laws/PEN/155.40 (last accessed October 5, 2024).
13. Grand larceny in the first degree, New York Penal Law, Section 155.42,

Chapter Notes

https://www.nysenate.gov/legislation/laws/PEN/155.42 (last accessed October 5, 2024).

14. *People vs. Colasanti*, Court of Appeals of the State of New York (1974), https://casetext.com/case/people-v-colasanti-1 (last accessed December 7, 2024).

15. Trespass, New York Penal Law, Section 140.015, https://www.nysenate.gov/legislation/laws/PEN/140.05 (last accessed October 2, 2024).

16. National Stolen Property Act, United States Code, Title 18, Section 2314, Transportation of stolen goods, securities, moneys, fraudulent State tax stamps, or articles used in counterfeiting, Legal Information Institute, Cornell Law School, https://www.law.cornell.edu/uscode/text/18/2314 (last accessed December 7, 2024).

17. Anna-Leigh Firth, "Arraigning the Grinch," The National Judicial College, December 20, 2019, https://www.judges.org/news-and-info/arraigning-the-grinch/ (last accessed October 5, 2024).

18. "Indictment: Burglars Stole Christmas Gifts, Other Items," *Appalachian News-Express* (Pikeville, KY), December 23, 2015, https://www.news-expressky.com/news/indictment-burglars-stole-christmas-gifts-other-items/article_c03ee34c-a8f5-11e5-9a17-6b741bbd584d.html (last accessed October 5, 2024).

19. Clarissa Schmidt, "Cops Replace Children's Stolen Christmas Gifts," News10—Dallas, December 15, 2016, https://www.news10.com/news/cops-replace-childrens-stolen-christmas-gifts/ (last accessed October 5, 2024).

20. Laura Morrison, "Watch: Police Department Replaces Family's Stolen Christmas Presents," WJW (Cleveland), December 25, 2022; updated December 26, 2022, https://fox8.com/news/watch-police-department-replaces-familys-stolen-christmas-presents/ (last accessed October 5, 2022).

21. Josephine Mayer, "Hooded Grinch Steals O.C. Family's Christmas Presents from Under Tree," *Los Angeles*, December 19, 2023, https://lamag.com/crimeinla/hooded-grinch-steals-oc-familys-christmas-presents (last accessed October 5, 2024).

22. Lexie Horvath, "Your Christmas Decorations Might Be Attracting Burglars," WTVC (Chattanooga), November 27, 2023, updated November 28, 2023, https://newschannel9.com/news/local/your-christmas-decorations-might-be-attracting-burglars (last accessed October 5, 2024).

23. "2022 Sutdy: America's Holiday Burglary Hotspots," Porch Research, November 4, 2022, https://porch.com/advice/burglary-hotspots-study-2022 (last accessed October 5, 2024).

24. Terry Collins, "Outdoor Christmas Decorations and Burglary Could Be Linked. Here's What to Know," *USA Today*, December 20, 2023, updated December 21, 2023, https://www.usatoday.com/story/news/nation/2023/12/20/outdoor-christmas-lights-target-theives-home-safety/71840831007/ (last accessed October 6, 2024).

25. Collins.

Chapter 18

1. *The Sopranos*, "Full Leather Jacket," HBO, March 5, 2000.

2. *The Sopranos*, "Funhouse," HBO, April 9, 2000.

3. *The Sopranos*, "To Save Us All from Satan's Power," HBO, April 29, 2001.

4. *The Sopranos*, "Funhouse."

5. Organized Crime Control Act, Public Law 91–452, Title V, Protected Facilities For Housing Government Witnesses, Section 501, October 14, 1970, https://www.govtrack.us/congress/bills/91/s30/text (last accessed December 7, 2024).

6. President Richard Nixon, Remarks on Signing the Organized Crime Control Act of 1970, October 15, 1970, The American Presidency Project, University of California, Santa Barbara, https://www.presidency.ucsb.edu/documents/remarks-signing-the-organized-crime-control-act-1970 (last accessed October 19, 2024).

7. Organized Crime Control Act, Public Law 91–452, Title V, Protected Facilities For Housing Government Witnesses, Section 502, October 14, 1970, https://www.govtrack.us/congress/bills/91/s30/text (last accessed December 7, 2024).

8. Pete Earley and Gerald Shur, Prologue, *WITSEC: Inside the Federal Witness Protection Program* (New York: Bantam Books, 2002), 5.

9. Lesley Visser, "Defendants Are Guilty in Fix Case," *Boston Globe*, November 24, 1981: 57.

10. Leslie Maitland, "Airport Cash Loot Was $5 Million; Bandits' Van Is Found in Canarsie," *New York Times*, December 14, 1978: A1.

11. Ed McDonald, "Ed McDonald Interview with Daniel Simone," YouTube, February 12, 2014, https://www.youtube.com/watch?v=vlwrMmdQ86E (last accessed October 22, 2024).

12. McDonald.

13. Nicholas Pileggi, *Wiseguy: Life in a Mafia Family* (New York: Simon & Schuster, 1985; New York: Simon & Schuster Paperbacks, 2011), 250. Citations refer to the paperback edition.

14. Pileggi, 251.

15. Henry Hill with Douglas S. Looney, "How I Put the Fix In: The Cast of Characters in the BC Caper," *Sports Illustrated*, February 16, 1981: 14.

16. Tracy Connor, "Henry Hill Dies at 69," *Daily News* (New York), June 13, 2012: 17; Robert Jablon and Andrew Dalton, "Henry Hill, 69, Life Was Basis for 'Goodfellas,'" *Star-Ledger* (Newark), June 14, 2012: 28.

17. David Martin, "Island Man Named as Part of Gotti Probe," *Staten Island Advance*, December 5, 1990: A16.

18. Peter Maas, *Underboss: Sammy the Bull Gravano's Story of Life in the Mafia* (New York: HarperCollins, 1997), 294.

19. Jerry Capeci, Gotti Aide to Testify Against the Don," *Daily News* (New York), November 12, 1991: 3; David Martin, "Island Mobster Might Squeal," *Staten Island Advance*, November 12, 1991: A13.

20. David Martin, "New Life Awaits Gravano Under Witness Protection Plan," *Staten Island Advance*, December 8,1991: A27.

21. "Gravano Sticks It to Feds," Associated Press, *Journal News* (Westchester, Rockland, and Putnam Counties, NY), June 3, 2001: A3.

22. "Julie Cart, "Former Mob Hit Man Pleads Guilty to Role in Ecstasy Ring," *Los Angeles Times*, June 30, 2001: A11; Gravano sticks it to feds."

Chapter 19

1. *L.A. Confidential*, Warner Brothers, 1997.

2. California Penal Code, Part 1 (of Crimes and Punishments), Title 15 (Miscellaneous Crimes), Chapter 2 (of Other and Miscellaneous Offenses), 647(b), https://leginfo.legislature.ca.gov/faces/codes_displaySection.xhtml?sectionNum=647.&lawCode=PEN (last accessed October 16, 2024).

3. California Penal Code, Part 1 (of Crimes and Punishments), Title 9 (of Crimes Against the Person Involving Sexual Assault, and Crimes Against Public Decency and Good Morals, Chapter 1 (Rape, Abduction, Carnal Abuse of Children, and Seduction), 266(h)(a), https://leginfo.legislature.ca.gov/faces/codes_displaySection.xhtml?lawCode=PEN&sectionNum=266h (last accessed October 17, 2024).

4. Evelle J. Younger, Attorney General, State of California, First Report of the Organized Crime Control Commission, National Criminal Justice Reference Service, Department of Justice, Organized Crime Control Commission, May, 1978, 20, https://www.ncjrs.gov/pdffiles1/Digitization/79411NCJRS.pdf (last accessed October 16, 2024).

5. "Cohen Tax Charge Dismissal Refused," *Los Angeles Times*, June 2, 1951: A1.

6. "Cohen's Wife Freed from Tax Charges," *Los Angeles Times*, June 14, 1951: 2; "Cohen Takes Stand In His Own Defense," *Los Angeles Times*, June 19, 1951: 1.

7. Dick Walton, "Cohen Found Guilty in Tax Fraud Case," *Citizen-News* (Hollywood), June 20, 1951: 1.

8. "Mickey Cohen Gets 5 Years, $10,000 Fine," *Los Angeles Times*, July 10, 1951: 1.

9. *People vs. Batwin*, California Court of Appeal, Second District, Division Three (1953) https://casetext.com/case/people-v-batwin (last accessed December 7, 2024).

10. *People vs. Batwin*.

11. California Penal Code, Part 1 (Of Crimes and Punishments), Title 8 (Of Crimes Against the Person), Chapter 1 (Homicide), 187(a), https://leginfo.legislature.ca.gov/faces/codes_displaySection.xhtml?sectionNum=187.&lawCode=PEN (last accessed October 17, 2024).

12. California Penal Code, Part 1 (of Crimes and Punishments), Title 7 (of Crimes Against Public Justice), Chapter 6

(Falsifying Evidence, and Bribing, Influencing, Intimidating or Threatening Witnesses), https://leginfo.legislature.ca.gov/faces/codes_displaySection.xhtml?sectionNum=141.&lawCode=PEN (last accessed October 18, 2024).
13. Cecilia Rasmussen, "The 'Bloody Christmas' of 1951," *Los Angeles Times*, December 21, 1997: B3.
14. Rasmussen; "Officer Gets Two-Year Term in Beating Case," *Los Angeles Times*, October 1, 1952: 2.
15. "Officer in Beating Case Gets Prison," *Los Angeles Times*, December 4, 1952: 2.
16. Chris Eggertsen, "'L.A. Confidential': The ultimate filming locations map," Curbed LA, September 29, 2017, https://la.curbed.com/maps/la-confidential-movie-kim-basinger (last accessed October 18, 2024).
17. Kenneth Turan, "Noir for the '90s," *Los Angeles Times*, September 19, 1997: F1.

Chapter 20

1. Martin Grams, Jr., *Car 54, Where Are You?* (Albany, GA: BearManor Media, 2009), 11.
2. *Car 54, Where Are You?*, "Christmas at the 53rd," NBC, December 24, 1961.
3. New York Police Department, "Neighborhood Policing: What's in a Sector?," https://www.nyc.gov/site/nypd/bureaus/patrol/neighborhood-coordination-officers.page (last accessed September 13, 2024).
4. United States Department of Justice, Community Oriented Policing Services (COPS), *Community Policing Defined*, "Organizational Transformation—Organizational Structure: Geographic assignment of officers," https://portal.cops.usdoj.gov/resourcecenter/RIC/Publications/cops-p157-pub.pdf (last accessed September 13, 2024).
5. "Community policing techniques undergoing a revival," Los Angeles Times—Washington Post News Service, *Rockland Journal-News*, December 27, 1991: B5.
6. Kerry Haglund, "Community Policing a Familiar Concept," *Austin American-Statesman*, August 30, 1992: A10.
7. Julio Laboy, "When Police Shift Focus," *Newsday*, February 13, 1994: Brooklyn Sunday, 1.
8. George L. Kelling, "It's Time to let Beat Cops Do Their Job," *Daily News* (New York), March 9, 1994: 27.
9. Jim Newton, "In South-Central, Concerns Rise on Community Policing," *Los Angeles Times*, June 13, 1994: A1.
10. "Neighborhoods Are Reclaimed When Citizens and the Police Work Together," *Fort Worth Star-Telegram*, October 13, 1997: B2.
11. Gary Chapman, "Net Plays Growing Role in Community Policing," *Los Angeles Times*, September 28, 1998: D7.
12. Gary Marx and Michael J. Berens, "City's COPS Program Has Its Critics," *Chicago Tribune*, May 16, 1999: 17.

Chapter 21

1. *White Christmas*, Paramount Pictures, 1954.
2. The Florida Senate, Title XLVI, Chapter 843, Section 2, Resisting officer without violence to his or her person, https://m.flsenate.gov/Statutes/843.02 (last accessed October 13, 2024).
3. The Florida Senate, Title XLVI, Chapter 777, Section 03(1a), Accessory after the fact, https://www.flsenate.gov/Laws/Statutes/2018/777.03 (last accessed October 13, 2024).
4. The Florida Senate, Title XLVII, Chapter 901, Section 2, Issuance of arrest warrants, https://www.flsenate.gov/Laws/Statutes/2018/901.02 (last accessed October 13, 2024).
5. The Florida Senate, Title VI, Chapter 83, Section 53(1), https://www.flsenate.gov/Laws/Statutes/2023/0083.53 (last accessed October 13, 2024).
6. The Florida Senate, Title VI, Chapter 83, Section 53(2), https://www.flsenate.gov/Laws/Statutes/2023/0083.53 (last accessed October 13, 2024).
7. U.S. Const. amend. IV.
8. U.S. Const. amend. V.
9. U.S. Const. amend. VI.
10. Marc A. Wites, Emotional Distress, Intentional Infliction, *Florida Litigation Guide*, https://floridalitigationguide.com/emotional-distress-intentional-infliction/ (last accessed October 13, 2024).
11. The Florida Bar, Fraud, Civil or

Criminal, https://www.floridabar.org/practice-areas/fraud-civil-or-criminal/ (last accessed October 14, 2024).
 12. Joanna Marsh, "Freight All Kinds: Getting the Show on the Road," FreightWaves, December 17, 2019, https://www.freightwaves.com/news/freight-all-kinds-getting-the-show-on-the-road (last accessed October 13, 2024).
 13. Bosley Crowther, "'White Christmas' Bows at the Music Hall," *New York Times*, October 15, 1954: 16.
 14. Philip K. Scheuer, "'White Christmas' Delivers Big, Brightly Hued Musical Package," *Los Angeles Times*, October 28, 1954: A8.
 15. Wriston Locklair, "'White Christmas' Playing Here," *Charlotte Observer*, October 30, 1954: 8A.
 16. Dale Freeman, "'White Christmas' Has What It Takes to Score a Success," *Springfield* [Missouri] *Leader and Press*, November 11, 1954: 30.

Chapter 22

 1. *A Christmas Story*, MGM, 1983.
 2. Indiana Code, Title 35, Article 42, Chapter 2, Section 1(c), Battery, https://iga.in.gov/laws/2023/ic/titles/35#35-42-2-1 (last accessed December 8, 2024).
 3. Indiana Code, Title 35, Article 41, Chapter 3, Section 2(c), Use of force to protect person or property, https://iga.in.gov/laws/2023/ic/titles/35#35-41-3-2 (last accessed October 7, 2024).
 4. *Jones vs. State*, No. 23A-CR-1722 (Ind. App. 2024), https://casetext.com/case/jones-v-state-44356 (last accessed December 8, 2024).
 5. *Jones vs. State*.
 6. Indiana Code, Title 35, Article 41, Chapter 3, Section 2(g), https://iga.in.gov/laws/2023/ic/titles/35#35-41 (last accessed December 8, 2024).
 7. Rule 404, Character Evidence; Crimes or Other Acts, Indiana Rules of Court, Rules of Evidence, https://www.in.gov/courts/rules/evidence/#_Toc373857058 (last accessed December 8, 2024).
 8. Rule 404.
 9. *Adrian Brand vs. State of Indiana*, Indiana Court of Appeals (2002), https://law.justia.com/cases/indiana/court-of-appeals/2002/04290201-mgr.html (last accessed December 8, 2024).
 10. Rule 406, Habit; Routine Practice, Indiana Rules of Court, Rules of Evidence, https://www.in.gov/courts/rules/evidence/#_Toc373857058 (last accessed October 8, 2024).
 11. Rule 405, Methods of Proving Character, Indiana Rules of Court, Rules of Evidence, https://www.in.gov/courts/rules/evidence/#_Toc373857058 (last accessed October 8, 2024).
 12. Indiana Code, title 35, Article 42, Chapter 2, Section 1(c)(1), Battery.
 13. Indiana Code, Title 35, Article 45, Chapter 10, Section 2, Harassment https://iga.in.gov/laws/2023/ic/titles/35#35-45-10-2 (last accessed October 9, 2024).
 14. Indiana Code, Title 35, Article 41, Chapter 2, Section 4, Aiding, inducing, or causing an offense, https://iga.in.gov/laws/2023/ic/titles/35#35-41-2 (last accessed October 9, 1990).
 15. Christine W. Young, "Respondeat Superior: A Clarification and Broadening of the Current Scope of Employment Test," *Santa Clara Law Review*, Volume 30, Number 2 (1990).
 16. Indiana Code, Title 35, Article 46, Chapter 3, Section 7(a)(1)(2), Abandonment or neglect of vertebrate animals; defense, https://iga.in.gov/laws/2021/ic/titles/35#35-46-3-7 (last accessed October 9, 2024).
 17. Rex Reed, "'Christmas Story' Is Kiddie Korn," *New York Post*, November 18, 1983: 45.
 18. Vincent Canby, "Film: 'Christmas Story,' Indiana Tale," *New York Times*, November 18, 1983: C36.
 19. Roxanne T. Mueller, "'Christmas Story' Is Full of Charm for Whole Family," *Plain Dealer*, November 19, 1983: C1.
 20. Gene Siskel, "'Christmas' Arrives Early, with Nostalgic Gifts for One and All," *Chicago Tribune*, November 21, 1983: C4.
 21. John A. Douglas, "A Nostalgic Trip, a Christmas Treat," *Grand Rapids Press*, November 23, 1983: C3.

Chapter 23

 1. *Love Actually*, Universal Pictures, 2003.

2. "Love Is All Around," Easy Song, https://www.easysong.com/search/songs/song-copyright-holder-information.aspx?s=18734 (last accessed October 15, 2024); History of HFA, Harry Fox Agency, https://www.harryfox.com/history (last accessed October 15, 2024).

3. "What Is a Mechanical License and How Do I Know If I Need One?," Harry Fox Agency, https://www.harryfox.com/blog/what-is-a-mechanical-license (last accessed October 15, 2024).

4. Michael Simon, Three Keys to 21st Century Rights Management Success, Harry Fox Agency, https://www.harryfox.com/blog/future-of-rights-management (last accessed October 15, 2024).

5. News Release, Delta Entertainment and the Harry Fox Agency Reach Settlement, July 21, 2003, https://cappellonoel.com/delta-entertainment-and-the-harry-fox-agency-reach-settlement/ (last accessed October 15, 2024).

6. *Goodman vs. the Harry Fox Agency*, United States District Court, District of New Jersey (2003), https://casetext.com/case/goodman-v-the-harry-fox-agency (last accessed December 8, 2024).

7. Sound Recording Act of 1971, Public Law 92–140, October 15, 1971; *Dowling vs. United States*, United States Supreme Court (1990).

8. *Goodman vs. the Harry Fox Agency*.

9. *Harry Fox Agency vs. Mills Music*, United States District Court, Southern District of New York (1982), https://law.justia.com/cases/federal/district-courts/FSupp/543/844/1460774/ (last accessed December 8, 2024); *Harry Fox Agency vs. Mills Music*, United States Court of Appeals, Second Circuit (1983), https://casetext.com/case/harry-fox-agency-inc-v-mills-music-inc (last accessed December 8, 2024), United States Copyright Act, Section 115, Scope of exclusive rights in nondramatic musical works: Compulsory license for making and distributing phonorecords(1976); United States Copyright Act, Section 1, Section 101 (1909).

10. HFA & the MLC, Harry Fox Agency, https://www.harryfox.com/hfa-and-the-mlc (last accessed October 15, 2024).

11. Governance and Bylaws, Mechanical Licensing Collective, https://www.themlc.com/governance (last accessed October 15, 2024).

12. Mechanical Licensing Collective, The MLC in 3 Years, 2023 Annual Report, page 1, https://www.themlc.com/hubfs/2023%20MLC%20Annual%20Report.pdf (last accessed October 15, 2024).

13. Mechanical Licensing Collective, A Conversation with Board Chair Alisa Coleman and CEO Kris Ahrend, 2023 Annual Report, 2, https://www.themlc.com/hubfs/2023%20MLC%20Annual%20Report.pdf (last accessed October 15, 2024).

14. Mechanical Licensing Collective, A Conversation with Board Chair Alisa Coleman and CEO Kris Ahrend, 2023 Annual Report, 2.

15. "Bill Nighy—The Interview," BBC, https://www.bbc.co.uk/nottingham/films/2003/11/bill_nighy_interview.shtml (last accessed October 15, 2024).

16. Ellie Harrison, "Bill Nighy Thinks Love Actually Quote Will Be at the Top of His Obituary," *The Independent*, November 13, 2022, https://www.independent.co.uk/arts-entertainment/films/news/bill-nighy-love-actually-living-b2224302.html (last accessed October 15, 2024).

17. Mark Caro, "'Actually' Plays It Too Cute," *Chicago Tribune*, November 7, 2003: Section 5, Page 2; Jocelyn Noveck, "'Love Actually': Love Is a Many Splendored Thing," Associated Press, *Manassas* [Virginia] *Journal Messenger*, November 13, 2003: C5; Kim Morgan, "Dizzy with love," *The Oregonian*, A&E Section, November 7, 2003: 36.

18. Rebecca Sullivan, "Yes, Alan Rickman's Character Did Have Sex with His Secretary in Love Actually," December 26, 2019, Now to Love, https://www.nowtolove.com.au/entertainment/movies/love-actually-alan-rickman-affair-61944/ (last accessed October 15, 2024).

Chapter 24

1. *Jack Frost*, Warner Brothers, 1998.

2. United States Copyright Act of 1976, Section 101, Definitions, https://www.copyright.gov/title17/title17.pdf (last accessed December 8, 2024).

3. General License Agreement—Restaurants, Bars, Nightclubs, and Similar Establishments, Limitations on License, ASCAP, https://www.ascap.com/~/media/files/pdf/

licensing/classes/licensing-agreements-current/bgt-pdf (last accessed September 28, 2024).

4. General License Agreement—Restaurants, Bars, Nightclubs, and Similar Establishments, Limitations on License; Definitions.

5. General License Agreement—Restaurants, Bars, Nightclubs, and Similar Establishments, License Fees and Payments.

6. General License Agreement—Restaurants, Bars, Nightclubs, and Similar Establishments, License Fees and Payments, Interference in ASCAP's Operations.

7. ASCAP Music Licensing, Frequently Asked Questions About ASCAP Licensing, Are there any types of business that can perform music without having to pay an ASCAP license?, https://www.ascap.com/help/ascap-licensing/why-ascap-licenses-bars-restaurants-music-venues (last accessed September 28, 2024).

8. ASCAP Music Licensing, Frequently Asked Questions About ASCAP Licensing, How do you pay your members for live performances?

9. United States Copyright Act of 1976, Section 103(b), Subject matter of copyright: Compilations and derivative works, https://www.copyright.gov/title17/title17.pdf (last accessed December 8, 2024).

10. ASCAP, Press Release, "ASCAP Unwraps Top 10 New Classic Holiday Songs Chart Featuring Kelly Clarkson, Justin Bieber, Katy Perry, Meghan Trainor, Jimmy Fallon and More," December 18, 2023, https://www.ascap.com/press/2023/12/12-18-top-holiday-songs (last accessed September 28, 2024).

The Top 25 ASCAP Holiday Songs of 2023, https://www.ascap.com/press/2023/12/12-18-top-holiday-songs (last accessed September 28, 2024).

11. United States Copyright Act of 1976, Section 115(a)(2), Scope of exclusive rights in nondramatic musical works: Compulsory license for making and distributing phonorecords, Availability and Scope of Compulsory License in General, Musical Arrangement, https://www.copyright.gov/title17/title17.pdf (last accessed December 8, 2024).

12. *Supreme Records vs. Decca Records*, United States District Court, Southern District of California, Central Division (1950), https://law.justia.com/cases/federal/district-courts/FSupp/90/904/1505284/ (last accessed December 8, 2024).

Chapter 25

1. *The Bishop's Wife*, The Samuel Goldwyn Company, 1947.

2. United States Copyright Act of 1909, Section 9, Santa Clara University School of Law, https://law.scu.edu/wp-content/uploads/hightech/1909%20Act%20as%20enacted.pdf (last accessed September 19, 2024).

3. United States Copyright Act of 1909, Section 1(e).

4. Statement of Marybeth Peters, The Register of Copyrights before the Subcommittee on Intellectual Property, Committee on the Judiciary, United States Senate, 109th Congress, 1st Session, July 12, 2005, https://copyright.gov/docs/regstat071205.html (last accessed December 8, 2024).

5. *White-Smith Music Pub. Co. vs. Apollo Co.*, United States Supreme Court (1908), https://supreme.justia.com/cases/federal/us/209/1/ (last accessed December 8, 2024).

6. *White-Smith Music Pub. Co. vs. Apollo Co.*

7. United States Copyright Act of 1909, Section 10.

8. United States Copyright Act of 1909, Sections 55, 61

9. United States Copyright Act of 1909, Section 1(e).

10. Kate Cameron, "'The Bishop's Wife' Is a Titillating Comedy," *Daily News* (New York), December 10, 1947: 76.

11. "'The Bishop's Wife,' Christmasy Movie, Will Rival 'Best Years,' Says Critic," Associated Press, *Gazette and Daily* (York, PA), December 8, 1947: 19; Philip K. Scheuer, "Angel Grant Helps Spread Holiday Glow," *Los Angeles Times*, December 26, 1947: 6.

12. Gene Handsaker, "Cary Grant Angel, but Looks Mortal," *Pasadena Star-News*, December 13, 1947: 7; Harold V. Cohen, "Grant, Young, Niven At the Fulton in 'The Bishop's Wife,'" *Pittsburgh Post-Gazette*, February 9, 1948: 20.

Chapter 26

1. *Scrooged*, Paramount Pictures, 1988.

2. Duane Byrge, "'Scrooged': THR's

1988 Review," *The Hollywood Reporter*, November 21, 1988, republished online December 13, 2014, https://www.hollywoodreporter.com/news/general-news/scrooged-review-1988-movie-757457/# (last accessed September 16, 2024).

3. United States Copyright Office, "Definitions—Where Is the Public Domain?," https://www.copyright.gov/help/faq-definitions.html (last accessed September 16, 2024).

4. U.S. Const., Article 1, Section 8.

5. United States Copyright Act of 1976, Section 106, https://www.copyright.gov/title17/title17.pdf (last accessed December 8, 2024).

6. United States Copyright Act of 1976, Section 102(a)(5).

Chapter 27

1. Franklin Delano Roosevelt, Inaugural Address, March 4, 1933, The Avalon Project (Documents in Law, History and Diplomacy, Yale Law School), https://avalon.law.yale.edu/20th_century/froos1.asp (last accessed December 8, 2024); John Fitzgerald Kennedy, Inaugural Address, January 20, 1961, The American Presidency Project, University of California, Santa Barbara, https://www.presidency.ucsb.edu/documents/inaugural-address-2 (last accessed December 8, 2024); Ronald Reagan, Farewell Address to the Nation, January 11, 1989, Ronald Reagan Presidential Library & Museum, https://www.reaganlibrary.gov/archives/speech/farewell-address-nation (last accessed December 8, 2024).

2. *Parks and Recreation*, "Citizen Knope," NBC, December 8, 2011.

3. Indiana Administrative Code, Section 42, 1–5–1, Section 1(a)(1–8); Gifts; travel expenses; waivers, https://casetext.com/regulation/indiana-administrative-code/title-42-office-of-the-inspector-general/article-1-indiana-code-of-ethics/rule-42-iac-1-5-ethics-rules/section-42-iac-1-5-1-gifts-travel-expenses-waivers (last accessed September 20, 2024).

4. Indiana Administrative Code, Section 42, 1–5–1, Section 1(b)(5).

5. *Parks and Recreation*, "Eagleton," NBC, May 5, 2011.

6. *Parks and Recreation*, "Flu Season," NBC, January 27, 2011.

7. *Parks and Recreation*, "Beauty Pageant," NBC, October 1, 2009.

8. Verne Gay, "In 'Parks,' Amy Poehler Is a Dork with a Heart," *Newsday*, September 16, 2009: B5.

9. Tom Shales, "A Show Not Worthy of Amy Poehler," *San Francisco Examiner*, April 12, 2009: A37.

10. Bill Keveney, "Amy Poehler Gets a Bigger Playground," *Reno Gazette-Journal*, April 6, 2009: 3C; *Parks and Recreation*, "One Last Ride—Part 2," NBC, February 24, 2015.

Chapter 28

1. *Family Ties*, "Be True to Your Preschool," NBC, September 25, 1986.

2. *Family Ties*, "Miracle in Columbus," NBC, December 20, 1987.

3. *Family Ties*, "Miracle in Columbus."

4. Ronald Reagan Presidential Library and Museum, "Presidential Gifts—Reasons for Not Retaining Gifts," https://www.reaganlibrary.gov/reagans/reagan-administration/presidential-gifts (last accessed September 14, 2024).

5. Code of Federal Regulations, Title 5, Chapter 16, Subchapter B—Gifts from Outside Sources, Definitions, Section 2635.203(d)(1), https://www.ecfr.gov/current/title-5/chapter-XVI/subchapter-B/part-2635/subpart-B (last accessed September 14, 2024).

6. Code of Federal Regulations, Title 5, Chapter 16, Subchapter B—Gifts from Outside Sources, Definitions, Section 2635.203(d)(2).

7. Code of Federal Regulations, Title 5, Chapter 16, Subchapter B—Gifts from Outside Sources, Definitions, Section 2635.203(d)(3).

8. Code of Federal Regulations, Title 5, Chapter 16, Subchapter B—Gifts from Outside Sources, Definitions, Section 2635.203(d)(4).

9. Code of Federal Regulations, Title 5, Chapter 16, Subchapter B—Gifts from Outside Sources, Definitions, Section 2635.203(d)(5).

10. Code of Federal Regulations, Title 5, Chapter 16, Subchapter B—Gifts from Outside Sources, Exceptions to the prohibition for acceptance of certain gifts, Gifts of $20 or less, Section 2635.204(a).

11. Code of Federal Regulations, Title 5, Chapter 16, Subchapter B—Gifts from Outside Sources, Exceptions to the prohibition for acceptance of certain gifts Section 2635.204.
12. Code of Federal Regulations, Title 5, Chapter 16, Subchapter B—Gifts from Outside Sources, Exceptions to the prohibition for acceptance of certain gifts, Gifts based on a personal relationship, Section 2635.203(b)(1–5) (inclusive)—Definitions, Gift.
13. United States Senate Select Committee on Ethics, Gifts, Gifts Rule Exceptions, Gifts of Certain Types, Items of Little Intrinsic Value, https://www.ethics.senate.gov/public/index.cfm/gifts (last accessed September 14, 2024).
14. United States Senate Select Committee on Ethics, Gifts, Gifts Rule Exceptions, Gifts of Certain Types, Donations of Home State Products.
15. United States Code, Title 18, Section 666(a)(2), Theft or bribery concerning programs receiving Federal funds, Legal Information Institute, Cornell Law School, https://www.law.cornell.edu/uscode/text/18/666 (last accessed September 14, 2024).
16. Jane Hulse, "A Past of Presents," *Los Angeles Times*, July 23, 1998: 130.
17. President Ronald Reagan, Address Before a Joint Session of Congress on the State of the Union, February 4, 1986, The American Presidency Project, University of California, Santa Barbara, https://www.presidency.ucsb.edu/documents/address-before-joint-session-congress-the-state-the-union (last accessed December 9, 2024).
18. *Spin City*, "Goodbye: Part 2," ABC, May 24, 2000. Charlie Sheen replaced Fox as the show's lead actor for the next two seasons.

Chapter 29

1. *Miracle on 34th Street*, Twentieth Century Fox, 1947.
2. United States Code, Title 18, Section 1701, Obstruction of mails generally, Legal Information Institute, Cornell Law School, https://www.law.cornell.edu/uscode/text/18/1701 (last accessed December 9, 2024).
3. "Benjamin Franklin," United States Postal Service, https://about.usps.com/who-we-are/postal-history/pmg-franklin.pdf (last accessed December 9, 2024).
4. Walter Isaacson, *Benjamin Franklin: An American Life* (New York: Simon & Schuster, 2003), 157.
5. Isaacson, 207.
6. Articles of Confederation, Article IX.
7. U.S. Const., Article 1, Section 8.
8. "A big day in the history of the United States Postal Service," National Constitution Center Staff, National Constitution Center, February 20, 2019, https://constitutioncenter.org/blog/a-big-day-in-the-history-of-the-united-states-postal-service (last accessed November 6, 2024); President George Washington, Third Annual Address to Congress, October 25, 1791, The American Presidency Project, University of California, Santa Barbara, https://www.presidency.ucsb.edu/documents/third-annual-address-congress-0 (last accessed November 6, 2024).
9. Smithsonian Institution, Post Office Act of 1792, https://postalmuseum.si.edu/object/npm_1984.1127.8 (last accessed November 6, 2024).
10. Devin Leonard, *Neither Snow Nor Rain: A History of the United States Postal Service* (New York: Grove Press, 2016), 19.
11. "Robert Hannegan Dies; Was Master Politician," Associated Press, *Springfield [MO] Daily News*, October 7, 1949: 15.
12. Harry S. Truman, Letter Accepting Resignation of Robert E. Hannegan as Postmaster General, The American Presidency Project, University of California, Santa Barbara, https://www.presidency.ucsb.edu/documents/letter-accepting-resignation-robert-e-hannegan-postmaster-general (last accessed November 6, 2024).
13. "The day the sun rose on USPS," United States Postal Service, August 9, 2024, updated August 13, 2024, https://news.usps.com/2024/08/09/the-day-the-sun-rose-on-usps/ (last accessed November 7, 2024); Public Law 91–375; United States Code, Title 39, Section 2, Chapter 1—Postal Policy And Definitions, Section 101, Postal policy, https://www.govinfo.gov/content/pkg/STATUTE-84/pdf/STATUTE-84-Pg719.pdf (last accessed December 9, 2024).
14. "Santa Claus Post Office," Santa

Claus, Indiana, https://santaclausind.org/listings/santa-claus-post-office (last accessed November 7, 2024).

15. "USPS Operation Santa Teams with Toys 'R' Us," United States Postal Service, September 18, 2024, updated September 24, 2024, https://news.usps.com/2024/09/18/usps-operation-santa-teams-with-toys-r-us/ (last accessed November 7, 2024).

16. Ann Helming, "'Miracle on 34th St.' Superior Film," *Citizen-News* (Hollywood), June 14, 1947: 4; Edwin Schallert, "'Miracle on 34th Street,' Decisively Out of World," *Los Angeles Times*, June 14, 1947: A5.

17. Edwin Howard, "'Miracle on 34th Street' Brings Santa in an Entertainment Gem," *Memphis Press-Scimitar*, July 4, 1947: 3.

18. Harry Martin, "Christmas In July Provided By 'Miracle on 34th Street,'" *Commercial Appeal* (Memphis), July 4, 1947: 6.

Chapter 30

1. *Seinfeld*, "The Maestro," NBC, October 5, 1995; *Seinfeld*, "The Jimmy," NBC, March 16, 1995; *Seinfeld*, "The Couch," NBC, October 27, 1994; *Seinfeld*, "The Boyfriend," NBC, February 12, 1992; *Seinfeld*, "The Alternate Side," NBC, December 4, 1991; *Seinfeld*, "The Shoes," NBC, February 4, 1993; *Seinfeld*, "The Stand In," NBC, February 24, 1994.

2. *Seinfeld*, "The Race," NBC, December 15, 1994.

3. "The permanent standing House Committee on Un-American Activities: January 3, 1945," History, Art & Archives, United States House of Representatives, https://history.house.gov/Historical-Highlights/1901-1950/The-permanent-standing-House-Committee-on-Un-American-Activities/ (last accessed November 28, 2024).

4. "McCarthy Charges 205 Reds Are Working in State Dept.," Associated Press, *Buffalo Evening News*, February 10, 1950: 2; Senator Joseph McCarthy, Address, Women's Republican Club, Wheeling, West Virginia, February 9, 1950, United States Senate, https://www.senate.gov/about/powers-procedures/investigations/mccarthy-hearings/communists-in-government-service.htm (last accessed October 24, 2024).

5. William T. Evjue, "McCarthy's Trick of Guilt by Association," *Capital Times* (Madison, WI), February 20, 1950: 18.

6. Edward R. Murrow, *See It Now*, CBS, April 13, 1954; American Rhetoric, https://www.americanrhetoric.com/speeches/edwardrmurrowtomccarthy.htm (last accessed October 24, 2024).

7. Joseph Welch, Committee on Government Operations' Permanent Subcommittee on Investigations, Army-McCarthy Hearings, Washington, D.C., June 9, 1954, "McCarthy-Welch Exchange"; American Rhetoric, https://www.americanrhetoric.com/speeches/welch-mccarthy.html (last accessed October 24, 2024).

8. "Joan's Bridal Coast Benny $60,000," *New York Journal-American*, March 10, 1954: 1; "H-Bomb Test Set for This Month," Associated Press, *New York Journal-American*, March 10, 1954: 7; Miles Kastendieck, "Bellini's 'Norma' Revived at Met," *New York Journal-American*, March 10, 1954: 22; Hugh Bradley, "Eager Rizzuto Tips 1571/2, Hopes To Play 154 Games This Year," *New York Journal-American*, March 10, 1954: 28; Rose Pelswick, "Entertaining Sports Film," *New York Journal-American*, March 10, 1954: 19.

9. Jack O'Brian, "An Analysis of Murrow's Portsided Political Pitching," *New York Journal-American*, March 10, 1954: 36.

10. A. M. Sperber, *Murrow: His Life and Times* (New York: Freundlich Books, 1986), 469.

11. "Senate Resolution 301: Censure of Senator Joseph McCarthy (1954)," National Archives, https://www.archives.gov/milestone-documents/censure-of-senator-joseph-mccarthy (last accessed December 9, 2024); Cecil Holland, "Lengthy Battle Over McCarthy Ends in Senate," *Evening Star* (Washington, D.C.), December 3, 1954: 1.

12. Scott Simon and Daniel Schorr, "George Clooney's Take on Murrow," Interview, National Public Radio, October 15, 2005, https://www.npr.org/2005/10/15/4960355/george-clooneys-take-on-murrow (last accessed October 24, 2024).

13. "3 Actors Label Hollywood Reds 'Active Minority,'" Associated Press, *Pittsburgh Sun-Telegraph*, October 23, 1947 (Final Night Extra): 1.

14. "Robert Taylor Tells of Movie-Land Pink Tints," Associated Press, *Standard-Sentinel* (Hazleton, PA), October 23, 1947: 1.

15. Thomas Doherty, "Reflections on Hollywood's Infamous Blacklist 70 Years Later (Guest Column)," *Hollywood Reporter*, November 24, 2017, https://www.hollywoodreporter.com/movies/movie-news/reflections-hollywoods-infamous-blacklist-70-years-guest-column-1060628/ (last accessed October 23, 2024).

16. "Comedian Zero Mostel Balks at Red Question," *Los Angeles Times*, October 15, 1955: 1.

17. Larry Parks, Testimony, March 21, 1951, HUAC Hearings on Communist Infiltration of the Motion-Picture Industry, 1951–52, University of Houston, https://www.digitalhistory.uh.edu/teachers/historyonline/huac_infiltration2.cfm (last accessed October 23, 2024).

18. "Larry Parks Says He Was Communist," United Press, *New York Times*, March 22, 1951: 1.

19. Thomas F. Brady, "Columbia Cancels Larry Parks Film," *New York Times*, March 23, 1951: 16; "Larry Parks Is Dead; Star of 'Jolson Story,'" Associated Press, *Buffalo Evening News*, April 14, 1975: 37.

20. Dorothy and Lloyd Bridges, Letter to the Editor, *Los Angeles Times*, April 28, 1975: 22.

21. Victor Navasky, *Naming Names* (New York: The Viking Press, 1980), 425.

22. *Red Channels: The Report of Communist Influence in Radio and Television* (New York: American Business Consultants, Publisher of Counterattack—The Newsletter of Facts to Combat Communism) (June 1950), 6–7; Primary Source Publications, 2017 (facsimile edition) (citation refers to the facsimile edition).

Bibliography

Books

American Business Consultants (Publishers of *Counterattack: The Newsletter of Facts to Combat Communism*). *Red Channels: The Report of Communist Influence in Radio and Television.* New York: American Business Consultants, 1950.
Arnold, Jeremy. *Christmas in the Movies* (Revised and Expanded Edition). New York: Running Press, 2023.
Arras, Paul. *Seinfeld: A Cultural History.* Lanham, MD: Rowman & Littlefield, 2020.
Crump, William D. *How the Movies Saved Christmas: 228 Rescues from Clausnappers, Sleigh Crashes, Lost Present and Holiday Disasters.* Jefferson, NC: McFarland, 2017.
Dickens, Charles. *A Christmas Carol. In Prose. Being a Ghost Story of Christmas.* Reprinted with Introduction by Lionel Barrymore and Illustrations by Everett Shinn. New York: Garden City Publishing Company, 1938. First published 1843.
Earley, Pete, and Gerald Shur. *WITSEC: Inside the Federal Witness Protection Program.* New York: Bantam Books, 2002.
Ebsen, Buddy. *The Other Side of Oz.* Newport Beach, CA: Donovan Publishing, 1994.
Ellroy, James, and Glynn Martin. *LAPD '53.* New York: Abrams Image, 2015.
Fitzgerald, Melissa, and Mary McCormack. *What's Next: A Backstage Pass to The West Wing, Its Case and Crew, and Its Enduring Legacy of Service.* New York: Dutton, 2024.
Fox, Michael J. *Lucky Man.* New York: Hachette Books, 2003.
Gottlieb, Sherry Gershon. *Hell No, We Won't Go! Resisting the Draft During the Vietnam War.* New York: Viking Penguin, 1991.
Grams, Martin, Jr. *Car 54, Where Are You?* Albany, GA: BearManor Media, 2009.
Hooker, Richard. *MASH: A Novel About Three Army Doctors.* New York: William Morrow and Company, 1968.
Imperioli, Michael, and Steve Schirripa. *Woke Up This Morning: The Definitive Oral History of* The Sopranos. New York: William Morrow, 2021.
Isaacson, Walter. *Benjamin Franklin: An American Life.* New York: Simon & Schuster, 2003.
Kalter, Suzy. *The Complete Book of M*A*S*H.* New York: Harry N. Abrams, 1985.
Leaffer, Marshall. *Understanding Copyright Law* (Seventh Edition). Durham: Carolina Academic Press, 2019.
Lear, Norman. *Even This I Get to Experience.* New York: Penguin, 2014.
Leonard, Devin. *Neither Snow Nor Rain: A History of the United States Postal Service.* New York: Grove Press, 2016.
Maas, Peter. *Underboss: Sammy the Bull Gravano's Story of Life in the Mafia.* New York: HarperCollins, 1997.
Navasky, Victor S. *Naming Names.* New York: The Viking Press, 1980.
O'Connor, Carroll. *I Think I'm Outta Here: A Memoir of All My Families.* New York: Simon & Schuster, 1998.
Pileggi, Nicholas. *Wiseguy: Life in a Mafia Family.* New York: Simon & Schuster, 1985.
Reiss, David S. *M*A*S*H: The Exclusive,*

Inside Story of TV's Most Popular Show. London: Arthur Barker Limited, 1980.

Seitz, Matt Zoller, and Alan Sepinwall. The Sopranos *Sessions*. New York: Abrams Press, 2019.

Shepherd, Jean. *In God We Trust, All Others Pay Cash*. New York: Doubleday, 1966.

Sperber, A.M. *Murrow: His Life and Times*. New York: Freundlich Books, 1986.

Stevens, Steve, and Craig Lockwood. *King of the Sunset Strip: Hangin' with Mickey Cohen and the Hollywood Mob*. Nashville: Cumberland House Publishing, 2006.

Tartikoff, Brandon. *The Last Great Ride*. New York: Turtle Bay Books, 1992.

Tereba, Tere. *Mickey Cohen: The Life and Crimes of L.A.'s Notorious Mobster*. Toronto: ECW Press, 2012.

Film and TV

All in the Family, CBS, 1971–1979.
The Andy Griffith Show, CBS, 1960–1968.
The Apartment, United Artists, 1960.
The Beverly Hillbillies, CBS, 1962–1971.
The Bishop's Wife, The Samuel Goldwyn Company, 1947.
Car 54, Where Are You?, NBC, 1961–1963.
Cheers, NBC, 1982–1993.
A Christmas Carol, Renown Pictures, 1951.
A Christmas Story, MGM, 1983.
Deck the Halls, Twentieth Century Fox, 2006.
Die Hard, Twentieth Century Fox, 1988.
Emmet Otter's Jug Band Christmas, CBC, 1977.
Family Ties, NBC, 1982–1989.
Home Alone, Twentieth Century Fox, 1990.
How the Grinch Stole Christmas!, CBS, 1966.
It's a Wonderful Life, Liberty Films, 1946.
Jack Frost, Warner Brothers, 1998.
L.A. Confidential, Warner Brothers, 1997.
Love Actually, Universal Pictures, 2003.
The Man Who Came to Dinner, Warner Brothers, 1942.
M*A*S*H, CBS, 1972–1983.
Miracle on 34th Street, Twentieth Century Fox, 1947.
Operation Christmas Drop, Netflix, 2020.
Parks and Recreation, NBC, 2009–2015.
Rich Little's A Christmas Carol, CBC, 1978.
Scrooge, Cinema Center Films, 1970.
Scrooge, Paramount Pictures, 1935.
Scrooged, Paramount Pictures, 1988.
Seinfeld, NBC, 1989–1998.
The Sopranos, HBO, 1999–2007.
Stalag 17, Paramount Pictures, 1953.
The West Wing, NBC, 1999–2006.
White Christmas, Paramount Pictures, 1954.

Index

Adrian Brand vs. State of Indiana 135
Ahrend, Kris 142–143
Air Force Historical Support Division 71
Alcohol and Tobacco Tax and Trade Bureau 95
All in the Family 66, 69–70
American Graves Registration Command 56
Andersen Air Force Base 72–73
Anderson, Harry 39
The Andy Griffith Show 93–96, 98
The Apartment 83–87
Arlington National Cemetery 49–50
Army-McCarthy Hearings 179–180
ASCAP 146–148
Association of Prosecuting Attorneys 91–92

Bank of United States 41–42
bank runs 41–43
Banking Act of 1933 43
Banking Act of 1935 44
Barnaby Jones 34
Barney Miller 69
Barrymore, Lionel 18–19
bearer bonds 22–23
Bevan, Donald 52
The Beverly Hillbillies 29–34
Bing Crosby Productions 57
The Bishop's Wife 150–155
blacklisting 178–183
"Bloody Christmas" 121
Bogart, Paul 69
Boggs, Wade 39
Borch III, Fred 55
Bridges, Dorothy 183
Bridges, Lloyd 183
Bureau of Alcohol, Tobacco, Firearms and Explosives 95
burglary 106, 107–108
Bush, George H.W. 71

California Bank building 122
California Law Review 38
Cappello, A. Barry 141
Car 54, Where Are You? 123–124, 127
Carter, Jimmy 68–69
Castle Doctrine 91–92
CenterPoint Energy 103
Cheers 35–39
A Christmas Carol 17–21, 156–157
A Christmas Story 133–138
Clooney, George 181
Code of Federal Regulations 166–167
Cohen, Mickey 117–118, 121
Coleman, Alisa 142–143
Coleman, Dabney 34
Communism 178–183
community policing 124–127
contests 25–27
Cooper, Alice 28
Copyright Clause in U.S. Constitution 157
Cornell Law School's Legal Information Institute 36
Crossroads of the World 121
Crowe, Cameron 53

Dallas 69
da Silva, Howard 181
Deck the Halls 99–100, 103
Defense of Home 89–92; *see also* Castle Doctrine
Delta Entertainment Corporation 141
De Palma, Brian 28
Deull family 131–132
Dickens, Charles 17–21
Die Hard 22–24
Dowling vs. United States 141
draft dodging 67–69
Dryer, Fred 39
Duffy, Julia 39
Dukakis, Michael 39
Durocher, Leo 69

Index

Early, Pete 111
Ebsen, Buddy 29, 33–34
Eisenhower, Dwight 64
EMI 147–148
Emmet Otter's Jug-Band Christmas 25, 27, 28
Epstein, Julius J. 82
Epstein, Philip G. 82
Ethier, Eric 53
Evjue, William 179

falsifying military records 60–62
Family Ties 165–169
Farsons on Contracts 37
FDIC 43–44, 46
Ford, Gerald 67
Fordham Urban Law Journal 86
Fox, Michael J. 165, 168–169
Franklin, Benjamin 172–173
Friendly, Fred 181
Friends 39
Frolic Room 121
"Frosty the Snowman" (song) 145, 148–149
Frosty the Snowman (TV special) 149

Garn, Jake 69
Gates, Thomas S. 67
Geneva Convention 53–55
Gettysburg Address 51
"Gift of the Magi" 25
Gifts to State Government Employees 159–164
Gifts to the President of the United States 166–169
Giuliani, Rudy 125
Goldwater, Barry 69
Goodfellas 112
Goodman, Richard "Dickie" 141–142
Gotti, John 114
Grams, Martin, Jr. 123
Gravano, Sammy 113–115
The Great Christmas Light Fight 101
Green Acres 33
USS *Greer* 57
Grey, Frank 53
Gulf War 71

Handy, Ned 53
Hannegan, Robert 174
harassment 87, 136
Harry Fox Agency 140–142
Harry Fox Agency vs. Mills Music 142
Hart, Moss 81
HBO 25
Henry, O. 25
Henson, Jim 25

Hill, Henry 112–114
Hoban, Russell 25
Hobby Distillers Association vs. Alcohol and Tobacco Tax and Trade Bureau 97–98
Hogan's Heroes 57–58
Holden, William 53
Holiday Inn 132
Hollenbeck, Don 180–181
Hollywood Ten 178
Home Alone 88–92
Hornberger, Richard 64
How the Grinch Stole Christmas! 104–107
Hunter 49

Indiana Code 136
Indiana's Rules of Evidence 135
Insurance Act of 1951 61
International Committee of the Red Cross 54
Interstate Commerce Commission 131
It's a Wonderful Life 18, 40–41

Jack Frost 145–149
Jackson, Robert S. 55

Kaufman, George S. 81
Kelling, George L. 126
Kennedy, Ethel 39
Kennedy, Ted 69
Kerry, John 39
King, Rodney 124–125
The King of Queens 39
Korean War, Armistice Agreement for the Restoration of the South Korean State 64; benefits for families of soldiers 61–62; drafting medical personnel 64; origins 63
Kudrow, Lisa 39

L.A. Confidential 116–121
Laird, Melvin 67
landlord-tenant relationship 129–131
Landt, Skip 28
larceny 44–45, 106
Lear, Norman 66
Lee County Electric Cooperative 102
The Legend of the Beverly Hillbillies 33
Leonard, Devin 173
Love Actually 140, 143–144
"Love Is All Around" 140, 143
Lovell House 122
Lowe, Rob 48
Lumley vs. Gye 38

Maas, Peter 114
Madsen, Virginia 73

Magnum, P.I. 69
Malmedy Massacre 55
The Man Who Came to Dinner 77–82
marijuana 118–119
Marques vs. Federal Reserve Bank of Chicago 22–23
Marquette National Bank of Minneapolis vs. First of Omaha Service Corporation 19
Martel's Christmas Wonderland 101
M*A*S*H: novel 64, 65; television show 59–61, 64, 65
Massachusetts Association of Realtors 37
Mayberry R.F.D. 33
McCarthy, Joe 178–181
McGoey, Andrew 125
McGovern, George 69
McHale, Kevin 39
Mechanical Licensing Collective 142–143
Michigan State University 125
military draft 67–68
military funerals 49–51
Minnesota Linseed Oil Co. vs. Collier White Lead Company 37
Miracle on 34th Street 170–171, 174–176
USS *Missouri* 56
Montgomery, Robert 181
Moonlighting 23
moonshining 93–98
Morley, Karen 181
Mostel, Zero 182
Mundt, Karl 63–64
The Munsters 69
murder 120
Murphy, George 181
Murray, Noel 28
Murrow, Edward R. 179
Music Modernization Act of 2018 142
Music Publishing Rights—Public Performance 145–149
Music Publishing Rights—Recorded Songs 139–144

Naming Names 183
National Center for Community Policing 125
National Defense Authorization Act 51
National Judicial College 107
National Stolen Property Act 106
Navasky, Victor 183
Negligence (Civil) 79–81
Neither Snow Nor Rain: A History of the United States Postal Service 173–174
New York City Bar Association 85
New York City Rent Guidelines Board 85
Night Court 39
Nighy, Bill 140, 143

Nixon, Richard 67, 110, 174
Nothing Lasts Forever 23
Nuremberg Trials 55
Nye, Clement 121

O'Brian, Jack 180–181
offer 36–37
Ohio Revised Code 80–81
Oklahoma Gas & Electric 101
Oncor 101
O'Neill, Tip 39
Operation Christmas Drop 72–77
Operation Christmas Drop 72–75
Operation Desert Storm 71
Operation Iraqi Freedom 71
Operation Rolling Thunder 71
Oppewall, Jeanne 122
Organized Crime Control Act 110–111
Overbey, Maj. Zach "Badger" 76

Pacific Gas & Electric 102–103
Paley, Bill 33–34
Paris Peace Accords 67, 68
Parker, William 121
Parks, Larry 182–183
Parks and Recreation 159–164
People vs. Batwin 118–119
Peters, Marybeth 152
Petticoat Junction 33
pimping 117
planting evidence 121
P.M. 180–181
Police Athletic League 125
Posner, Richard 23
Post, Markie 39
Postal Reorganization Act 174
private banking 30–32
prostitution 116–117
provocation 136
public domain 156–157

Reagan, Ronald 24, 166–168, 181
Red Channels: The Report of Communist Influence in Radio and Television 183
Red Scare 182
Rehm, Diane 48
Reidman, Harold 123
Remini, Leah 39
resisting arrest 128–129
Respondeat superior 137
Return of the Beverly Hillbillies 33
Richards, Michael 39
Rockefeller Institute of Government 91
Ronald Reagan Presidential Library 166
Roosevelt, Franklin D. 43, 56–57
Route 66 69
Rules of Land Warfare 56

safe electricity 103
Santa Clara Law Review 137
Santa Claus, Indiana 175
Scheibel vs. Lipton 79
Schiff, Richard 48–49
Scrooged 156–157
See It Now 179
Seinfeld 39, 177–178
Selective Service and Training Act 67
self-defense 133–135
Semayne's Case 91
sexual assault 87
Shepherd, Cybill 23
Shinn, Everett 18
Shur, Gerald 111
Simon, Michael 140–141
The Sopranos 109–110, 115
Stalag 17 52–54, 57–58
Stompanato, Johnny 121
Strathairn, David 181
subletting 84–86
Supreme Records vs. Decca Records 149
S.W.A.T. 69

Tartikoff, Brandon 39
Taylor, Robert 181
Temple, Renny 69–70
theft of electricity 100–103
Themal, Harry F. 23
Thorp, Roderick 23
Tiant, Luis 39
Till Death Do Us Part 66
Toys "R" Us 175
trespass 106
The Troggs 140
Trop vs. Dulles 97–99
Truman, Harry S. 55, 63
Truman Library Institute 56
Trzcinsky, Edmund 52
Turan, Kenneth 122

U-652 57
Underboss: Sammy the Bull Gravano's Story of Life in the Mafia 114
Uniform Code of Military Justice 60
United Nations Security Council 63, 71
U.S. Code 62, 75, 168
U.S. Constitution 56, 63, 130–132, 157
U.S. Copyright Act (1831) 152
U.S. Copyright Act (1909) 141, 142, 151–154
U.S. Copyright Act (1976) 142, 145–146, 148
U.S. Copyright Office 156

U.S. Court of Appeals 62
U.S. Department of Defense 74–75
U.S. Department of Justice 124
U.S. Department of Justice Organized Crime Control Commission 117
U.S. Department of Justice Organized Crime Strike Force for the Eastern District of New York 113
U.S. Department of Veterans Affairs 61–62
U.S. House of Representatives Un-American Activities Committee 178–179, 181–183
U.S. Marine Corps (Second Battalion, Seventh Marines) 49
U.S. Navy 49–50
U.S. Office of Government Ethics 166
U.S. Post Office 171–176
U.S. Senate Committee on Government Operations' Permanent Subcommittee on Investigations 179
US. Senate Select Committee on Ethics 167
U.S. Supreme Court 19, 152–153
U.S. Transportation Command 74
United States vs. Spicer 60
unpublished works 151–153
Urich, Robert 39
usury 19

Vanity Fair 53
Varney, Jim 34
Vietnam War 66–69, 71

Waldorf Declaration 181–182
warrant 129
Welch, Joseph 179–180
The West Wing 47–48
West Wing Weekly 48–49
White Christmas 128–132
Wilder, Billy 53
William Mitchell Law Review 38
Williams, Paul 25, 28
Witness Protection Program 110–115
WITSEC: Inside the Federal Witness Protection Program 111
Woolley, Monty 77
World War II: D-Day 71; German and Russian soldiers 55–56; Germany surrenders 56; Japan surrenders 56; Japanese treatment of American prisoners 56; Malmedy Massacre 55; origins 56–57